Working with Clarion™

Gary Liming

To Stephen, Kim, Bob, and Monty for their valued friendship, and, of course, to Sandi and the boys for their patience.

NOTICES

Clarion Professional Developer	Clarion Software Corporation
dBASEII, dBASE III	Ashton-Tate
DIF	DIF Clearing House
Plink86	Phoenix Technologies, Inc.

Windcrest books are published by Windcrest Books, an imprint of TAB BOOKS. The name "Windcrest" is a registered trademark of TAB BOOKS.

FIRST EDITION
SECOND PRINTING

Library of Congress Cataloging-in-Publication Data

Liming, Gary.
    Working with Clarion / by Gary Liming.
       p. cm.
    ISBN 0-8306-3403-7 (pbk.)—ISBN 0-8306-9403-X
    1. Clarion Professional developer (Computer program) I. Title.
QA76.9.D3L565 1990
005.75′65—dc20
                                       89-29158
                                            CIP

TAB BOOKS offers software for sale. For information and a catalog, please contact TAB Software Department, Blue Ridge Summit, PA 17294-0850.

Questions regarding the content of this book should be addressed to:

Windcrest Books
Imprint of TAB BOOKS
Blue Ridge Summit, PA 17294-0850

Acquisitions Editor: Stephen Moore
Book Editor: Kellie Hagan
Production: Katherine G. Brown
Book Design: Jaclyn J. Boone
Cover Design: Lori E. Schlosser

Contents

————————————PART ONE————————————
The Clarion environment

3   What is a Clarion program?   37

4   Designer — ready, set, go!   51

PART TWO
The Clarion language
---

5   Simple programs   95

_____PART THREE_____

Application strategies

About the author

Gary Liming was one of the system programmers of the Clarion Professional Developer, versions 1 and 2. He implemented the database features of the language, and many of the utilities. He also developed course materials and was an instructor for the seminar, *Using the Clarion Professional Developer*.

Gary has worked in the computer industry since 1974 and has written numerous articles on microcomputers. Prior to Clarion, he was a software manager with Digital Equipment Corporation and a telecommunications analyst with McDonnell Douglas. Gary holds a B.S. degree in Physics from Illinois State University.

Gary is currently Vice President of Engineering for Meridian Technology Corporation, a research and development company specializing in computer networks.

Who should use this book

This book is for those who want to use the best tool available to create programs for the IBM PC. That tool is the Clarion Professional Developer. I realize this might sound like a rather strong statement to make. However, if you invest some time in this book, you'll see why thousands of Clarion developers agree.

Clarion is very easy to use. Its many built-in features do much of the work for you. This ease of use, however, does not sacrifice depth and power. Even though simple programs can be done very quickly, you can still write very complex applications. Because of its general-purpose nature, you can create programs that will do exactly what you want.

If you are new to programming, I truly envy you. You will be learning a set of tools and a language that is both very powerful and also very elegant. To be able to create sophisticated, friendly programs without the tedium of counting row and column numbers of screens and reports is a luxury that I wish I had many years ago.

If you have experience with a database program, but not with procedural programming, do not despair. Clarion allows you to create very complex applications without a single line of code by using the Designer utility. This alone can be a great way to ease into the language — letting a utility write the code that provides your own working example.

If you have a traditional programming background, I believe you are in for a pleasant surprise. You'll find that you already know much about Clarion due to its familiar syntax. Many products talk about programming productivity, but are ultimately disappointing. A poor programming tool can severely limit your application designs.

Clarion was specifically designed to provide very high level support for creating user-friendly features with a minimum of effort. At the same time, it allows for complete control over every keystroke, every character and color on the screen, every byte in a disk file, and every location in memory.

If you are a current Clarion user, whether a seasoned version 1.0 "wizard" or a version 2.0 novice, this book will give you greater understanding of how to use both the utilities and the language to create your applications. *Working with Clarion* is not a replacement for the Clarion Professional Developer manuals, but a resource that provides you with information about how to get more out of Clarion.

Regardless of your experience, I welcome you to *Working with Clarion*—an investment that will be well worth the effort.

Gary Liming
St. Louis, MO

Introduction

In the not-so-distant past, most computer programs were simply hard to use. They often required a high level of experience or training on the part of the user. Because the tools available to the program creators were also hard to use, the significant amount of time required to make them "user friendly" was often not considered worth the effort or cost. For this reason, a program is often a reflection of the tools used to create it.

Today's computer users, however, are much more demanding about the type of software they want to use, and rightly so. They want application designs that make the software fast, safe, and easy to use. Accordingly, the tools used to create this type of software should also be easy to use, powerful, and support the type of features that users have come to expect. Clarion is such a tool.

Just what is Clarion?

Most programming tools help you write programs: that is, step-by-step instructions of what the computer is supposed to perform. But this is only part of the picture—what most users need are complete *applications*. An application refers to the set of programs, database files, and help screens that together represent a complete software solution for the user.

There are many methods and tools that you can use to create these application components. Clarion integrates a complete set of these tools into a single working environment. Tools such as screen generators, report generators, help generators, editors, compilers, debuggers, and even an entire application generator all come together to create a new way of developing software.

The Clarion Professional Developer is not only a new set of tools, but also a powerful, complete language. Clarion is a full, rich software language in the tradition of Pascal, C, and BASIC. Unlike those languages, however, Clarion is specifically developed to provide you with high-level support for things like pop-up windows, menus, indexed database operations, reports, arrays, and tables.

The Clarion Professional Developer is often referred to as *fourth generation language* (4GL). Simply put, 4GLs are software tools that assist you in writing programs at a very high level. This usually means a powerful language with statements that replace many lines of traditional programming, or even a method of generating code without any programming.

Clarion is a 4GL because of its ability to create applications quickly and simply, with much (if not all) of the code automatically generated for you. While Clarion certainly has these high level commands and even a nonprogramming code generator, it is also much more.

The Clarion Professional Developer has received awards for its capability as a database management system (DBMS). Although there are several strict definitions of a DBMS, the microcomputer industry uses this term loosely to include products like dBASE III and others. These products can create programs, but their strength lies in their ability to store and retrieve large amounts of data from storage devices. Clarion provides these data control capabilities for you, but also gives you the freedom to design an application that closely matches the needs of the user.

This is why Clarion can more properly be called an *applications development environment*. It is an integrated collection of software development tools and a high level language that makes the development of complete applications simpler and faster than any previous development tool.

The type of applications you can create with Clarion is virtually limitless. Because of its general-purpose language, you have control over every keystroke that is pressed, every character and video attribute sent to the screen, and every character sent to the printer. You can also read or write information to any file on a hard or floppy disk, or anywhere on a network.

Clarion users have been able to create a very wide range of applications, including business and accounting, scientific instrument data acquisition, telecommunications, optical scanning and storage control, and robot control systems.

If you've gotten the impression that there is a lot of capability in the Clarion Professional Developer, you're right. You will also find out that this capability is much easier to use than you might think.

What is in this book?

This book covers the principles involved in using the Clarion Professional Developer, version 2.0, and is based on batch 2008 of the product. If you have an older batch version, there might be some features described in this book that were subsequently added. Also, Clarion is constantly improving the product. If you have a version later than 2.0, it might contain new features not described. The basic ideas presented in this book, however, are applicable to any version of Clarion.

Working with Clarion contains thirteen chapters, divided into three parts. The three parts deal, respectively, with the Clarion environment, language, and application strategies.

Part One is an introduction to the Clarion environment, an overview of Clarion terms and application components, and a guided tour of each utility. If you are new to Clarion, you should pay careful attention to this part before going on. Even if you have been using Clarion for some time, I still recommend you review this part to understand the definition of terms used with the product and throughout this book.

Chapter 1 presents basic concepts about creating applications. It covers the program development cycle, and introduces the various Clarion utilities and explains how they are used. It also includes some philosophy about why Clarion was designed to work in ways to make you productive.

Chapter 2 explores the Clarion environment, giving a description of the function and use of each of the Clarion utilities.

Chapter 3 provides definitions for basic concepts that are used throughout the application development process, including programs, procedures, data declarations, and data file definitions.

Chapter 4 is a step-by-step introduction to creating applications with Designer. The example is a simple inventory program for a bookstore that displays books on the shelf and prints various reports.

Part Two presents the Clarion language. It provides a description of each major part of the language, and examples of their use.

Chapter 5 covers the format of Clarion programs, describing data types and how they are declared, processed, and formatted. It also shows you how you can break up a large program into smaller, more manageable units.

Chapter 6 describes the ways you can alter program execution, describing basic programming statements like IF-THEN-ELSE, CASE, and LOOP. The ability to call other programs from Clarion is also described, along with basic input/output statements.

Chapter 7 shows how data files are declared and how you can access and process data. It also describes Clarion data file utilities.

Chapter 8 covers the screen formatter, used to create high-level screen structures in your programs. The language statements used to process these screens are also covered.

Chapter 9 explains how to create reports for your application with the report formatter, and describes the language statements that process them.

Chapter 10 discusses memory tables, a powerful feature of Clarion that lets you process data in free memory.

Part Three of this book discusses various strategies that can be used to put whole applications together.

Chapter 11 provides practical advice about planning your applications, including user interface considerations, file layout, and screen design principles.

Chapter 12 discusses how a combination of Designer and the Editor can be used to create part of an application, and provides information about modifying the model file.

Chapter 13 discusses the options available for the distribution of Clarion applications.

PART ONE
The Clarion environment

1
CHAPTER

Welcome to the fourth generation

In this chapter, you'll find a brief introduction to the capabilities of the Clarion Professional Developer, along with a description of the contents of the package. If you are new to Clarion, you'll learn how to quickly get started using it.

The Clarion Professional Developer is an application development environment designed to let you create high quality applications, quickly and easily. It consists of several design utilities that let you create applications at a very high level by simply describing their appearance and operation. It also includes many implementation utilities that make your job as a developer easier, and yet maintain the versatility you need for those truly unique applications. Finally, it provides database utilities that help you manage the data stored for your applications.

Before you get started on the various parts of the Clarion environment, it will be helpful to review some of the basic steps involved in creating application software.

Writing programs

The most traditional way of writing programs consists of typing computer instructions, expressed in a particular software language, into a utility program. This utility program, most often called an *editor*, is used to record your instructions in a file for later use by the computer. The resulting file (or output) is called the source file. To change the way a program works, you make changes to, or edit, the source file. Clarion provides an excellent Editor to do this job.

Because a computer processes information at a very simple level (using only binary numbers), your language statements must be converted into commands that the computer understands. Some development systems allow for the scanning, or interpreting, of your program statements for execution by the computer. These systems are referred to as *interpreters.*

Other systems use a separate utility to read your source file and produce another file that contains the encoded, computer-ready operations. This process is called compilation, and the utility is called a *compiler.* The major advantage of using a compiler over an interpreter is that the interpretation of your language statements (a slow process) needs to be done only once by the compiler, not each time your program is run. Clarion provides such a compiler to do this job.

Most higher languages include pre-written and pre-compiled procedures and functions that you can include in your programs. These pre-written program segments are combined into one or more files called a library. The process of collecting your compiled statements and the code you want to include from a library into a single, ready-to-run file is called linking, and the utility used to do it is called a *linker.* Linking an application requires quite a bit of file manipulation, and can therefore be quite slow.

The steps in the process of program development are shown in Fig. 1-1. Source files come from the Editor (where you spend time writing the actual program), and are compiled, linked, and then run to see if they perform correctly. At each step, you might discover errors which might necessitate changing a source file. Notice that, while performing these steps, you spend time thinking about your program while using the Editor, and then waiting on the computer to see if your program is running correctly.

Now that you've seen the traditional approach, I'll tell you what Clarion has to offer. The basic steps in developing programs with Clarion, shown in Fig. 1-2, give you more options. Clarion provides another utility, Designer, that can also creates source files for the Compiler.

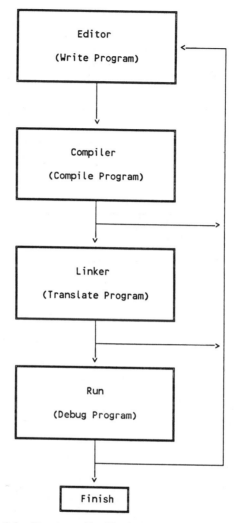

1-1. The steps of traditional program development

Designer is a utility that generates source files by letting you describe the data the program will use, how the program looks when it runs, and what happens to the data when it runs. This descriptive information is stored in a file with an .APP extension, and is referred to as the application file.

At the end of a Designer session, Clarion will ask you if you want to generate source files for your application. If you answer yes, it "merges"

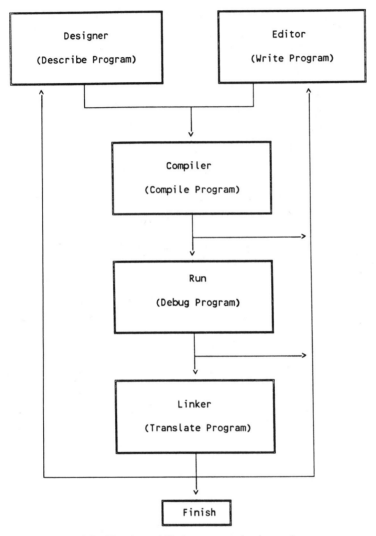

1-2. The steps of Clarion program development

the application file with a model source file to generate the source. There are two model files supplied with the package — the standard model file, which creates applications for single-user operations, and the network model file, which produces applications that run with simultaneous users. Model files will be covered in more detail in Chapter 2.

Besides the Designer, there is one other major difference between Clarion and traditional program development — you can run and debug your program directly after compiling with Clarion. Only after the program is complete and working will you have to use the Linker. This major distinction allows Clarion to make you more productive.

Both the Designer and the Editor have an additional time saving feature that differs from traditional development — they both have screen and report formatters built into them. These formatters can completely specify the layout and form of both video screens and reports in a "what you see is what you get" (WYSIWYG) manner. This means that you can create and maintain all the screens and reports in your application by just drawing a picture of the screens and reports, including data fields and their formats, and then let the formatter write the code for you.

This is an overview of the steps to create an application with Clarion, but only a few of the ways Clarion will save you time over other development systems.

What is in the package?

The package you receive when you purchase Clarion consists of two major manuals, the *Language Reference* manual, which describes all of the components and syntax descriptions of the Clarion language, and the *Utilities Guide*, which describes the environment and the use of each utility. These two manuals are indispensable for writing Clarion applications.

In addition to these manuals, documentation is also provided to aid in the learning process. The *Getting Started* manual is a step-by-step introduction to using Designer for your first application. This first application is a basic name, address, and phone number list which will illustrate the creation of files, tables, update screens, menus, and reports. The *Annotated Examples* manual provides several sample programs of increasing complexity. The program listings include commentary on how they work. The sample programs are also provided in source form on the software distribution disk, and can be compiled and run.

Clarion also gives you a function key template for your keyboard. You can use this to overlay descriptions of how the function keys are used, while creating applications.

How to get started with Clarion

If you are new to the Clarion Professional Developer, the best way to get started is to follow these steps:

1. Perform the installation procedure if you have not already done so. Step-by-step instructions are given in the *Getting Started* manual. The full installation process will require approximately 3½

megabytes of hard-disk space. It will save time if you verify that you have enough room on your disk before you begin. Invoke the installation procedure by placing the first distribution disk in your diskette drive, and type A:INSTALL from a DOS command line.

Pay careful attention to the READ.ME file that is automatically displayed. The READ.ME file contains up-to-date information about the utilities, language statements, and their use. I strongly recommended that you print a copy of this file for future reference. If you cannot make a hard copy of the file, read it carefully to remember what topics are discussed in it in case you need to refer to it later.

The installation procedure will create a directory on your hard disk in which to put the various Clarion files. Unless you specify a different name, it will create the \CLARION directory. In general, it is a good idea to stay with default values unless you know your way around both Clarion and your disk. Under the \CLARION directory, the procedure will create the \CLARION\EXAMPLE directory, where it will put all the example programs and application files referenced by the documentation. This book assumes that Clarion is installed in the default \CLARION directory.

The installation procedure will also ask you to change your AUTOEXEC.BAT and CONFIG.SYS files, which are used by DOS to configure resources for your machine when it starts up. If you are already familiar with these files as well as the BUFFER and FILE statements used by DOS, you can change the parameters. If you are not familiar with these files or statements, just take the defaults for now.

2. After (or during) installation, scan through the various manuals just to get an idea of where things are located. Also, make sure you fill out and mail the registration card. This card ensures that you are eligible for support services, and that you will receive any publications, announcements, or notices from Clarion Software.

3. Go through the tutorial provided with the package. There is a lot of information provided in this tutorial, and it will give you a good idea about how to use the utilities and the language. Note that this tutorial is longer than the one available as a "demo" diskette, and contains much more information about the language. To run it, change your default directory to \CLARION, and type TUTOR CLARION from DOS.

4. Complete the example Designer application described in the *Getting Started* manual. This will give you step-by-step instructions for creating a simple application with Designer. It also shows you how to compile and run completed programs. Once you have com-

pleted the example, experiment. Change the application by modifying screens, reports, adding more files, etc.

5. Compile and execute the programs in the *Annotated Example* manual. These programs are already provided for you on your disk. As you run each example program, follow along with the manual to see what effect the language statements have on the execution of the program. Use the *Language Reference* manual for a description of the effect of any particular statement. Once you have an understanding of how each program works, try experimenting by changing or adding your own features.

6. Create your own application with Designer, adding special procedures, as needed, to begin using the language.

2
CHAPTER

Exploring
the environment

This chapter will provide you with a fast overview of the Clarion environment, a description of how the different parts of the environment are used
to create application programs, and a description of each utility program
that makes up the environment. Before going into the details of any one
part of Clarion, however, I think a quick tour of the whole environment
will give you a feel for how Clarion can be used to create application
programs.

The Clarion menu system

As described earlier, The Clarion Professional Developer is a collection of
utilities. Each one of these utilities can be run from a DOS command line.
For instance, you can invoke the Editor from a DOS prompt by typing
CEDT. Using the utilities from DOS is covered in the Clarion *Utilities
Guide*.

Using the utilities from the DOS prompt is the traditional approach to invoking the Editor or Designer, Compiler, and Processor utilities separately to develop your programs. However, Clarion also provides a menu system that not only allows you to choose a utility with one of several methods, but also provides other features that makes program development as smooth as possible.

To invoke the Clarion Main Menu, simply type CLARION at a DOS command line. The menu will then appear as shown in Fig. 2-1. If you have successfully completed the installation procedure, the \Clarion directory should be specified in your path statement, which means Clarion can be invoked from any directory. CLARION.COM is the filename for the program that runs and displays the Clarion Main Menu. You can now select any utility by one of three methods:

- Use the arrow keys to move the highlighted selector bar to the name of the utility you wish to use, and press the Enter key.
- Press the corresponding key for the first letter of the name of the utility you want to invoke, and the selector bar will move to that utility. You can then press Enter to invoke it. For utilities that have the same first letter, the first time you press the key, one of the utilities will be selected. The second time you press the key, another utility with the same first letter will be selected. You can continue to select the letter until the utility is selected, and then press Enter.

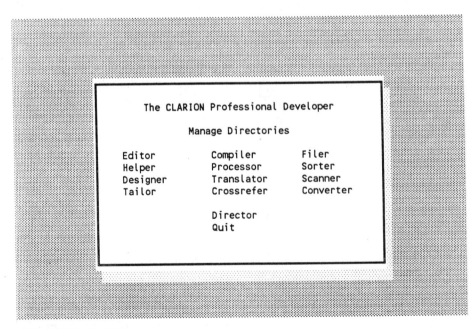

2-1. Clarion Main Menu

- There are several function keys that have been assigned to invoke the most often-used utilities with a single keystroke. These are shown in Table 2-1. For instance, while in the Main Menu, simply pressing the F5 function key will invoke the Editor.

Table 2-1. Function keys for the Clarion environment

Key	Function
F1	Context Sensitive Help
F2	Clarion Main Menu
F3	Designer*
F4	Helper*
F5	Editor*
F6	Compiler*
F7	Compiler and Processor*
F8	Processor*
F9	Translator*
F10	Director

*Utilities that automatically use the selected file

One function key, F1, has been assigned to provide immediate, context-sensitive help screens to give you information about using Clarion anywhere within the environment. *Context-sensitive* means that you will get help that is relative to what you were doing when F1 is pressed. For instance, pressing F1 while in a menu will give you information about using the menu, while pressing F1 in the Director will give you information about the Director, and so on.

It is interesting to note that all the help techniques and features you see while using Clarion can also be used in the programs you write with Clarion. This is a result of the Helper utility, which you can use to create your own help screens. Helper, in fact, was used to create the Clarion's help screens. It is worthwhile to use the F1 key not only to get help on how to use Clarion, but also to see what is possible with the Helper utility.

Automatic file selection

One of the most important features of the Clarion menu system is its ability to remember what files you are working with. Suppose you select the Editor, edit a file, exit the Editor, exit Clarion, and turn off your computer. The next time you invoke Clarion and select the Editor, it will have the name of the file you last edited already specified for you. When a utility remembers the last file you used in this way, it is said to be *selected*.

Designer will also remember the application name, the data file utilities will remember the last data filename you used, and so on. It is the Clarion menu system that provides this feature; running a utility from DOS will not provide the ability to use selected filenames. Many utilities can also predict the name of files that will be used. For instance, if you compile a source program with the compiler, it will automatically pass the name of the program to run to the processor, so that you don't need to specify a filename that Clarion already knows.

Default parameter selection

Another feature of the Clarion menu system is its ability to remember many of the default parameters used throughout the environment. These parameters are provided when they are not specified, but required. This allows you to specify a particular parameter once, and from then on the menu will provide these parameters to whatever utility needs them.

The default parameters are set with the Tailor utility, which you select from the Clarion Main Menu. Selecting this utility will display a screen as shown in Fig. 2-2.

```
                    The CLARION Tailor

    Change Colors      :No      Yes   No     Default
    Window Shadows     :Yes     Yes   No
    Set Keyboard Locks:Yes      Yes   No
    Error Beep         :Yes     Yes   No
    Enhanced Keyboard :No       Yes   No
    Video Timeout Mins: 10

    Compiler Listings :No       Yes   No
      Lines on Page    :58
      Control Before   :
      Control After    :
    Conditional Stream:No       Yes   No

    Statement Column  :14
      Column Indention: 2
    Keyword Case      :UPPER    Caps  UPPER  lower
    Non-Keyword Case:UPPER      Caps  UPPER  lower  As is
    Translate Tracks:No         Yes   No
```

2-2.   Tailor's options window

The video timeout feature, for instance, lets you control how long a Clarion utility screen will remain visible without any keyboard activity. This is done to prevent "phosphor burn" on your monitor. If you want the utilities to remain on the screen indefinitely, simply set this parameter to zero. A description of each parameter is given by pressing F1 while in the Tailor utility. A more complete description is given in the *Utilities Guide* that accompanies the product documentation.

Remember that setting these parameters only affects the environment while you are developing your programs; they have nothing to do with how the programs you create will run. They are provided to make your programming effort more convenient.

When a utility is invoked from the Main Menu, it normally displays a "base page" screen. This screen is where you tell the utility which files to operate with and any other parameters that might be needed. The Clarion Main Menu allows an even faster way to invoke each utility by using "selected" filenames and bypassing the base page screen.

Function speed keys

This fast method is accomplished by using "shifted" function keys. For instance, while on the Main Menu, press Shift–F5 (hold down the Shift key and strike the F5 key). This will invoke the Editor, use the last selected source filename for the input file, and accept the defaults for the rest of the base page. What you will see is simply the last file you edited, ready for new Editor commands.

This simple keystroke access to utilities is provided for the most common operations used during program development. An example of this occurs when you are finished editing a file. Normally, you would exit the Editor, select the Compiler from the Main Menu, fill out the Compiler base page, and compile your program. The same operation can be accomplished by pressing Shift–F6 while still in the Editor. The next thing you will see is your program being compiled!

All the utilities that can be invoked with "shifted" function keys are marked in Table 2-1 with an asterisk. One of these shifted function keys, Shift–F7, merits further description.

In Chapter 1, the steps in program development were described as edit, compile, and run. The Shift–F7 key is all you need to use to step through this entire cycle. For example, when you have finished a session with Designer, you can simply type Shift–F7 and Designer will then generate your source files, invoke the compiler, compile your source, and run your program with the processor.

If you have just finished editing your program with the Editor, Shift–

F7 will invoke the compiler. If there are no errors from the compiler, the processor will then execute your program. If there are errors, however, the compiler will display them and ask you if you want to correct them. If you select yes, you will be sent to the Editor, the cursor will be placed on the line that caused the error, the error message will be displayed, and an arrow will point to the part of the line that caused the error.

Specifying files

Most of the utilities in Clarion ask you to specify filenames on their base page. There are several ways you can do this. If the file you want to use is already displayed, you can simply press the Enter key. If you want to clear the field to specify a different filename, press Ctrl–End and the field will be erased from the current cursor position. If the cursor is not already at the beginning of the line, Ctrl–Home will place it there.

You can now type the filename (up to eight characters) that you wish to use. When you press Enter, the default file extension, along with the current drive and full directory path, will be added to your filename. The complete string of drive, directory path, name, and extension is referred to as a *file specification*.

You can also type an asterisk on an empty field of the base page, press Enter, and you will see a scrolling list of available filenames in the current directory. At this point, you can use the arrow keys to point to the file you want and press Enter to select it. You can also select another directory in order to select files not in the current directory.

I will now give you a brief tour of each Clarion utility. More details about each utility can be found in the Clarion *Utilities Guide*.

Designer
a model of a program

As described in Chapter 1, with the Designer utility you can create the source code for a complete application program. While this utility does not provide the same flexibility as a programming language, it also does not require much specialized knowledge about programming, and can be used to create simple programs very quickly.

You create Designer programs by describing three basic things about your application: the data you want to use, the kinds of operations you want to perform on the data, and the appearance of the screens and reports you want to produce. Designer will then generate your source files, which can be compiled and executed to create a running program.

After you have been introduced to some basic terms and concepts, you will learn how to use Designer in Chapter 4. For now, however, I will discuss what you can do with Designer and a little of how Designer works.

Designer is a source code generator that can be used in several ways. Designer stores all the information you provide about your application — the screen, report, file, and procedure layouts — in a single file, called the application file. This file uses a default extension of .APP. To create a new application, tell Designer the name of this file and enter all your layouts. If you quit Designer, you can come back later and modify or further develop your application by simply naming your application file again.

Designer generates source files from a model file, or template, that determines how your screen, report, and file layouts will be used in a program.

When you invoke Designer from the Main Menu, it displays its base page window, as shown in Fig. 2-3. Here you enter the name of your application, which model file you wish to use, the name of the help file where you will store your help screens, and the name of the procedure that will be called when your program is run.

```
┌────────────────────────────────────────────────┐
│            The CLARION Designer                 │
│                                                 │
│   Application    :C:\BOOK\BOOK.APP              │
│   Model File     :C:\CLARION\STANDARD.MDL       │
│   Help File      :BOOK.HLP                      │
│   Base Procedure:START                          │
│                                                 │
└────────────────────────────────────────────────┘
```

2-3. Designer's base page

As with all Clarion utilities that are invoked from the Main Menu, the name of the last file you were working with will be in the application name field. Once the name of the application has been entered, the rest of the fields will also default to the last ones you used. You can also press Ctrl–Enter on any field to accept the rest of the screen as it is displayed.

When you quit making changes to your application and exit Designer, you will be asked if you want to generate the source for your application. If yes is selected, Designer will then save the changes to the application file, and open the model file which was named on the base page. It will then merge these two files to produce the source files.

The model file determines how most of the source statements will be created. Two different model files are provided with the package, STANDARD.MDL and NETWORK.MDL. The STANDARD.MDL file produces programs that are designed to run on stand-alone systems, or ones that do not have their data files shared on a network. The NETWORK.MDL model file produces programs that have the appropriate source statements to allow the program to share data files on a network.

Note that to change a program already created with Designer so that it will run on a network, you only have to specify the NETWORK.MDL file as your model, and Designer will then generate the same application, but will allow your data files to be shared with other programs on a network.

Although programs generated with the network model will also run on a single user system, there is a disadvantage to doing so. Programs generated for networks must allow for file sharing, which causes slower performance than single-user programs.

You can also easily include Clarion source files written with the Editor in your application. Thus, things outside of the range of Designer's capabilities can also be included in Designer-created programs.

One further point — because the model file is written in Clarion, once you become familiar with the language you can also change the way Designer generates code. You do this by creating your own model files. This topic will be covered in Chapter 12.

Editor
power under the hood

The Editor is a general-purpose text editor, and contains many of the features found in other commercial quality editors: the ability to edit two files at once, character and line modes for manipulating text, assignable macro keys, and automatic column insert, to name just a few.

However, the Editor also has several features that are unique to Clarion. The most important Clarion-specific features are a built-in screen formatter and a report formatter. The Editor can also communicate with the Compiler about compilation errors that might have occurred in this file. These are important features, and represent a major difference from traditional editors. Even though you use the Editor to write in a procedural language by typing in statements, the Editor still has the higher-level screen design and report design formatters that generate the tedious row, column, and field placement statements for you.

The Editor's base page is shown in Fig. 2-4. The first field is the input filename, or the name of the source file you wish to edit, and the second field is the output filename, or the name of your saved file when you are finished. The output filename defaults to the name of the input filename.

If you enter a filename that doesn't exist, the message ''File will be created'' is displayed, telling you that you will be working with a new (empty) file.

The last field on the base page lets you enter the name of the edit file. The edit file stores all the options and default settings that you might need along with all the keyboard macro definitions. The default filename

```
┌─────────────────────────────────────────────────────────┐
│                   The CLARION Editor                     │
│                                                          │
│   Input File :C:\BOOK\BOOK.CLA                           │
│   Output File:C:\BOOK\BOOK.CLA                           │
│   Edit File  :C:\CLARION\CLA.EDT                         │
│                                                          │
└─────────────────────────────────────────────────────────┘
```

2-4. Editor's base page

is the same as the input file, with the default extension of .EDT. This allows you to use an edit file for any type of file you edit.

The files CEDT.EDT and CLA.EDT are provided with keyboard macros for many of the common operations used in Clarion. It is well worth your time to become familiar with them. Consider the following example:

After completing the base page on a new file, you see an empty file screen. This screen shows a ruler at both the beginning and end of the file. If you press Alt−P (all macros use the Alt key to invoke them), the specified macro will get a starter file and place it in your file. This provides you with the shell of a Clarion program, all with one keystroke.

The Editor's control keys are shown in Fig. 2-5. These keys provide very useful functions, such as moving, copying, and deleting blocks of text from the file. They also provide many of the same functions that are included in Designer and Helper.

```
┌─────────────────────────────────────────────────────────────────┐
│                      Editor Control Keys                         │
├─────────────────────────────────────┬───────────────────────────┤
│ ^B  toggle Block mode LIN/CHR        │ ^N  go to Next search string │
│ ^C  Copy block                       │ ^O  set editing Options      │
│ ^D  Delete block                     │ ^P  Put block to a file      │
│ ^E  jump to compiler Error           │ ^Q  Quit edit session        │
│ ^F  Format screen or report          │ ^R  toggle Ruler lines       │
│ ^G  Get a copy of another file       │ ^S  set Search/replace string │
│ ^I  toggle Indention mode            │ ^T  Track mode               │
│ ^J  Jump to a string or line #       │ ^U  Undelete last deletion   │
│ ^K  create Keyboard macros           │ ^W  get/toggle Worksheet     │
│ ^L  List block to printer            │ ^X  eXecute a DOS command    │
│ ^M  Move block                       │ ^Z  toggle Zone insert mode  │
├─────────────────────────────────────┴───────────────────────────┤
│              ^ means pressed with Ctrl key                       │
├──────────────────────────────────────────────────────────────────┤
│      Press Enter for more help or Esc to return to Editor        │
└──────────────────────────────────────────────────────────────────┘
```

2-5. Editor's control keys

Helper
just a keystroke away

The Helper utility is provided to let you create context-sensitive, on-line help windows for your application. You do this by naming each window, and simply drawing the windows exactly like you want them. It has several useful features that should be noted:

- Help windows are stored in a separate file, but can be retrieved very quickly. They can be developed and modified independently from the rest of the program.
- Help windows can be chained together, allowing the user to select window after window until the needed information is given. Help windows can also present menus that allow the user to select the next desired window.
- When help windows are displayed, they can be made to float, or be positioned at run-time so that the area of the screen requiring explanation will not be covered by the help window. They can also be fixed on the screen.
- Areas of the help window can be made transparent, so that the underlying data on the screen shows through. This allows you to draw arrows that point to different fields, or let "live" data from the screen show through.
- This utility can be invoked from the Processor, so that you can design or change your help screens while your program runs. This lets you see the background screens you are providing help for while you create them—a very useful feature. See the discussion of the Processor later in this chapter.

The Helper's base page is shown in Fig. 2-6. The first field asks for the name of the help file in which to store the help screens. If you name a file that doesn't exist, you will see the message "Help file will be created," and you can then begin a new file.

The next field asks you for the name (or Help ID) of the window you want to design. A Help ID can be eight characters long, and is used to identify a particular window in this file.

The next field asks you if you want the window chained to another window. In your application, if the user presses F1 on a field that has declared a Help ID, that window will be displayed. If there is a chained window named, the user can press the Enter or Pg Dn (page down) key to display it, and so on. The user must always press the Esc key to return to the application. In this way, you can chain a long series of explanatory text windows, allowing the user to display as much help data as he wants.

```
                    The CLARION Helper

    Help file :C:\BOOK\BOOK.HLP

    Window      :MAINMENU

    Chained to:

    Position :Float        Float  Fix

    Attribute :White On Black
```

2-6. Helper's base page

The next field on the Helper's base page lets you select whether the window will be fixed on the screen, or if its position will be determined when the screen is displayed. If the help window is small, you might want to let it float so that the field you are supplying help for will not be covered when the window is displayed.

If you are using transparent painting to let the data underneath the window show through, you will want to fix this window at a particular place on the screen.

The next field is completed to determine the default foreground and background colors of the help window. The combination of foreground and background colors is called the base attribute, and is selected by pointing to the color combination in the color selection window, shown in Fig. 2-7.

2-7.   The color selection window

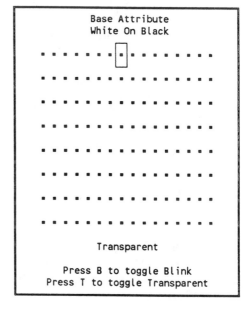

The selected base attribute can always be painted over with a different color; the base attribute you select here is simply the default colors that will be used if no other color is later specified.

Once the base window has been completed, you enter Helper's worksheet screen. Once in this screen, you can size the window, type in text, draw line characters (tracking), or paint new color combinations.

Moving the cursor around is done with the cursor position keys. You can always get a list of these keys while in Helper by pressing F1. Use these keys to indicate where characters are typed, where an item like track characters or menu items are placed, or the starting position of a block of the screen.

The control keys are used to start the main operations on the help window. They are shown in Fig. 2-8. These keys are best learned by trying each of them on a "scratch" screen. A full description of each key is provided in the *Utilities Guide*.

```
                            Control Keys

  ^A    change the Attribute at the cursor
  ^B    Browse through menu items in the current help window
  ^C    Copy a block to another location (^C again for multiple copies)
  ^D    Delete a block from the window
  ^F    Flush (erase) a window from the help file
  ^G    Get a copy of another window
  ^I    call the Item menu window to define the choices in a menu
  ^L    List this window to the printer
  ^M    Move a block to another location
  ^O    call the Options window
  ^P    Paint an area of the screen (^V to alter paint video attributes)
  ^Q    Quit and abort from Helper's worksheet
  ^R    toggle the Ruler lines on or off
  ^S    Set indention to column number where the cursor is
  ^T    Track mode (^T to alter parameters, ^V to alter video attributes)
  ^V    Video attributes window to change keyin, track and paint attributes
  ^W    change Window dimensions
  ^X    eXecute DOS command
                    ^ means pressed with Ctrl key
            Press Enter for the help menu or Esc to return to Helper
```

2-8. Helper's control keys

Compiler
the source of it all

The Compiler takes Clarion language source files, produced either with the Editor or Designer, and compiles these statements into very compact modules. These output files have the extension of .PRO, because they are executed by the Processor.

While the compiler is reading your source programs, it also does extensive checking to see if your language statements "make sense," or could cause an error. If errors exist, you will be given error messages from the compiler explaining why there is a problem. If the program is generated by Designer and you haven't included any of your own statements, you can expect your source files to be free from errors.

The Compiler's base page is shown in Fig. 2-9. The first line asks you for the name of the source file you want to compile. As described before, this will usually be completed in advance with the selected file and uses .CLA for a default file extension. The Compiler will then ask you if you would like a listing file produced for this source file.

```
                    The CLARION Compiler

        Source File:C:\BOOK\BOOK.CLA
        Listing    :No          Yes  No
```

2-9. Compiler's base page

A *listing file* is a complete copy of your program, including formatting, line numbers, and code levels. *Code levels* are numbers that indicate how deeply "nested" your code has become. This will be explained further in Part 2 of this book and is an important feature of the listing.

Once you've specified the source filename and the listing status, the compiler will then compile your program. It will produce the program file for the processor (.PRO), a file with program symbol names (.SYM), and a listing file if you've asked for one (.LST). Also, if you have any errors, a scrolling window will appear that displays the errors. Errors are written to an error file (.ERR) in a special format for the Editor to use.

If you are compiling the main part of your program (the source file with the PROGRAM statement) and you have other source files that are part of your program, you will be asked if you want to *Stream Compile* the rest of your source files for this program. This lets you recompile your entire program while letting the Compiler find all the source files that your program needs.

What if only some of the source files need to be compiled? You will also be asked if you want the compilation to be conditional. If yes, the Compiler will determine if each of the source files needs compilation. if no, all of the source files for the program will be compiled. A complete description of the method the Compiler uses to determine this need is given in the *Utilities Guide*. A good rule of thumb is "when in doubt, compile it."

Processor
bugs? let me at them

The Clarion Processor directly executes the output of the Compiler. The Processor has two separate forms, one that is used for development, and one that can be distributed to the end user of your programs. The Processor accessed from the Clarion menu is the developmental version and has several features that are highly useful; its DOS name is CPRO.EXE. The DOS name of the other runtime version of the Processor is CRUN.EXE.

When you invoke CPRO from the Main Menu, the Processor's base page simply asks you for the name of the program you wish to run. This is usually already filled out with the name of the last selected .PRO file. Pressing Enter on this completed field causes your program to be loaded into memory and executed. All the .PRO files for this program must be available to the Processor for the program to run.

Once your program is running, the Processor will take whatever actions you have specified in the Clarion language with either the Editor, or with the language statements produced with the Designer. There are several things, however, you can also do with the Processor.

The Processor contains an on-line symbolic debugger. This means that you can look at the value of variables while your program runs, or even change the value of the variables to see how it might affect program execution. Also, you can trace the steps of your program execution, and specify locations where you would like the program to stop.

You can invoke this debugger by one of two methods: you can Press Ctrl–Break while the program is running, or you can place a STOP statement in your program source with the Editor, and then compile and execute your program. When the STOP statement is executed, the debugger window will be displayed.

The Processor's debugger window is shown in Fig. 2-10. The first line of the window gives the reason the window was displayed; if the window was displayed by pressing Ctrl–Break, then that reason will appear on this line. If a STOP statement was the reason, any message from that statement will also appear here.

The Debugger window also shows the procedure name and line number where the program has been stopped, along with the procedure name and line number that called the current procedure. While in this window, you can press Ctrl–S to scroll the source file for the current program,

```
┌──────────────────────────────────────────────────────────────────┐
│                      The CLARION Debugger                          │
│                                                                    │
│ Stopped for:Ctrl-Break                                             │
│ Stopped at :ORDER/PROCESS/264                  (Ctrl-S for source) │
│ Called from:ORDER/ORDER_MENU/142               (Ctrl-F for source) │
│ Memory left:53K                                (Ctrl-X to execute) │
├──────────────────────────────────────────────────────────────────┤
│ Trace   :Off                       Off   Step  Display    Dump     │
│ Jump to :   0                      (225  thru 513)                 │
│ Break at:                                                          │
├──────────────────────────────────────────────────────────────────┤
│ Variables                                                          │
│ CUS:NAME             =John Jones                                   │
│ CUS:ADDRESS          =123 Pine St.                                 │
│ CUS:ZIP              =33333                                         │
│                      =                                             │
│                      =                                             │
│                      =                                             │
│                                                                    │
│        Press Ctrl-Enter to resume or Ctrl-Break to exit            │
│        Press Ctrl-P to peek then any key to debug                  │
└──────────────────────────────────────────────────────────────────┘
```

2-10. Processor's debugger window

starting at the line where the program was stopped. Pressing Ctrl−F will scroll the source file that the current procedure was called from. The source files must be available to the Processor in order for Ctrl−S or Ctrl−F to display them.

The Trace function causes the debugger to display all the program "jumps," so that you can follow the exact execution of your program statements. You can also directly "jump to" a particular line number, or specify a new line number to stop via the active debugger window.

The lower portion of the screen allows you to specify up to six different variables used by your program. As soon as you name these variables (remember, you can use Ctrl−S or Ctrl−F to look up their names in the source file) their current values are displayed on the screen. You can change the values of these variables, and continue program execution.

While in the debugger window, you can press Ctrl−U, which displays much more information about the machine environment, status of the current window, current directory path, and other information that might be helpful in debugging programs. You can also press Ctrl−F for a scrolling display of all filenames you have opened from your program, and whether they have been opened normally or shared.

The debugger window offers some powerful methods to determine exactly why your program is behaving in a particular way. If you suspect some procedure or function is not working correctly, you can place breakpoints right after the procedure to determine which variables are not correct. You can also use the STOP statement to display the ERROR() function in order to determine if there are any errors in your program.

Because the debugger references locations in your program by line numbers, it is useful to have a listing of your program beside you while debugging.

There is one other major feature about the Clarion Processor—its ability to design help screens while your program is in operation. Most of the Helper utility has been included with CPRO so that not only can you display help windows you have defined, but you can change them as well.

In the Editor (using the HELP statement) or in the Designer, you must specify the name of a help file in order to store your help screens. You can also specify the names of particular help screens (Help IDs) throughout your program. Then, anytime your program is running and asks you for keyboard input, you can press F1. You will see either a help screen that you have already created with Helper, or you will see the message "No help is available." At this time, you can press Shift–F1, which will load the help design overlay of CPRO, and allow you to change or create this help window. The same key commands available in Helper are now available to you to create your help windows.

The advantage of creating your help screens while the program is running is that you usually have a much better idea of what the help screen should say if you know exactly what the program is doing when it is displayed. You can also make some of the help screen transparent, so that the underlying screen shows through. This allows you to draw arrows or point at "live" data on the screen.

Because CRUN does not have the debugger or help design features with it, it is much smaller. Also, CRUN is one of the utilities that is provided for distribution without royalties or license fees.

Translator
easy linking

The Translator utility takes the output of the Compiler and creates all the files necessary to invoke a linker utility (not supplied in the Clarion package). The linker will then create a stand-alone version of your program (an .EXE file) that you can run under DOS without the Processor. The base page for the Translator is shown in Fig. 2-11.

The first file name Translator asks for is the name of the program. After specifying this, it will ask you what kind of *automatic response file* (.ARF) to create. This file provides the linker with all the filenames and directions needed to create the .EXE file, and is specific to the type of linker you will use. You can select Link (the most common linking program, often supplied with DOS), Plink 86, or none at all. Other linkers, compatible with the DOS linker, can be used by selecting Link.

```
┌─────────────────────────────────────────────────────────────┐
│                    The CLARION Translator                    │
│                                                              │
│                                                              │
│   Program      :C:\BOOK\BOOK.PRO                             │
│                                                              │
│                                                              │
│   Create ARF  :No          Link  Plink86  No                │
│   ARF Filename:C:\BOOK\BOOK.ARF                             │
│   ARF Switches:                                             │
│                                                              │
│   Run Linker  :No          Yes  No                          │
│   Linker Name :C:\DOS\LINK.EXE                              │
│                                                              │
│   Line Numbers:No          Yes  No                          │
│                                                              │
└─────────────────────────────────────────────────────────────┘
```

2-11. Translator's base page

You will also be asked for the name of the .ARF file, which will default to the program filename with an .ARF extension. After this, you have an opportunity to pass options to the linker, called *switches*. These are parameters that the linker uses to implement various features, specific to a particular linker. Examples of these switches are shown in the *Utilities Guide*. Also, consult your linker reference manual for more information on these options.

You can now select whether you want to invoke the linker, and specify a different name than the supplied default. You can also specify that the linker include line numbers in your .EXE if you want to use a low level symbolic debugger. Including line numbers will make your .EXE larger.

As soon as you complete the base page (remember, you can press Ctrl–Enter to complete the screen with defaults at any time) the Translator will then access all the .PRO and .SYM files for your program, creating object files (.OBJ) for each .PRO file in your program.

If there are any errors, the Translator will display them at this time. If there are no errors, then it will create an .ARF file that names all the newly created .OBJ files and the Clarion library files. The Translator will then invoke your chosen linker. If you get any linker error messages, consult your linker reference manual for more information. After the linker completes, you have a completed program in a self-contained .EXE file.

One last note: if you see a simple, unimaginative screen while your linker is running, don't be alarmed. It's just that some linkers don't seem to be concerned about what the programmer sees. You'll soon be back in the Clarion environment.

Crossrefer
who was that masked variable?

The Crossrefer utility produces a listing of how your program allocates memory and how your program is organized into modules, procedures, and functions. It will list all the global variables, procedures, functions, and modules that are used by your program.

Crossrefer's base page simply asks for the name of your program. Once specified, it will then look for the program's .PRO and .SYM files, along with any other .PRO and .SYM files for all the modules used by your program. It then creates a file, using the name of your program and a .XRF extension.

The Crossrefer report is useful to verify the sizes of data structures and procedures so that you can determine what portions of your program could be reduced in size, or overlaid. One of its most useful features is that it will mark any variables that are not used (referenced) anywhere in the program, and might therefore be removed.

Director
the DOS shell game

The Director utility is a DOS "shell" that enables you to handle files, directories, and DOS commands without leaving the environment. Its screen is shown in Fig. 2-12.

When the Director screen is displayed, the cursor is on the DOS command line, in which you can type any DOS command. The Director also displays the current directory files in one of several ways. You can display the files sorted by name, extension, size, time, or date.

You can also use the up and down arrow keys (or page up and page down keys) to point at a particular file in the directory. Once you have highlighted the file you have in mind, you can perform some operation on it. There are several control keys defined to perform common file operations, like Ctrl-C to copy, Ctrl-T to type the file to the screen, Ctrl-P to print, and so on. All these keys are shown on the Director screen for quick reference. Two of these need some further explanation.

Ctrl-M marks files. When you use the arrow keys to point to a single file and press Ctrl-M, you will notice a mark next to the file appears on the screen. You can then point at other files and mark them as well. If you change your mind, you can press Ctrl-U to unmark a file. Once you have a group of files marked, you can perform operations on them as a group.

```
  7/05/89                   The CLARION Director                    2:22PM

  DOS Command:

  Pattern    :*.*
  Sort by    :Name     As is       Name     Ext    Size    Date·   Time
  Sort Order :
  Show Hidden:No        Yes No  ┌─C:\CLARION────────────────────────────────┐
  DOS Pause  :No        Yes No  │ \..                   (Parent)            │
                                │ \EXAMPLE            (Sub-dir)  6-22-88  1:37p │
  ┌─────────────────────────┐  │ \TUTORIAL           (Sub-dir) 12-09-88  4:12p │
  │  63 Files :  4,678,936  │  │ ALT_KEYS CLA          1,960   2-08-89  2:00a │
  │   0 Marked:          0  │  │ CCMP     EXE        220,241   5-05-89  4:06p │
  │ Capacity  : 31,768,576  │  │ CCMP     HLP          8,545  10-26-88  8:00p │
  │ In Use    : 29,779,968  │  │ CCVT     EXE        125,577   5-12-89  4:36p │
  │ Available :  1,988,608  │  │ CCVT     HLP          6,470   5-24-89  9:37a │
  └─────────────────────────┘  │ CDES     EXE        313,147   5-24-89  9:26a │
  ┌─────────────────────────┐  │ CDES     HLP        169,617   4-17-89  5:16p │
  │ ^Copy        ^Print     │  │ CDIR     EXE         65,127   5-02-89 11:32a │
  │ ^Delete      ^Rename    │  │ CDIR     HLP         10,673  10-26-88  8:00p │
  │ ^Flashback   ^Select    │  │ CDSM     EXE         75,191   5-02-88  2:36p │
  │ ^Go to       ^Type      │  │ CEDT     EDT          4,199  12-06-88 11:15a │
  │ ^List        ^Unmark    │  └────────────────────────────────────────────┘
  │ ^Mark        ^eXecute   │
  └─────────────────────────┘
```

2-12.   Director's screen

Ctrl–C will copy all of them, Ctrl–D will delete all of them, and so on. Once the operation completes, the files are no longer marked.

Another useful key is Ctrl–S. Ctrl–S allows you to make the currently highlighted file the "selected" file. Remember, a selected file will be used as the default filename parameter for a utility. For example, if you are in Director, looking for a particular file to edit, you can use the arrow keys to point the source file, press Ctrl–S to make it the selected file, and then press Shift–F5 to invoke the editor with that file. The next thing you'll see is the file you want to edit.

Filer
goodbye, fudge programs

The Filer utility is used to change a Clarion data file to match a new file definition. It can also be used to create a new, empty Clarion file.

For instance, suppose you have a working application that uses Clarion data files that contain many records. If you need to change the layout of these files, such as adding new fields, changing their data types, adding or changing key definitions, and so on, you would first make these changes to the source file. Changes can be made directly with the Editor, or by changing their definition with Designer and then generating the source.

Now that there is a new source file that indicates your changes, use the Filer to make each data file match the source program. Filer's base page is shown in Fig. 2-13. The first parameter is the name of the source file that has your new file definition.

```
                    The CLARION Filer
              Record layout has not changed
    Source File:C:\CLARION\EXAMPLE\VIDEO1.CLA
    Label     :MOVIES
    Input File :C:\CLARION\EXAMPLE\MOVIES.DAT
    Output File:C:\CLARION\EXAMPLE\MOVIES.DAT

    Get Output Field          From Input Field

        1  CODE                1  CODE
        2  TITLE               2  TITLE
        3  CATEGORY            3  CATEGORY
        4  DATE_ADDED          4  DATE_ADDED
        5  LAST_RENTAL         5  LAST_RENTAL
        6  TOTALS              6  TOTALS
        7  RENTS_MONTH         7  RENTS_MONTH
        8  RENTS_YEAR          8  RENTS_YEAR
        9  RENTS_TOTAL         9  RENTS_TOTAL

        Press Enter to Change Input Field
           Press Ctrl-Enter to Convert
```

2-13. Filer's base page

The second parameter is the label of the FILE statement in your source program. If the code was generated by the Designer, this will also be the name of the file. You don't have to type this parameter—if you press Enter on an empty field, Filer will look through your source file, looking for a file structure. If it finds only one, it will use it. If it finds more than one, it will present you with a scrolling selection list.

The next parameter is the name of the input data file. This will normally be filled out for you by what Filer found as the name of the file declared in the source. The next parameter asks for the name of the output file. This parameter defaults to the same name as the input file.

Once these parameters have been specified, Filer will then display two lists of field names. One list, on the right side of the base page, shows what all the field names are in the input file (the data file you want to convert to the new definition). On the left side of the screen, you will see a list of field names as they appear in the new source file definition (how they will occur in the new data file).

These fields normally match up, unless you have added new fields, or changed field names. If you have added new fields, the name "new field" will occur as the input field name for each new field you've added to the output file. If you've changed many field names, Filer might not have enough information to match input fields with output fields. This window allows you to assign any input field to any output field in order to remove ambiguity.

If you haven't changed any field names, you can just press Ctrl–Enter on this window. Filer will then convert your records and rebuild any keys.

It is very important to remember that if you make *any* change to your file definitions, you must use Filer to convert your files to match your current source definitions. This includes any changes to fields, records, keys, or memos. These file features will be described further in the next chapter.

Filer can be used from a DOS batch file, or run from within a Clarion program. If you supply all the parameters it needs, using the /V switch will cause it to run without the base page or any message appearing on the screen. Filer can be distributed with your application so that you can write and distribute Clarion programs to support data file conversion.

Sorter
data, any way you want it

The Sorter utility sorts the records of Clarion data files in a particular order. On Sorter's base page, shown in Fig. 2-14, you specify all of the parameters Sorter needs to complete its operation, including the name of the input file and the output file.

```
                     The CLARION Sorter

  Input            :C:\CLARION\EXAMPLE\MOVIES.DAT
  Output           :C:\CLARION\EXAMPLE\MOVIES.DAT

  Sort Key         :MOV:CODE

  Compress File    :No          Yes  No
  Retain Deletions:No           Yes  No
  Remove Key Files:No           Yes  No
```

2-14. Sorter's base page

If the named output file already exists, a temporary file will be created to hold the incomplete data that will become the new file. After the temporary file is complete, the output file is deleted and the temporary file is renamed to the output filename. This is done to ensure that the original file will always be available should a power failure occur during the sort operation.

The next parameter asks you to specify the sort sequence to be used. If no parameter is specified, no sorting will occur. In this field, you can type a series of field names used in the data file, separated by '+' or '−' characters. The '+' character (the default) indicates that the following field will be sorted in ascending sequence, and a '−' character indicates descending sequence. For instance, the sort parameter

FIL:DEPT-FIL:SALARY

will sort the records first by ascending alphabetical order of department name (FIL:DEPT is the name of the field and the + was defaulted). Then, if any records have the same department name, those records will be sorted by salary in descending order (highest to lowest).

If you don't remember any of the field names used in the file, you can simply type a + or − character where you want the field name, and a scrolling list of field names will appear for your selection.

The next field asks you if you want the output file to be compressed. A compressed data file is one that has all the records compressed and has no key files with it. This allows you to put the compressed data file (and memo file, if any) on a backup or distribution media without any keys files. A compressed file requires considerably less disk space.

A compressed file can be read only by Sorter. If you specify a compressed file as the input file, Sorter will automatically decompress the input records, perform any sort operations, and rebuild any key files.

The next field asks you if you want to retain deleted records. To answer this question, you must first understand a little about the layout of Clarion data files. Data in Clarion files is stored in fixed length records. As your programs adds new records to the file, the file grows in size. However, as you delete records from the file, they remain in the file until they are removed. There are two ways to remove these records—under program control (see the PACK statement) or by using Sorter. More information about Clarion data files will be presented in the next chapter.

If you select no (the default) to retain deleted records, the Sorter will process the input file and leave any deleted records out of the output file. Normally, you will want to remove these deleted records to recover disk space for your files. Alternatively, you can write programs that make use of the fact that some records are deleted, and you might wish to retain them for that reason.

The last parameter that Sorter uses is the Remove Key Files option. If you sort a data file to be used for a report or other special processing, you might not need any other key files with it. You could then make a new data file by specifying a new output filename to Sorter, sort the records with your sort parameter, and select yes for the Remove Key Files option. Normally, however, you will select no for this option (the default).

A very useful feature of the Sorter is its ability to be called from another Clarion program. By using the /V switch to turn off the video, you can run the Sorter without any base page or message appearing on the screen. Because Sorter is one of the utilities that have no license fee requirements, you are free to distribute it with your application.

Scanner
what's in those files, anyway?

The Clarion Scanner utility lets you look at the contents of files. Scanner's base page is shown in Fig. 2-15. The first parameter it requires is the name of the file you want to see.

```
                    The CLARION Scanner

  Input File:C:\CLARION\EXAMPLE\MOVIES.DAT
  Sequence  :CODE_KEY
  ──────────────────┤Press Enter to scan file├──────────────
  Active Recs  :        24        File Size  :      2,153
  Deleted Recs :         0        Change Date:    2/26/88
  Record Length:        75        Change Time:     3:17PM


                      FILE,PRE(MOV)
        CODE_KEY          KEY(MOV:CODE)
        RECORD            RECORD
        CODE                LONG
        TITLE             STRING(40)
        CATEGORY          STRING(12)
        DATE_ADDED          LONG
        LAST_RENTAL         LONG
```

2-15.   Scanner's base page

The Scanner operates in one of two very different modes. If the file you specify is not a Clarion data file, you will see the message "Entering DOS mode" displayed, and you will then see each byte in the file displayed in a *hex dump* format. This format shows each byte in both hexadecimal and ASCII text forms.

This format also allows you to change any byte anywhere in any file in either text or hexadecimal format. This mode is useful for verifying

Exploring the environment

what data is really in the file. Because any byte in any file on the disk can
be changed, this mode is not recommended for use by anyone other than
a programmer.

Scanner is even more interesting when you provide the name of a
Clarion data file. In this mode you will see the data file in a table, or
spreadsheet format—where each record in the file is a row on the
screen, and each field in the file is a column.

After you specify the name of a Clarion data file that has key files
defined for it, Scanner will then ask you for the order that you want to see
the record displayed. In this field, you can specify either any of the keys
that have been defined for the file, or *record order*. Record order is simply
the order that the records appear in the file.

After specifying the order, Scanner will then present some statistics
about the file, and a scrolling list of the statements that make up the file
definition for the file. Note that Scanner doesn't know about the source
file that has the file definition; this definition is displayed from information contained in the file header.

After pressing Enter, you will be taken into a worksheet screen that
displays the records. An example file is shown in Fig. 2-16.

CODE	TITLE	CATEGORY	DATE ADDED
31	THE AMITYVILLE HORROR	HORROR	4/02/86
41	PALE RIDER	WESTERN	4/02/86
51	BATTLESTAR GALACTICA	SCI-FI	4/02/86
61	BLAZING SADDLES	COMEDY	4/02/86
71	BORN FREE	OTHER	4/02/86
81	DAS BOOT	FOREIGN	4/02/86
91	GONE WITH THE WIND	CLASSIC	4/02/86
101	MURDER, ANYONE?	MYSTERY	4/02/86
111	THE MIRROR CRACK'D	MYSTERY	4/02/86
121	LOVE STORY	ROMANCE	4/02/86
131	STAR TREK	SCI-FI	4/02/86
n-4	s40	s12	d1
141	THE RETURN OF THE PINK PANTHER	COMEDY	4/02/86
151	THE TEN COMMANDMENTS	CLASSIC	4/02/86
161	TRUE GRIT	WESTERN	4/02/86
171	THE WIZARD OF OZ	CHILD	4/02/86
181	TOOTSIE	COMEDY	4/02/86
191	THE SPY WHO LOVED ME	ACTION	4/02/86
201	PSYCHO	ROMANCE	4/02/86
211	REWUOTUIORHJKGHKDF	CLASSIC	2/09/88
221	GJIDFSHGHJDFKHGJKHDFJK	CHILD	2/09/88
451	DFSG	ACTION	2/09/88

MOVIES.DAT   Record:13   Status:Active   Order:CODE_KEY

2-16. Scanner's worksheet

Besides the normal scrolling keys of up and down arrows, Page up
and Page down, and Ctrl–Page up and Ctrl–Page down, the Scanner also

lets you locate records by record number (Ctrl−J for jump) and by the contents of a particular field. For instance, if you are looking for a record with "Born Free" in the TITLE field, use the right or left arrow keys to place the highlighted cursor on the TITLE column, and press Ctrl−S for Search. A window will appear that asks you for the search parameter, where you can type "Born Free." It will also ask you if you want to replace that parameter with another and uses the search parameter as a default (no change). After completing this window, Scanner will locate the first record that matches the search parameter for that field.

There are many other functions that the Scanner provides, such as Ctrl−A to add a record, Ctrl−C to change a field, and Ctrl−D to delete a record. F1 shows all these functions and their keystrokes. One important thing to remember about Scanner is that it is a debugging tool. It allows you to determine if records are being added, changed, and deleted after your program runs. It also lets you enter test data into a record to see if your program is handling these cases correctly.

Scanner does not make backup copies of your data! If you want to protect your data, make a copy of it first. Scanner does not make backups automatically in order to ensure that data files can be viewed on a full disk.

Converter
your import/export license

The Converter utility is used to import data files from one of several formats into the Clarion data file format. It will also export a Clarion data file into one of several different formats. The base page for the Converter is shown in Fig. 2-17.

```
              The CLARION Converter

  Input Type    :Clarion    Clarion dBase DIF  BASIC
  Input File    :C:\CLARION\EXAMPLE\MOVIES.DAT


  Output Type   :dBaseIII   dBaseII dBaseIII DIF  BASIC
  Output File   :C:\CLARION\MOVIES.DBF

  Source File   :
```

2-17. Converter's base page

The first parameter Converter asks for is the input type. Select this by using the arrow keys to highlight Clarion, dBASE, DIF, or BASIC file formats. If you select Clarion, you will be converting an existing Clarion data file into one of the other formats. If you select dBASE, DIF, or BASIC, you will be importing a file of one of these formats into a Clarion file.

The next parameter is the input filename. Once you specify this name, the file will be opened. The next parameter is the output type. The choices for this parameter will be limited based on which input type you select. If you select dBase, DIF, or BASIC, your only choice for output file type will be Clarion. If you select Clarion as the input file type, you can choose from dBASEII, DBASEIII, DIF, or BASIC output file types.

The next parameter required is the name of the output file. Because data will be transformed from one format to another, you should not use an output filename that is the same as the input filename.

If you are importing a file into the Clarion format, Converter will also create a source file that has all the Clarion statements in it to define the new Clarion data file. This source file can be included in your program with the Editor (using Ctrl–G), or you can use the data file itself to add its file definition to Designer (using Ctrl–G also).

Conclusion

This completes the brief tour of the Clarion environment and utilities. As you learn the purpose of each utility, it will become one more tool that you can apply to create the best applications you can. Each of the utilities have many features—more than you can learn at one sitting. While using them, especially the Designer or the Editor, if you find yourself thinking "there must be an easier way to do this," there probably is. Simply remind yourself to press the F1 key for help. You will probably find an alternative, which will add to your capabilities.

3
CHAPTER

The anatomy of a Clarion application

This chapter presents basic terms that are necessary to understand whether you should use the Designer or the Editor to create your programs. The building blocks of a Clarion program are defined, as well as the way data is stored, both within a program and on disk.

The parts of a Clarion program

There are many parts of a Clarion application, and also several ways that you can view one. For instance, you could look at an application from the viewpoint of what is seen on disk — source files, processor files, executable files, data files, index files, help files, etc. These are all parts of the application, and you could describe the application in terms of how these files change over time.

You could look at an application from the viewpoint of the user — which keys perform what functions, which screens cause data to be changed or searched, or how reports are printed. This is a result-oriented viewpoint that the programmer must keep in mind while planning and developing the application.

You could also look at an application from a logical viewpoint, seeing each part of the application, its structure, and how one part relates to the others. This is the most common viewpoint a programmer considers while writing the programs that make up an application.

Whether you are going to use the Designer or the Editor to create your programs, you will need to use the logical viewpoint to see how the application is structured in terms of each of its parts. First, however, a few terms must be defined.

Programs, procedures, and modules

Clarion programs can be divided into separate parts called procedures. There are, typically, many procedures that make up a program. However, there must be one procedure that is different from the rest — the one invoked when the program is first run. This procedure is called the *program procedure*. All Clarion programs have one (and only one) program procedure. While the program is running, it can then "call" other procedures, which can also "call" other procedures, and so on. When a procedure is called, the program executes that procedure and then returns to the procedure that called it.

Procedures are kept in source files called modules. Choosing which procedures reside in a given source file is up to you — your application might have twenty procedures that reside in one module, or each procedure might be in its own module. See Fig. 3-1.

In this figure, you can see a program procedure that calls two separate procedures and one function. Each of these can reside in its own source file, or module. As each procedure or function is named in the program, control is transferred to the procedure or function being called. When a RETURN statement is reached, control is transferred back to the program that called it.

Designer has four pre-defined types of procedures that can be selected: the Menu, Table, Form, and Report procedures. The Editor has no pre-defined procedure types, and procedures can be created to perform any task. Also, as mentioned in Chapter 2, Designer also allows you to include procedures created with the Editor. These are called Other procedures and, with them, you can mix the procedures pre-defined by Designer with those you create with the Editor.

Each procedure is divided into two parts: the data section and the

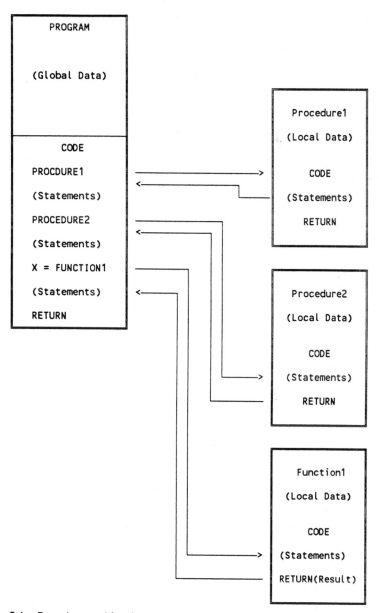

3-1. Procedures and functions

code section. The data section of a procedure is where the data for that procedure is declared, and the code section holds the language statements that manipulate the declared data.

Two more important terms—the data declared in the program procedure (remember, you can have only one program procedure per program) is accessible by all of the procedures and functions used throughout the program, and is called *global data*. Data that is declared in procedures other than the program procedure is only accessible by the procedure or function that declared it, and is called *local data*.

How does Clarion store data?

In either the Editor or Designer, you will need to declare the way the data is stored. Clarion stores data in a variety of ways, but the two main types are character data and numeric data.

Character data is stored in strings, and can include any combination of up to 256 bytes. Strings usually hold alphanumeric data, like names, addresses, part numbers, and so on.

Numeric data is strictly numbers. There are a variety of ways to store numbers in computer memory, and Clarion supports many of them. They are: byte, short, long, decimal, and real.

A byte stores simple integers in the range of zero to 255. Note that no negative numbers or fractions are allowed. Although this might seem limiting, a byte is the smallest single unit of storage in both memory and on disk. It is used to minimize storage requirements.

A short represents integer numbers from −32,768 to 32,767. This is the range of positive and negative numbers that can be represented in the space of two bytes. Although it allows negative numbers, it does not allow fractions.

A long is also an integer number and requires the space of four bytes. It provides for numbers in the range of −2,147,483,648 to 2,147,483,647.

A decimal is a variable length number that can contain decimal places. It is specified by two numbers: the total length of the number, and the number of decimal places. For instance, a decimal data type of 10,2 means that 10 total digits will be accommodated, with 2 of them used as decimal fractions. This format is useful for storing data about money. A decimal of 10,2 would then store 8 places of dollars and two places of cents, or a range of −99,999,999.99 to 99,999,999.99. A decimal of 5,1 would store −9999.9 to 9999.9, and so on.

Each digit for a decimal requires one half of a byte (four bits, sometimes called a nibble.) Also, one nibble is required for the positive or negative sign. Therefore, a 10,2 Decimal requires 6 bytes. Because there is one nibble left over for the sign, this is also the same storage required for a decimal of 11,2.

The maximum size of a decimal data type is 15 digits, or 8 bytes of storage.

A real data type stores double-precision floating point numbers. This number is stored in the Intel 8087 format and requires 8 bytes of storage. It is used to store numbers of a very large range, from $4.19 * 10^{-307}$ to $1.67 * 10^{308}$. This format allows for 15 significant digits.

One nice feature of Clarion is that if you use real numbers in your program and your program runs on a machine with a 8087 (or 80287) numeric processor, the real arithmetic will be much faster. If the processor is not present, the arithmetic will be performed by software routines.

Given these six basic data types to choose from, how do you choose which one to use to store your data? For alphanumeric data, you should always use strings. For numerics, the basic idea is to select the smallest data type that will store the range of numbers your application needs to accommodate. However, if there is any doubt, select the next largest data type so that you will not run into problems later on if the numbers get larger.

If you need to store fractions, you will need to select either the decimal or real data type. Beware of rounding-off problems that can occur with real numbers, however. You don't want a monetary amount to come out to $15.3333333333333! The decimal is a good choice for numbers that represent money.

A summary of each data type, their size, and range is shown in Table 3-1.

Table 3-1. Summary of data types

Name	Size	Use
BYTE	1	Integers from 0 - 255
SHORT	2	Integers from -32,768 to 32,767
LONG	4	Integers from -2,147,483,648 to 2,147,483,647
REAL	8	Floating Point numbers from 4.19 * 10**-307 to 1.67*10 **308
DECIMAL	8 (max)	Numbers with fixed decimal places
STRING	255 (max)	Alphanumeric Data
GROUP	65,534 (max)	Any combination of above.

There is one more very useful data type that allows you to choose several of the above types and combine them into a single new type. This type is called a group, because you can group other data types together. For instance, a group might look like the following:

```
NAME        GROUP
FNAME         STRING (20)
INITIAL       STRING (1)
LNAME         STRING (20)
```

In this group, called NAME, there are other strings declared, called FNAME, INITIAL and LNAME. This grouping allows you to use each part of the name in the program, but also allows you to refer to the NAME group, which includes the whole name.

When a statement consists of several other statements, it is called a *structure*. Groups are similar to structures in other languages, like C or Pascal. Groups and other structures are covered in more detail in Part 2 of this book.

All of these types of declared data will always hold some value. Because the value of any data type can change over time, data type declarations are often referred to as variables.

The data section of a Clarion procedure can also store other types of data structures—those used for screens, reports, memory tables, or data files, for example. In order to use Designer, you must have a good understanding of data files.

Formatting data with pictures

Thus far, you have seen how Clarion stores data. Clarion also offers many ways to display data. These two ideas are very distinct from each other. You can store numeric data in four bytes as a long, for instance, but display it in the form 11/28/89 as a date. In Clarion, you use picture codes to declare how the data will be displayed.

You will be asked for a picture code in either the Designer or the Editor wherever you define data to be displayed on either a screen or report. All picture codes begin with a @ character. These picture codes are divided into string, numeric, scientific, date, time, and free-form categories. You don't have to memorize these codes to use them—whenever Clarion asks you for a picture code, you can always press F1 for a list of all of the codes you might want to use.

String picture codes display alphanumeric data and declare the length of the string to be displayed. Therefore, a picture code of @S10 will display a data type as a string, with a maximum length of 10 characters. Note that the data type to be formatted using this picture code can be of any type—type like a long or real will be converted to a string and displayed.

Numeric picture codes are very powerful for displaying numbers in a variety of ways. You can use them to automatically insert commas or leading zeros, for instance. Consider Tables 3-2 through 3-6.

These tables show the results of values that are displayed using example picture tokens. A date picture code, like @D1, will most likely use a standard date, stored in a long, as the data type to be displayed.

Table 3-2. Numeric picture codes

Picture	Value	Result
@N05	123	00123
@N05	67,321	67321
@N05	342,345	*****
@N_5	123	123
@N_5	67,321	67321
@N_5	342,345	*****
@N6	123	123
@N6	67,321	67,321
@N6	342,345	******
@N8.2	123.45	123.45
@N8.2	9,876.54	9,876.54
@N8.2	17,654.32	********
@N_9.2	9,876.54	9876.54
@N_9.2	17,654.32	17654.32
@N09.2	17,654.32	017654.32
@N09.2	123.45	000123.45
@N_9	0	0 *
@N9B	0	
@N$9.2	2,345.67	$2,345.67
@N$9.2	18,765.43	*********
@N-10.2	-3,123.45	-3,123.45
@N10.2-	-3,123.45	3,123.45-
@N(10.2)	-3,123.45	(3,123.45)
@N(10.2)	-23,456.78	**********

* 'B' as the last character means show blanks when zero.

Table 3-3. Scientific picture codes

Picture	Value	Result
@E9.0	1,967,865	.20e+007
@E12.1	1,967,865	1.9679e+006
@E12.1	-1,967,865	-1.9679e+006
@E12.1	.000000032	3.2000e-008 *
@E12.1B	0	

* 'B' as the last character means show blanks when zero.

Table 3-4.   Date picture codes

Picture	Result	Picture	Result
@D1	3/13/89	@D1.	3.13.89
@D2	3/13/1989	@D2-	3-13-1989 *
@D3	MAR 13,1989	@D1_	3 13 89 *
@D4	March 13, 1989	@D2,	3,13,1989
@D5	13/03/89	@D5.	13.03.89
@D6	13/03/1989	@D6-	13-03-1989 *
@D7	13 MAR 89	@D5_	13 03 89 *
@D8	13 MAR 1989	@D6_	13 03 1989
@D9	89/03/13	@D9.	89.03.13
@D10	1989/03/13	@D9-	89-03-13
@D11	890313		
@D12	19890313		

* These formats cannot be used as an ENTRY picture.

Table 3-5.   Time picture codes

Picture	Result	Picture	Result
@T1	15:12	@T1.	15.12
@T2	1512	@T1_	15 12 *
@T3	3:12PM	@T3`	3`12PM
@T4	15:12:30	@T4-	15-12-30

- produces dashes   ` (grave accent) produces commas
. produces periods   _ (underscore) produces spaces

Table 3-6.   Free-form picture codes

Picture	Value	Result
@P<#/##/##P	20,987	2/09/87
@P<#/##/##P	120,987	12/09/87
@P<#:## AMP	146	1:46 AM
@p<#:## PMp	1,146	11:46 PM
@P###-##-####P	246,732,453	246-73-2453
@P###/###-####P	3,059,417,665	305/941-7665
@P(###)###-####P	9,417,665	(000)941-7665
@P4##A-#P	112	411A-2
@P#' <#"P	511	5' 11"
@P<# lb <# ozP	902	9 lb 2 oz

Likewise, a time picture code, like @T3, will usually require a standard time, also stored in a long, as its data type.

There are two important things to keep in mind while using picture codes. One is that you must allocate enough room for the data to be displayed, or you will see asterisks formatted in place of data. If you ever see a field on a screen or report with asterisks in it, therefore, it is probably because your picture code simply needs to be larger. The other thing to remember is that to display negative values, the picture code must have some type of negative sign indicator, specified either with a leading or trailing negative sign in the picture code, or with parentheses.

Picture codes can save you a lot of work, relative to most traditional programming methods. Take a moment to familiarize yourself with them and you will be able to display data in the most common formats with ease.

Files

Clarion allows you to store data in files on disk, and does so by providing for two types of files—DOS files and Clarion files. A DOS file is simply any file on disk. With DOS files you can read or write any number of bytes anywhere within any file. However, DOS files require you to keep track of where to get at your data, and provide no way of putting that data in a particular order.

For this reason, Designer allows only Clarion files to be defined (DOS files can be used in Other procedures, as mentioned earlier).

Clarion lets you define as many files as you need for your application, as long as you do not have more than 252 files (of any type) open at any one time. This is strictly a DOS limitation—Clarion does not have any architectural limit. You control the maximum number of open files by changing the CONFIG.SYS file, accessed when your system is powered up.

Clarion files provide you with a way to group data in a logically related way. This grouping is called a *record*, and is very similar to the group data structure defined earlier. For instance, consider the following record structure:

```
CUSTOMER      RECORD
NAME          STRING (20)
ADDRESS       STRING (20)
CITY          STRING (15)
STATE         STRING (2)
ZIP           LONG
```

In this structure, you have all of the data about a customer you might want to keep. When you add a new customer, you simply add this entire record to the file. If you were to add up the size of all these fields, you would find the length of this record to be 61 bytes.

The data types declared in this record are also referred to as fields of the record.

If you want to see the data for a particular customer, simply retrieve the record from the file, and all of the fields in that record will contain the data. The format of Clarion files is shown in Fig. 3-2.

The first part of a Clarion file is a variable-length file definition called the *header*. The length of the header depends upon the complexity of the file definition. The header is followed by each fixed length record in the file. Clarion creates these file structures on disk for you and maintains accurate information about your files as you add and revise records. Clarion files can have up to four billion records and 65,000 bytes per record.

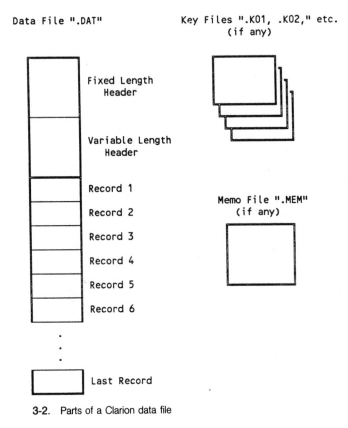

3-2. Parts of a Clarion data file

Keys

Clarion also lets you specify the order in which you want to retrieve the records, called a *key*. It does this by letting you name the fields that determine the order. If you use the Name field as a key, you can then access the customer records in ascending alphabetical order by name. If

Table 3-7. Key File Sizes

Data Type	Length of Key	Key File Size (k bytes) With R Records in File		
		R=100	R=1000	R=10000
CHR	1	1.0	6.5	53
NDX	2	2.0	7.5	62.5
INT	4	2.0	9.5	83.4
FLT	8	2.5	11.5	126
STR,PIC,GRP	1	1.0	6.5	53
	2	2.0	7.5	62.5
	3	2.0	8.5	72.5
	4	2.0	9.5	83.4
	5	2.0	10.5	94
	6	2.5	11.5	106
	7	2.5	12.5	115
	8	2.5	13.5	126
	9	2.5	14.5	136.5
	10	2.5	15.5	148.5
	11	3.0	16.5	158
	12	3.0	18.5	168
	13	3.0	19.5	179.5
	14	3.0	21.0	193.5
	15	3.0	21.5	201
	16	3.5	23.0	218.5
	17	3.5	24.0	228
	18	3.5	25.5	239
	19	3.5	26.5	252
	20	3.5	27.5	264.5
	21-22	4.0	29.0	279.5
	23	4.0	31.0	295.5
	24-25	4.0	32.5	314.5
	26-27	4.5	34.5	335
Data Type	Length of Key	R=100	R=1000	R=10000
	28-29	4.5	37.0	358.5
	30-31	5.0	40.0	386.5
	32-34	5.0	42.5	418.5
	35-37	5.5	46.5	456
	38-41	6.0	51.0	501.5
	42-45	6.0	56.0	556
	46-51	8.0	64.0	627
	52-58	8.5	72.5	716
	59-67	10.0	84.5	835.5
	68-79	11.0	101.0	1002
	80-95	13.5	126.0	1251
	96-120	17.0	167.5	1668.5
	121-162	26.0	250.5	2503
	163-245	50.5	501.0	5003

you use the ZIP field as a key, you can access records in ascending numerical order by ZIP code. Note that the data type for the key determines the order sequence—a string field will be in alphabetical order and a numeric field will be in numeric order.

Keys can also consist of more than one field. If there are any records with duplicate data in the first field, then those records will be ordered by the second key named, and so on. Because a key can consist of several fields, the fields are referred to as *key components*, and the keys are referred to as *composite keys*.

There is a maximum size for a key—245 bytes. However, the larger the size of the key, the more disk operations will be required to access records and maintain the key. Also, the size of the key can dramatically affect the size of the key file. How the size of a key influences the size of a key file is shown in Table 3-7. From this you can see how large the file will be as the key size increases for a given number of records.

You can also define more than one key for each data file. Each key you define creates another file that stores the information necessary to access records in the keyed order. Thus, the maximum number of keys you can have for a particular file is subject to the open file limit of 252, stated earlier. However, there is additional disk activity and space required for each key you create, so it is best to keep the number of keys to a minimum.

Memos

There is one more type of data storage that Clarion provides: the *memo field*. A memo field allows storage of large amounts of text data with each record. This data is stored in a separate file, called the *memo file*. One of the most common uses for a memo field is to provide a comment about a particular record. For instance, you might want to provide a way to store some comments about a customer that you can see whenever that customer's record is retrieved.

You could provide this storage as a group of strings that are part of the record definition, but then that group would take up disk space for each record whether there was any comment for that customer or not. A memo field will only take up disk space if there is any text to be stored for that record. Also, a memo field can be up to 65,000 bytes long.

Text in memo fields is stored in 252-byte blocks. If there is any text in the memo field, it will be stored in increments of 252-byte blocks until there is no more text in the field. After all the text is stored, no disk space is allocated for any blank areas at the end of the memo field. This is true regardless of how large you define the memo field.

Whenever a record is read from the data file, its memo will also be read from the disk. If a record is added to the file, a memo (if there is any text in the memo field) will also be added. Reading a record, changing the memo field, and putting a record back will also update the memo file.

As you have seen, there can be many files on disk to represent a Clarion data file: the data file itself, which holds the records, any key files you might have defined, and any memo file you might need.

Conclusion

You have seen that Clarion programs can be broken up into procedures, and that these procedures can reside in one or more source files, called modules. The program procedure is the procedure that is called when the program is first run. Each procedure can also declare data that is used by the program.

You can declare byte, short, long, decimal, real, or string data types in these procedures, and you can group these together to form new data structures. One type of structure is used to store data on disk—the file structure.

Armed with this basic information, you are now ready to create an application with Designer.

4
CHAPTER

Designer—
ready, set, go!

In this chapter, you will learn how to create a simple working application using Designer, and how to later expand the application.

Before you jump into an application, you should understand the basic components of Designer. All applications that are created with Designer are comprised of five basic building blocks, called procedures. There are four pre-defined types: *Menu*, *Table*, *Form*, and *Report*. A fifth type, the *Other* procedure, is one that Designer doesn't generate, but that you can create with the Editor. Designer allows you to build complex applications by specifying combinations of these procedures.

Menus are used to call other procedures. Menus let the user select from a list to invoke further procedures. Menus can call other menus, tables, reports, or Other procedures.

Tables present a scrolling list of data from records in one or more files. They let the user "browse" through a file to see records in a particular order. The user can select one of these records to call another procedure in order to change or delete the record, or add new records. The procedure type to change records is the Form. Tables can also let the user see and select data from a file, and place this data in the field of another procedure.

   Forms are the procedures that update records in a file. They can add, revise, or delete the record they display. They are called from Tables, and typically have all of the fields in the record displayed and available for the user to change them.

   Reports are the procedures that produce printed reports. They can show some or all of the records in a file, and can also contain fields from records in related files. They can have page headers and footers and contain many different types and formats of data.

   The building blocks used in an example program are shown in Fig. 4-1.

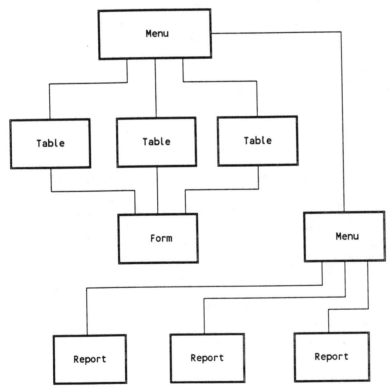

4-1. Example application block diagram

The other major part of Designer is the definition of the files for application data storage. When a file is defined, the definition specifies not only how the data will be stored on disk, but how that data will be formatted and displayed throughout the application.

An example application

Designer can easily create an application to monitor the books of a bookstore. The first thing you need to do is determine what the application needs to do and define what data it will need to store. This program should allow the user to quickly locate any book by subject, title, or author. It should also provide a listing of these books — by subject, title, and author.

For each book, you should store the following information: author, title, subject, type of book, publisher, number of pages, quantity on the shelf, price, and date published. Although there could be other information a particular bookstore might want to store about a book, you should start with this basic information.

Because you are starting a new application; first create a new directory on the disk, using Director. At the DOS command prompt, issue the DOS commands MD \BOOK and Enter, followed by CD \BOOK and Enter to create the BOOK directory and set that to be the default. As you develop the application, this will keep all of the files about this application in the BOOK directory.

Then select the Designer from the main Clarion menu. Designer's base page will then be displayed, and you will need to fill out the base page, as shown in Fig. 4-2. As the base page indicates, you'll name both the application and the help file BOOKS, and select the STANDARD.MDL model file. You should also call the base procedure START.

After completing the base page, you will see the application summary window, shown in Fig. 4-3. Note that it shows START as a procedure (the only one you've named so far), described as "ToDo." This means that it has yet to be defined. You'll define it later.

For now, you should define your data file to store the information about the books. To do this, place the cursor bar on the left hand side of the screen, under the "Files" heading, and press Enter. This column shows all of the files that have been defined for the application so far. Note that there is already a "MEMORY" file defined. This is where memory variables are kept, because Designer lets you perform operations on these variables as if they were a file. These variables are actually global variables that are accessible by all procedures in the application.

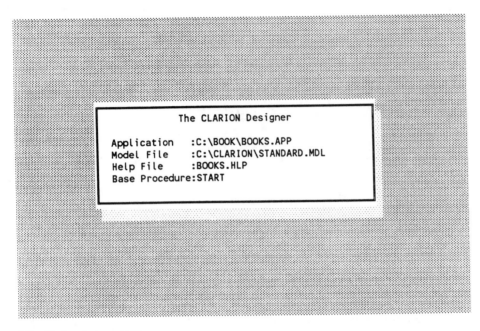

The CLARION Designer

Application   :C:\BOOK\BOOKS.APP
Model File   :C:\CLARION\STANDARD.MDL
Help File   :BOOKS.HLP
Base Procedure:START

4-2.   Designer's base page

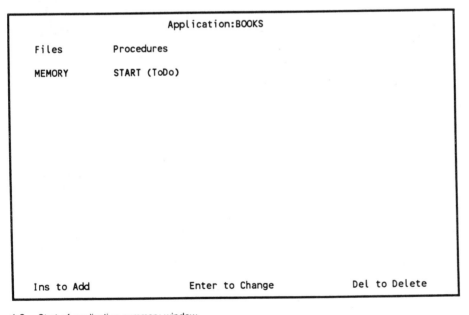

Application:BOOKS

Files   Procedures

MEMORY   START (ToDo)

Ins to Add   Enter to Change   Del to Delete

4-3.   Start of application summary window

File definition

To create a new file, press the Ins (insert) key. You will see the file options window (see Fig. 4-4).

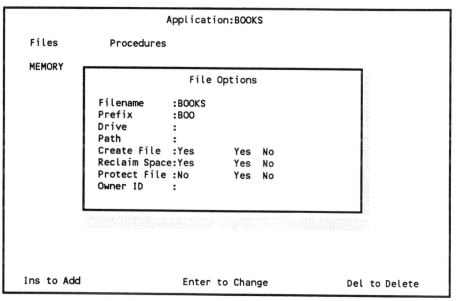

```
                        Application:BOOKS

      Files          Procedures

      MEMORY
                  ┌─────────────────────────────────────────┐
                  │             File Options                 │
                  │                                          │
                  │   Filename    :BOOKS                     │
                  │   Prefix      :BOO                       │
                  │   Drive       :                          │
                  │   Path        :                          │
                  │   Create File :Yes        Yes  No        │
                  │   Reclaim Space:Yes       Yes  No        │
                  │   Protect File :No        Yes  No        │
                  │   Owner ID    :                          │
                  │                                          │
                  └─────────────────────────────────────────┘

   Ins to Add              Enter to Change        Del to Delete
```

4-4.   File options window

File options

This window allows you to specify options about the Clarion data file you are going to create. The first line asks for the name of the data file. You should call this file BOOKS, as well. (Remember, the default extension for this file will be .DAT.)

Designer then asks you for the name of the prefix. The default is the first three characters of the filename, so accept BOO as the prefix. The prefix will cause the names of all of the variables in the file to start with these three characters. For instance, you'll certainly have a Title field in the record of the file. However, there will be many places in the application that will specify a title—the title that appears on a screen, on a report, or in the file. The BOO prefix on the title field will remind you that you are specifying the title field, and not one of the other fields.

The next two prompts, Drive and Path, ask you for the drive (like C:) and directory path in which to look for the file when the application runs. If you leave these blank, the application will look for the file in whatever the default drive and directory are at runtime. Leave these blank.

You will next be asked if you want the application to create the data file. If you answer yes, the application will look for the data file based on the information in the Drive and Path lines. If it finds it, the application will continue. If it doesn't find it, the application will create an empty data file, and then continue. If you answer this no, and the application is unable to find the file, the application will halt with a "File Not Found" error message. Answer this yes.

The next line asks you if you want to reclaim space in the file. When records are deleted in a Clarion file, those deleted records cause "holes" in the files that represent unused space. If you select yes, those deleted records will be reused to hold new records when they are added to reclaim this space. Answer yes to this line.

The next line asks you if you want to protect the file. If you select yes, it means that other Clarion utilities will not be able to modify this file. Select no.

The next line asks you for an owner ID. If you enter in a string here, the file will be encrypted so that the data in the records is unreadable except by this application. It does this by taking the string of characters you specify and uses it as an encryption key. Because the data in this file is not sensitive, leave it blank.

File Summary

After you enter the last line, you should see the file summary window (see Fig. 4-5). In this window, you will define the fields in the record, along with the keys that will allow you to access the records in the order in which you need them.

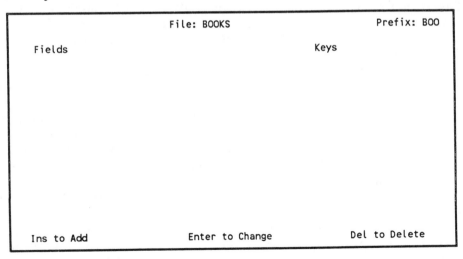

4-5. File summary window

To add the first field, place the cursor bar under the "Fields" column, and press the Ins (insert) key. You will then see the field window (see Fig. 4-6). The first line is the name you will use for this field, and you should call it TITLE. The next line asks you for a description of this field. This is a simple description of the field, up to 30 characters, and it only helps to identify the field during development — it does not affect the application in any way. You can enter Title of book here.

```
                          Field

         Field Name :TITLE
         Description:Title of Book
         Type       :String
         Length     : 30
         Picture    :@s15
         Choices    :
         Dimensioned:
         Type Mode  :AsIs        Ins  Ovr  AsIs
         Required   :No          Yes  No
         Immediate  :No          Yes  No
         Num Lock   :No          Yes  No
         Left Just  :Yes         Yes  No
         Upper Case :No          Yes  No
         Help ID    :'TITLE'
```

4-6. Field window for TITLE

The next line will display a data type selection window, allowing you to select the data type for this field (Data types are described in Chapter 3). Select String here.

Now that you've selected a data type, the rest of the field window is filled out with specifications about your string data. If you had chosen another data type, the field window would be filled out in a different way. For reference, a complete chart of parameters for the different data types is given on page 5-22 of the *Utilities Guide.*

The next line asks you for a length. The length is the size of the string you will define to hold titles in the records on disk. You should make this 30 characters.

The next line asks you for a picture code. This code will be used to display the data elsewhere in your application, like on a screen or report. Note that the length of the displayed data can be different than how it is stored on disk. For strings, the picture code defaults to an @S picture (called a string picture), with the same length specified in the previous line. You can change this, however. If you make this picture an @S15, only 15 of the first 30 characters will be displayed. This is a real advantage because it allows you to put more fields on a report or screen, but still only require the user to enter in (and see) 30 characters. You should use @S15 here.

The next line asks you for Choices. If you want to restrict the string to one of a few types of strings, you can type them in here. You will see an example of this when you define the Type field. For now, leave this line blank.

The line asks you if you want to specify a dimension; this lets you create an array of strings in this field. Although Designer does not allow you to reference dimensioned data in its procedures, you could define them here for use with Other procedures. Dimensioned variables are a little advanced at this point, however, so leave this line blank.

The remaining lines prompt you for information on how data can be entered by the user for this field. You could just press Ctrl–Enter to select the defaults for all these choices, but a description of them is in order.

The Type Mode line asks you to select from Ins, Ovr, or As Is. These modes determine the default way a user will enter data in this string field. If you select Ins, or Insert mode, as the user enters data in this field, any characters present in the field to the right of the cursor will shift to the right, creating room for the typed-in characters. The Ovr, or overwrite mode, lets the user write over any data that might already be there. Regardless of which default you choose, the user can always change this by pressing the Ins key when the application runs. The As Is choice doesn't force the mode either way, but leaves the insert or overwrite default in the last state the user chose. For this line, select As Is.

The Required line asks you if this field is required, which means that you can make sure the user enters something in this field. If the user presses Enter on a blank Required field when the application runs, the program will beep and the cursor will remain on this field. Select no here.

The Immediate line asks you what to do if the user enters in all 30 characters. Do you want the application to immediately jump to the next field, without requiring an Enter? This is occasionally a good idea if you are defining an application for rapid data entry, but since this application is for casual users, select no here.

The Num Lock line asks you if you want to activate the Num Lock mode for the user. Since this is not numeric data, and since the user can always toggle the key if he needs to, select no.

The Left Just line asks if you want to left justify the data. This is especially important for keyed fields (and you'll key this one later), so select yes.

The Upper Case line asks you if you want to specify that the data is made all upper case when the user presses Enter. Select no for this field.

The last line asks for a Help ID. If you want to have a specific help window for this field, you can simply name it here, and define the window later. Since you might want several lines of text explaining how to enter a title (like always enter the "The" that occurs at the beginning of a title at the end of the field), enter a Help ID called 'TITLE'. As soon as you enter this field, you will go back to the file summary window, but this time it will show the Title field defined.

In a similar manner, you should define the Author, Subject, and Publisher fields. Give them a length of 20 characters and use a @S20 picture. You can also use the name of the field for a Help ID. The order in which the fields appear in the record does not matter.

The next field to define is the Type field. The book type will also be a String field, but this time you will use the Choices line. For the type of book, the user should select from the abbreviations HB for hardback, PB for paperback, TR for trade book, and GF for gift book. You will also use these abbreviations on the Choices line in the field window.

When you create the Type field, use a length of 2 and a @S2 picture, and on the Choices line enter PB HB TR GF. The spaces between the abbreviations are used to separate the items. When the application runs, the user will be given a choice to select one of these items to complete the field (see Fig. 4-7).

4-7. Field window for TYPE

```
                        Field

Field Name :TYPE
Description:Type of Book
Type       :String
Length     : 2
Picture    :@s2
Choices    :PB HB TR GF
Dimensioned:
Type Mode  :AsIs        Ins  Ovr  AsIs
Required   :No          Yes  No
Immediate  :No          Yes  No
Num Lock   :No          Yes  No
Left Just  :Yes         Yes  No
Upper Case :No          Yes  No
Help ID    :
```

Because the Price, Quantity, Published, and Pages fields are numeric, they are entered differently.

To create the Price field, place the cursor bar below the last field and press the Ins key to get the Field window (see Fig. 4-8). After completing the Name and Description lines, you need to select the data type. Since Price will be used to represent money, select the Decimal data type. After selecting this type, you need to specify the size of the decimal and the number of places. For the Price field, enter a length of 6 and 2 decimal places. This will allow the user to enter the price of a book up to $9,999.99.

```
                        Field

 Field Name :PRICE
 Description:Selling Price of Book
 Type       :Decimal $<<<#.##
 Length     : 6
 Places     : 2
 Picture    :@n$8.2
 Lower Range:    $0.00
 Upper Range:$9999.99
 Dimensioned:
 Type Mode  :AsIs      Ins  Ovr  AsIs
 Required   :No        Yes  No
 Immediate  :No        Yes  No
 Num Lock   :Yes       Yes  No
 Help ID    :PRICE
```

4-8. Field window for PRICE

In the picture field, note that the Designer defaults the picture code to @n7.2. It does this to make the picture accommodate the decimal point. Remember, the length specified in the picture is the total length of the resulting data. In this example, you could include a dollar sign in the picture, so enter @n$8.2 for the picture code. You should make the length 8 to include room for the dollar sign.

Note that because you are defining a numeric field, you are shown two prompts—The Upper and Lower Range. This allows you to restrict the user to enter values that fall between these ranges. For the Price field, use zero for the lower range (no negative numbers) and 9,999.99 for the upper range. You should take the defaults for the rest of the lines in this window.

Likewise, you can create the fields Pages and Quantity by using a Short data type with simple @n4 pictures.

The Published field will be a date, so you should select a Long data type. This is because date data in Clarion is stored as a certain number of days since a fixed date in the past (December 28, 1800). Storing dates this way allows for very simple arithmetic, like determining the number of days that have elapsed—just subtract one date from another. You do not have to be concerned with getting a calendar date from this number— there are a variety of picture codes to do this for you.

After filling in the Name, Description, and Data Type lines in the field window, select a @D1 picture to display this date on screens and reports. To see what other picture codes are possible for dates, simply press F1 while on the Picture line in the field window. You can default the rest of the lines for the Published field.

At this point, you have all of your fields completed for the record definition. Now you need to define the keys for this file. In the file options window, position the cursor bar over under the Keys column, and press the Ins key. This will bring up the key window as shown in Fig. 4-9.

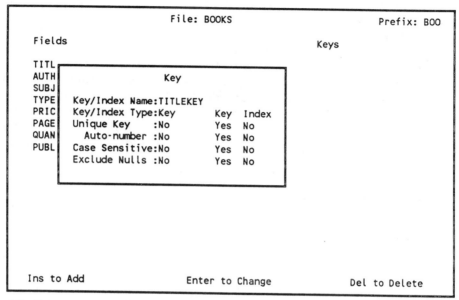

```
                        File: BOOKS                      Prefix: BOO

      Fields                                    Keys

      TITL
      AUTH                     Key
      SUBJ
      TYPE    Key/Index Name:TITLEKEY
      PRIC    Key/Index Type:Key        Key   Index
      PAGE    Unique Key    :No         Yes   No
      QUAN      Auto-number :No         Yes   No
      PUBL    Case Sensitive:No         Yes   No
              Exclude Nulls :No         Yes   No



      Ins to Add                Enter to Change          Del to Delete
```

4-9.   Key window for TITLEKEY

Keys

The first line in the key window asks for the name of the first key. As stated earlier, you will key on the Title field, so you should name this key TITLEKEY.

The next line asks for the type of key field, either a key or an index. A key is a file that is updated whenever the keyed fields in the record change. This makes the key always available to access the records in key order, but also requires some disk activity (overhead) each time the record is changed. In contrast, an index is never updated, so there is no overhead incurred when the data in the record changes. An index, however, must be built before it is used.

When would you use an index? If you have a report that is printed rarely, like at the end of the month, and prints the records in an order that is not already keyed for other reasons, you can use an index. This means that there will be no disk overhead during the month as the records are changed, but it will take longer to create the report because the index must first be built. You should not use an index for screen display of information. This example will not use an index, so select Key as the file type.

The next line asks if you want the key file to include records that have duplicates in the keyed fields. If you select yes for the Unique Key prompt, it will not allow you to add records for books with duplicate titles. Since some of the books in the bookstore may have the same title, and because many will certainly have the same subject and author, you should allow duplicates by selecting no to the Unique Key prompt.

If you were to have a unique key, the next line asks if you would like to auto-number the keyed fields. Suppose you were creating an application to manage a checkbook. You might want to show each check by check number, and when you write a new check, you might want the data screen (a form) to automatically default the check number to the next highest number. If you answer yes here, it will auto-number the check field. This will only work, however, if the last (or only) field of the key is a numeric data type, and if the key is unique. Auto-numbered fields must be keyed.

The next line asks you to select yes or no to the Case Sensitive prompt. This makes the order in which the records are displayed and retrieved alphabetical, regardless of whether the characters have been entered in upper or lower case. For instance, if the key is not case sensitive, either JOE SMITH or Joe Smith will always appear before JOHN SMITH or John Smith. You should select no for this, so you won't have to worry about how the user has set the Caps Lock key when entering data. This will still allow the user to record upper and lower case characters.

The last line has the Exclude Nulls prompt, meaning that if the key field in a record is blank (or zero, if the keyed field is numeric) that record will not be included in the key file. The record will still be in the data file, but it will not be seen while accessing the file in the keyed order. Select no for this line.

When would you select yes for Exclude Nulls? If you had an application with a key field that contained blank records, you would normally see all of the records in key order with blank values. This is because blanks always sort before any other typed characters. In order to prevent those records from being displayed, you could select yes to Exclude Nulls. Because the key fields in the application will have data in them, you should select no.

After completing the key window, you will see the file summary window, with the key name now displayed under the Keys column. However, you still have not specified which field in the file will be the key component. To do this, place the cursor bar on the key name and press the Ins key. This will cause a window to appear that will ask you for the name of the field you want to include in this key. Type in the name of the field to be used for TITLEKEY, which is Title. Or, you can just press Enter while the field is blank. Designer will present a list of all the fields defined in this file to select from. You should select Title. The key name now points to the Title field on the file summary window, showing how the key is defined.

To define the next key, you must place the cursor bar under the lines now used for the TITLEKEY, and press the Ins key. Again, you will see the Key window. You can now define the key you need for authors, and you might name it AUTHORKEY. It will use the Author field as its key component. You should answer the prompts in the key window the same way.

The subject key will have many duplicates; that is, there will be many books with the subjects of fiction, science, or diet. For those records with the same subject, how do you want those records ordered? As discussed in Chapter 3, keys can have more than one field component. In this case, it might be a good idea to have the Title field as the secondary component. This would cause any duplicates by subject to be alphabetized by title.

To create this key, fill out the key window as before, naming the key SUBJKEY. Use the same parameters you specified for TITLEKEY. When you name the field components, place Subkey first. Then, keep the cursor bar on the Subject field name under the SUBJKEY, and press Ins. You will see the same Key field window as before, but now enter the Title field and press Enter. Note that the file summary window will show you all the field components for this key. These key components can be any data type, and the key will still be maintained in the correct order.

The completed file summary window is shown in Fig. 4-10. Press Ctrl−Enter to complete the file definition screen, and return to the application summary window.

```
┌─────────────────────────────────────────────────────────────────┐
│            File: BOOKS                          Prefix: BOO       │
│                                                                   │
│   Fields                                        Keys              │
│                                                                   │
│   TITLE (String 30) - Title of Book s15         TITLEKEY (Key)    │
│   AUTHOR (String 20) - Author of Book           └TITLE            │
│   SUBJECT (String 20) - Subject of Book                           │
│   TYPE (String 2) - Type of Book                AUTHORKEY (Key)   │
│   PRICE (Decimal 6.2) - Selling Price of Book $ └AUTHOR           │
│   PAGES (Short) - Number of Pages <<<#                            │
│   QUANTITY (Short) - Books on Hand <<<#         SUBJKEY (Key)     │
│   PUBLISHED (Long) - Date Published mm/dd/yy    ├SUBJECT          │
│                                                 └TITLE            │
│                                                                   │
│                                                                   │
│                                                                   │
│                                                                   │
│                                                                   │
│   Ins to Add              Enter to Change           Del to Delete │
└─────────────────────────────────────────────────────────────────┘
```

4-10. Completed file summary window

Menus

If you go back to the application summary window, you will still see the START procedure defined as "ToDo." To define this procedure, place the cursor bar on START, and press Enter. You are then presented with a pop-up menu of procedure types to select from, shown in Fig. 4-11.

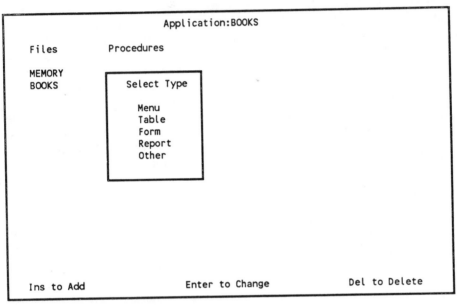

```
                    Application:BOOKS

    Files       Procedures

    MEMORY
    BOOKS            Select Type

                     Menu
                     Table
                     Form
                     Report
                     Other




    Ins to Add            Enter to Change        Del to Delete
```

4-11. Procedure selection window

The menu type allows the user to select from a menu of items, with each item linked to another procedure. A menu can call a table, a report, or even another menu. Because the application should give the user a choice of seeing the books listed by subject, author, or title, your first procedure should be a menu. Select menu from the list.

Menu options

The next window you see is the menu options window, shown in Fig. 4-12. This window will ask you for information about the menu. Note that the first line, the Procedure Name, is already filled in with START.

The next line on the window asks for a title of the menu. This is used for two purposes. It will be shown after the procedure name on the application summary window, much like the description of fields was used in the file summary window. It will also be used for the initial title of the

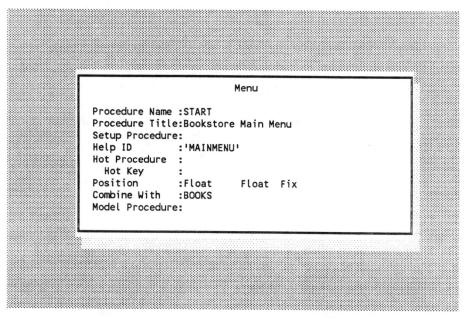

```
                        Menu

Procedure Name :START
Procedure Title:Bookstore Main Menu
Setup Procedure:
Help ID        :'MAINMENU'
Hot Procedure  :
  Hot Key      :
Position       :Float      Float  Fix
Combine With   :BOOKS
Model Procedure:
```

4-12.   Menu options window

menu, which will appear in the menu screen design worksheet. Type Bookstore Main Menu here.

The next line asks you for the name of the setup procedure. The setup procedure lets you insert code in the menu procedure after the menu screen is displayed, but before the user can take any action. You can write a line of Clarion code to set a memory variable here, or call another Designer procedure, or call an Other procedure that you have written with the Editor.

The setup procedure is one of many places in Designer where you can call another procedure to do something unique. These places, sometimes called "hooks," allow you to provide a higher degree of customization. They work by taking whatever you type in for this line and simply inserting it into the code. Normally, you can just name a procedure, and because naming a procedure in the Clarion language is the same as calling it, that procedure will be executed. You can actually type in 255 characters on this line, which is room enough for several Clarion statements. In this example, however, there is nothing to setup, so leave this line blank.

The next line asks for the name of the Help ID for this screen. Although you have already provided Help IDs for each field you have defined in the data file, here you can specify the name of the help screen to be displayed if there is no other Help ID available when the user presses F1.

Note that these Help IDs must enclosed in apostrophes. Enter 'MAINMENU' here.

After the Help ID line, there are two lines that ask you about a hot procedure. A *hot procedure* is a procedure that can be invoked any time with a hot key. For instance, you can define a report procedure and name it here. You can also specify the F5 key (or any other key) as the hot key for this report. This means that while the user is on this screen, he can press F5 to produce this report. This procedure can be a Designer procedure or an Other procedure created with the Editor. Up to three hot procedures can be defined for this window. Since there isn't any need for hot procedures in this application, leave these fields blank.

The next line is the Combine With line. This line lets you control into which source file this procedure will be placed. The default is the name of the application (BOOKS). If you take the default for every procedure you create, all of the source for the entire application will reside in one source file the name of the application with a .CLA extension.

You can also specify another name in this line, allowing the source for the procedure to be stored in its own source file. If you specify START here, this procedure will appear in a separate source file. The source for other procedures can be combined with this new source file, or each procedure can reside in its own source file. Note that you do not name the source file, only the name of the procedures which will contain the source file. Designer will name the source files when it generates the code. In all these example procedures, you should take the default so that each procedure will in the same source file.

The next line asks for name of the procedure in the model file that will generate the source for this procedure. This line is only used if you have created your own model file and wish to specify something other than the default. No default name is shown; if you leave it blank, Designer will use the procedures that are supplied with Clarion. Since you are using the model file supplied with the package, you should always leave this line blank.

Screen initialization

After completing the menu window, you will see a screen initialization window. This window, shown in Fig. 4-13, lets you set the colors and border around the screen. As soon as the initialization window appears, another window also appears that lets you select the foreground and background colors for the screen. This is the same color selection window you saw in Chapter 1 with the description of Tailor. Simply point to the color combination you want, and press Enter. This is the color combination that will be used to paint the whole screen. It will also become the

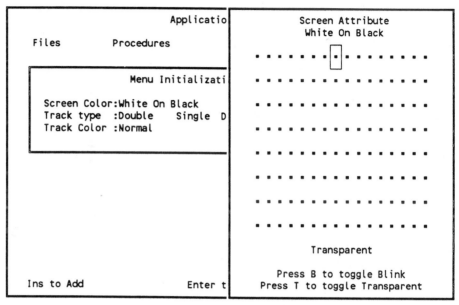

4-13. Screen initialization window

normal color. The *normal color* is the color that will be used for this screen if no other colors are specified.

After you select the normal color, you are prompted for what kind of track characters you want to use for the border of the screen. You can select from single, double, or block tracking characters. You can also change or erase them when you are on the worksheet.

After selecting double track characters, you are then asked for the color combination for the track border. A good starting suggestion is make the tracks the normal color, but you can select any color you want.

Screen worksheet

After completing the initialization window, you will see the screen worksheet, shown in Fig. 4-14. This worksheet is a picture of how the menu will appear when the program runs. Note that the worksheet already has a given size, track border, and title. The size, track border, title, and even color can be changed in the worksheet.

Now you need to define the menu. The choices you should provide to the user are Show Books by Title, Show Books by Author, and Show Books by Subject. You should also provide a way to print reports and exit the program. A few lines under the title, position the cursor about a fourth of the

4-14. Bookstore Main Menu worksheet

way from the left side of the screen. The exact position doesn't matter. Press Ctrl–F for field, and you'll see Select field type window, as shown in Fig. 4-15. This allows two types of fields: entry fields, in which the user is asked to input something, and display fields, which will simply display data on the screen.

Display fields provides several different methods for displaying data. The simple String field will display the current contents of any field that has already been defined, either from a file or a variable in the MEMORY file.

The Computed field allows you to display the result of an arithmetic expression. This expression can be any calculation you want to perform using any fields in files or memory variables. It can also simply be a function call to one of the many functions provided in Clarion's function library. For instance, if you wanted to show the current date on your menu, you could position the cursor where you wanted the date, press Ctrl–F and select a Computed field. You would then define a screen variable for the date, called SCR:DATE, and for an expression, called the TODAY function. This function returns the current date, which can be displayed through a @D1 picture. Try it, it's simple.

The Lookup field allows you to display a field from a record in another file by specifying the relationship between the files. Although you can

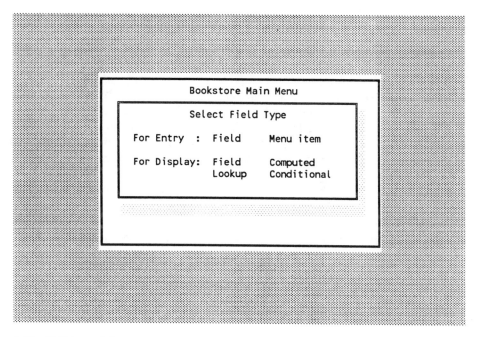

4-15. Field type window

place a Lookup field in the menu screen. Lookup fields will be explained in the discussion of tables, later in this chapter.

A Conditional field will display some variable if a special condition that you can specify is met. Conditional fields can be placed on a menu, table, form, or report procedure. The use of the conditional field will be explained in the discussion of tables.

You should do the menu items first, so select the menu item choice in the field type window. This brings up the menu item window, shown in Fig. 4-16. The first line asks you for a string. This is the string literal, or text, that will show on the screen for this item. Type 'Show Books by Title' here.

The next line asks for the name of this procedure. This is the name of

4-16. Menu item window

```
              Menu Item

String   :'Show Books By Title'
Procedure:SHO_TITLE
Attribute:Normal
  Select :Reversed
```

the procedure that will be called if the user selects this item, so you should name it SHO_TITLE.

The next line asks you for the color attribute used when the menu item string is displayed. Again, you will see a color selection window, from which you should choose Normal for now.

The next line asks for the colors to be used when the menu item is selected. If you choose Reversed here, you will get a cursor bar, like the one you've been using in Designer. You could choose to display the selected menu item string in a different color, make it blink, or use any other combination of video attributes. Just make the selected string Reversed for now.

After completing the last line, you are shown the menu worksheet again, but now the first menu item is on the screen. It might not be centered, but all you have to do to center it is put the cursor anywhere on the line with the menu item, and press Ctrl–^. This will center the line between the tracking characters. In a similar manner, create the following menu items:

String:	'Show Books By Author'
Procedure:	SHO_AUTHOR
String:	'Show Books By Subject'
Procedure:	SHO_SUBJ
String:	'Print Reports'
Procedure:	PRT_RPTS
STRING:	'Quit'
Procedure:	RETURN

and use the same parameters you used in the menu item field for SHO_TITLE. On the Quit menu item, specify the name of a pre-defined procedure named RETURN. Since there is no calling procedure for the Main Menu, the program will return to DOS if the user selects Quit.

Remember to center each item, and you should have a finished screen like the one in Fig. 4-17.

Now press Ctrl–Enter to return to the application summary window, which now looks like Fig. 4-18. Notice that because START (the Main Menu procedure) now calls the procedures you named as menu items, they are shown as ToDo procedures.

It is important to remember that you can always go back and change anything about the menu screen you have just defined, for instance, add other types of fields to the screen, change the colors, the size of the window, or add new menu items.

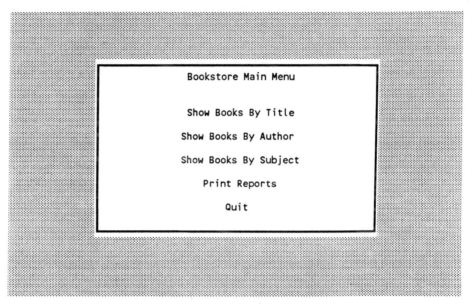

4-17. Completed Main Menu worksheet

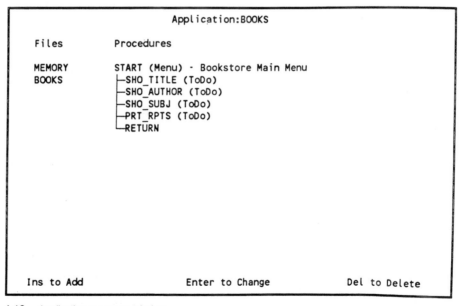

4-18. Application summary window

The SHO_TITLE, SHO_AUTHOR, and SHO_SUBJ procedures are going to show the user information about each record, allow the user to rapidly find a particular book, and see any of the details of any book's record. Such a procedure should be defined as a table.

Tables

A table shows a series of fields from records in one or more data files. Once the screen has displayed as many records as will fit on the screen, the user can use the up and down arrow keys, the PgUp and PgDn keys, or the Ctrl–PgUp or Ctrl–PgDn keys to "browse" through the data.

A particular record is always highlighted with the cursor bar. The user can then display, change, or add records by pressing one of three keys. All three keys cause a form procedure to be called, which displays the fields for that record.

If the user presses Enter while positioned on a record, the data for that record will be displayed and can be changed by the user. If the user presses the Ins (insert) key, the data is again displayed and the user can add a new record. If the user presses Del (delete) key, the user can delete the displayed record.

To create the example table, go to the application summary window, position the cursor bar on the SHO_TITLE procedure and press Enter. Because this is a ToDo procedure, you will see the list of possible procedure types, and you should select Table.

Table options

The next window you will see is the table options window (see Fig. 4-19). The first line of this window asks you for the name of the procedure, which is already filled out with the name you have chosen, so simply press Enter.

The next line is for the title of the screen. This is just like the title in a menu screen—it will be centered on the worksheet and will also be used as a comment on the application summary window. You should type in Books by Title here, and press Enter.

The next line asks for the name of a setup procedure. Since you have no procedure to be called here, leave it blank.

The next line asks for the name of the update procedure. Because this window will show data about books on the screen, you can give the user the ability to change a book's record by letting them point to a desired book, and change it with a form procedure. All you have to do is enter the name of the form procedure that will allow the update on this line. Enter UPD_BOOK here.

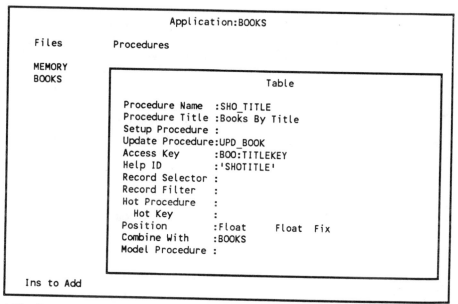

```
                       Application:BOOKS

        Files        Procedures

        MEMORY
        BOOKS                                   Table

               Procedure Name  :SHO_TITLE
               Procedure Title :Books By Title
               Setup Procedure :
               Update Procedure:UPD_BOOK
               Access Key      :BOO:TITLEKEY
               Help ID         :'SHOTITLE'
               Record Selector :
               Record Filter   :
               Hot Procedure   :
                 Hot Key       :
               Position        :Float     Float  Fix
               Combine With    :BOOKS
               Model Procedure :


        Ins to Add
```

4-19. Table options window

The next line asks for the name of the access key. This must be one of the keys defined for any file in the File column of the application summary window. This key will determine the order that the records in this table are displayed. Because this table will show books by title, all you need to do is enter the name of the key that uses the Title field as its key component.

You could just type in TITLEKEY here. However, if you leave the line blank and press Enter, Designer will display a list of all the keys that have been defined, and let you select the key by pointing to it and pressing Enter.

The next line asks for the name of the Help ID. Type in 'SHOTITLE' here.

The next line asks you for the name of the record selector — the name of a field which is part of the key being used to display the table. When the table is displayed, this field will isolate those records in the file that match its value. For instance, if you are using the AUTHORKEY, and specify the Author field here, you can create an entry field that lets the user enter an author's name. The table will then display only books written by that author. For now, since the user should see all of the books when the table is displayed, leave this field blank.

The next line asks for the name of the record filter. In this line, you can type in an expression to specify that only those records that match the expression be displayed. A filter is like a selector in that it shows only a subset of the available records in the display. A filter, however, can be used with any field (not just those that have been keyed) and can use a complex expression to determine which records are displayed. For instance, if you type in INV:PUBLISHED > TODAY() − 365, this table will show only those books that have been published in the last year. This works because you will have only those records whose date published is greater than today's date, TODAY(), minus one year. This is an example of an expression, and will be further discussed in Chapter 5. Because the user should see all of these titles on this table, leave this field blank.

The rest of the lines are identical to the ones you saw on the Menu window. Just take the defaults to complete this window.

The next screen you will see is the screen initialization window, just like the one you completed for the menu. Select the same colors for "normal" as you did for the menu, and a single track border for now.

Table worksheet

The next screen is a worksheet for the table. The same window editing keys that you used to paint, track, copy, move, and delete in the menu screen are now active. You can change the title of this screen, and make other cosmetic changes.

Now you need to add the scrolling fields that will let you see the data fields for each record. Because the default window is too narrow to hold some of the fields, expand it (using Ctrl−W and then the arrow keys) to the size shown in Fig. 4-20. Place the cursor six lines down from the top of the window and 2 spaces to the right of the border. This is where you'll place the first scrolling field. Press Ctrl−F to display the field type window (see Fig. 4-21). There are two basic types of fields that you can select: a field in the fixed portion, and a field in the scrolling portion.

Each table you define has two areas on the screen. One area is where fields from records are scrolled by letting the user press the up and down arrow keys, the PgUp and PgDn keys, and the Ctrl−PgUp and Ctrl−PgDn keys. As the user presses these keys, a different record is highlighted. The other area on the screen is everywhere else; in this area you can place string literals like titles, tracking, instructions, and any of the field types in the fixed portion part of the field type window. The screen to be developed is shown in Fig. 4-22.

Since the cursor is placed at the start of the first scrolling field, you should select the Scrolling portion of the menu. Here you want to place the Title field. Designer will ask you for the name of field. As always, you can either type in the name of the field (BOO:TITLE), or leave it blank to get a list of the available fields. Likewise, across the same line, place the Author, Subject, Price, and Quantity fields.

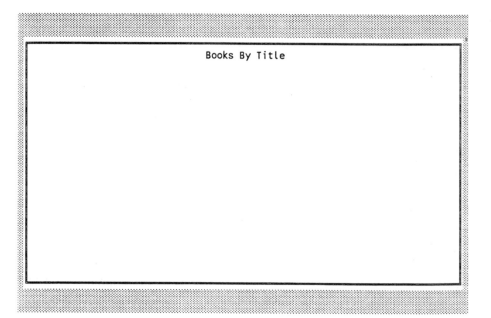

4-20. Table worksheet

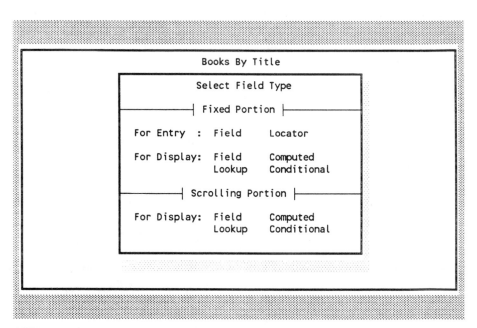

4-21. Table field type window

```
                        Books By Title

                Locate: ••••••••••••••••

  Title            Author            Subject              Price    Quan.
  ••••••••••••••   •••••••••••••••••••  ••••••••••••••••••••• $<<<#.## <<<#
```

```
  Enter the Title of the Book to Locate, and use Arrow Keys to Point,
  Press Enter to Select, Ins to Add New Book, and Del to Delete Book.
```

4-22. Complete table for TITLE

It is important to understand that wherever you place the first scrolling field is where the scrolling area starts. The scrolling area will continue down the screen until Designer finds the first non-blank character. In this example, you will place all the fields on the same line so that the cursor bar that highlights the selected record will also be one line, and each displayed record will require one line. However, you can also display more than one line per record by simply placing more fields on the next line.

There is one more field to place—the Locate: field. It is a locator field. You can place this by positioning the cursor where Fig. 4-22 indicates, and pressing Ctrl–F. You can now select Locator from the fixed portion part of the menu, and name the field BOO:TITLE as before. A locator will let the user rapidly locate the book they are looking for by typing in the title, character by character, until it appears on the screen.

For instance, with the locator field, when the table is first displayed, the cursor will be on the locator field. If the user types an R, the table will be redisplayed with those books that start with R. As the user continues to type characters, the table will be redisplayed, starting with the title of the book that is the closest match to the title. This lets the user rapidly locate a specific book.

For a big file, the user might be able to type faster than the time it takes to redisplay the table. If you want to let the user type in a whole field and do the table display only after he presses Enter, you can make the field a simple entry field, and, type DO FIND_RECORD on the line that calls for an edit procedure.

All of the text you see on the screen was done by simply positioning the cursor and typing the characters. You should also draw, with the Ctrl–T tracking function, an extra line across the bottom, 3 lines up from the bottom. This will form a box in which you can place the instructional text for the user.

After you have completed the table procedure, as shown in Fig. 4-22, press Ctrl–Enter to exit the screen worksheet, and you will return to the application summary window.

Although you have completed this table procedure to simply display the records of the BOOK file, there is a field type that greatly enhances Designer's capabilities. This is the lookup display field.

A lookup display field lets you specify fields from records in more than one file at a time. Suppose you have two files defined, one that has a record for each order placed, and one that has customer information. Also, both of these files have keyed fields for the customer's name. When you create a table to display fields from the order file, you can use the common field (customer's name) to "look up" the fields for the record with the same customer's name in the customer file. Once this relationship is established, you can display any of the fields from the customer file along with the fields from the order file.

You can also have more than one lookup field for each scrolling item on the screen. This means you can have fields from several different files on the screen. You can also have lookup entry fields, so that a data item to be entered by the user can be selected from data in another file. This type of field will be discussed in the next section on forms.

In the same way that you defined the SHO_TITLE procedure, you can define the SHO_AUTHOR and SHO_SUBJ tables. Although you could design very different screens for these, in this example the operator should get a feeling of consistency, so you should make the screens very similar. All you have to do is specify a different access key (AUTHORKEY for SHO_AUTHOR, for example) and different Help IDs in the table options window. On the screen worksheet, you will need to make the locator field specify the right field for the access key, like BOO:AUTHOR for AUTHORKEY, etc.

In fact, rather than duplicate each effort, Designer lets you copy a whole procedure into a new one. To do this, place the cursor bar on the SHO_AUTHOR procedure, which is still a ToDo, and press Ctrl–G for "get." You will be prompted for the name of the application to get the procedure (in this case, BOOKS) and the name of the procedure (in this case, SHO_TITLE). It then asks you for the name of the new procedure (in this case, SHO_AUTHOR). Immediately, you will see the SHO_AUTHOR procedure defined as a Table, but it will work exactly like SHO_TITLE. If you are going to use this feature, you must remember to make all the necessary changes to make it act like SHO_AUTHOR.

Forms

A form procedure allows the user to change the data in a specified file. When the form procedure is called from a table, a variable that is created by Designer (called Action) is set to a value that indicates whether the user pressed the Enter, Ins, or Del key. This variable is then used to determine if the record on the form will be changed (put back to the file) or deleted, or if a new record is to be added.

On the Application Summary window, there is a new ToDo procedure called from the last table, the UPD_BOOK procedure (see Fig. 4-23). This procedure was specified as the update procedure for your table, and this procedure will be a form. Press Enter on this procedure, and select Form from the list of procedure types. The form options window is shown in Fig. 4-24.

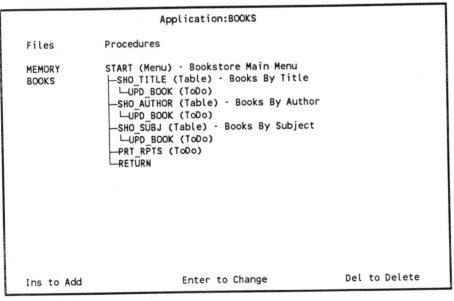

```
                    Application:BOOKS

    Files           Procedures

    MEMORY          START (Menu) - Bookstore Main Menu
    BOOKS           ├─SHO_TITLE (Table) - Books By Title
                    │ └─UPD_BOOK (ToDo)
                    ├─SHO_AUTHOR (Table) - Books By Author
                    │ └─UPD_BOOK (ToDo)
                    ├─SHO_SUBJ (Table) - Books By Subject
                    │ └─UPD_BOOK (ToDo)
                    ├─PRT_RPTS (ToDo)
                    └─RETURN




    Ins to Add              Enter to Change          Del to Delete
```

4-23. Application summary window

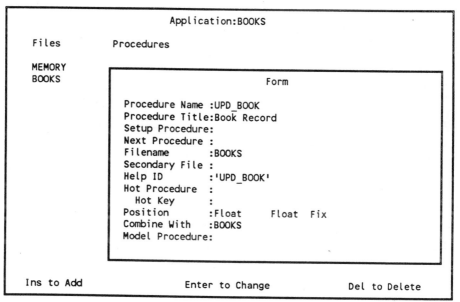

```
                    Application:BOOKS

 Files          Procedures

 MEMORY
 BOOKS                                        Form

            Procedure Name :UPD_BOOK
            Procedure Title:Book Record
            Setup Procedure:
            Next Procedure :
            Filename       :BOOKS
            Secondary File :
            Help ID        :'UPD_BOOK'
            Hot Procedure  :
              Hot Key      :
            Position       :Float      Float  Fix
            Combine With   :BOOKS
            Model Procedure:


 Ins to Add             Enter to Change          Del to Delete
```

4-24.   Form options window

Form options

The first line in this window shows you the name of the form procedure, and the next line asks you for the title of this procedure. Just as in the menu and table procedures, this title will be used for both a description and the initial title that will appear on the screen worksheet. You should use Book Record as the title here.

The Setup Procedure line, and the lines with the Help ID, Hot Procedure, Hot Key, Combine With, and Model Name prompts are just like those described in the sections on menu and table procedures. There is no need for a setup procedure here, so leave it blank.

The first new type of line is the Next Procedure line. This is another of the programming "hooks" that allow you to place a procedure call or a line of source code that will be executed after the file update for this form procedure is completed. Since there isn't any need to do this, you should leave it blank.

The next line asks you for the filename for this form. This must be the name of one of the files already defined. As always, you can leave it blank and press enter for a list of the files, or you can type in BOOKS.

If you had any secondary files to update, you could specify them next. This assumes that through some other procedure, the records for those files are in memory and ready for update. Since there are no secondary files, leave this blank.

You can use 'UPD_BOOK' for the Help ID, and use the defaults (press Enter) for the rest of these lines.

Form initialization

After completing the form window, and selecting your colors and tracking, you will see the initialization window, as shown in Fig. 4-25. This window presents the same screen initialization options as in the previous screens, but also asks you if you want to "populate" the form. If you select yes, it will automatically place each field defined in the BOOK file on the worksheet as entry fields, along with the field names for prompts. This is usually a good idea because it is easier to move or change the fields and prompts than it is to place each one from scratch. Select yes for this.

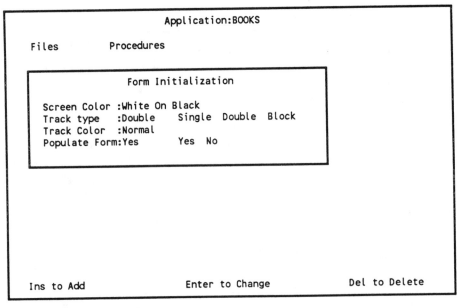

4-25. Form initialization window

Form worksheet

The next thing you'll see is the worksheet for the form, as shown in Fig. 4-26. Notice that there is a display string field placed under the title. This will be used to tell the user what is happening on this screen. If the user presses the Ins key to bring up this form, the message "Record Will Be Added" is displayed. If the user presses the Enter key, the message "Record Will Be Changed" is displayed. The Del key indicates "Record

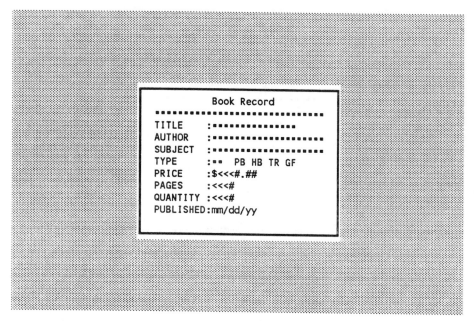

```
                  Book Record
■■■■■■■■■■■■■■■■■■■■■■■■■■■■■■■■■■■
TITLE    :■■■■■■■■■■■■■
AUTHOR   :■■■■■■■■■■■■■■■■■
SUBJECT  :■■■■■■■■■■■■■■■■■
TYPE     :■■  PB HB TR GF
PRICE    :$<<<#.##
PAGES    :<<<#
QUANTITY :<<<#
PUBLISHED:mm/dd/yy
```

4-26. Initial form worksheet

Will Be Deleted." Also notice that Designer generates a small menu of choices for the user that was specified for "Choices" in the Type field.

Designer tries to create the smallest window that will contain all of the fields. You can make the window larger by pressing Ctrl–W and using the arrow keys. You can also move (using Ctrl–M) the prompts and fields around to make a more pleasing display. For this example, use Ctrl–M and Ctrl–W to create a form that looks like Fig. 4-27.

Besides the fields that were "auto-populated," there are several other type fields that can be placed on the screen. If you place the cursor on a blank position of the screen and press Ctrl–F, you will see the field window, as shown in Fig. 4-28.

An entry field is one that allows the user to enter data. All of the fields on this example form are entry fields. A pause field gives the user the chance to review the data on the screen before the record is updated. You usually place a pause field at the bottom of the screen. When a user enters a Pause field, a message is displayed and the program waits until the user presses the Enter key to update the record, or the Esc key, which places the cursor on the previous field so that the user can change the data. A display field simply displays a file or memory variable. Whatever value is in this field when the window is opened will appear in this field. Computed, conditional, and lookup fields work the same as they do with menu screens.

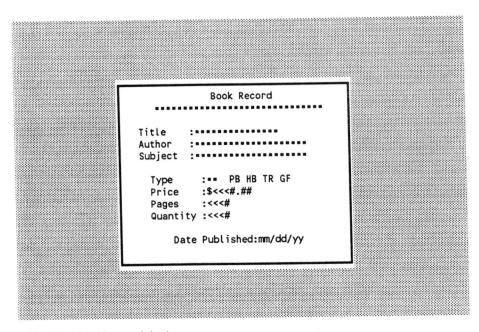

4-27. Completed form worksheet

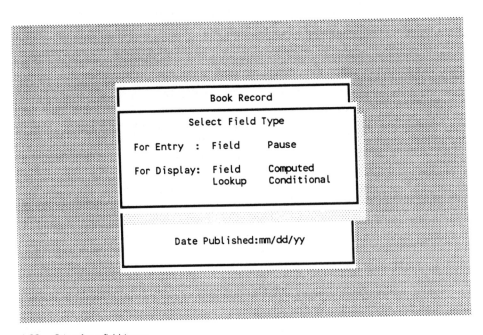

4-28. Other form field types

This completes the form to update the records in the BOOKS file, and completes an example menu, table, and form for the program. Press Ctrl–Enter to return to the application summary window, as shown in Fig. 4-29. As you can see, the reports for the bookstore remain. However, before you begin the reports, allow the user to select which report by defining the PRT_RPTS procedure to be a menu, with each report procedure called from there. Fig. 4-30 shows this menu.

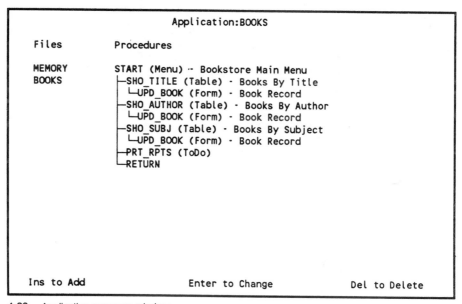

```
                     Application:BOOKS

       Files          Procedures

       MEMORY         START (Menu) ·· Bookstore Main Menu
       BOOKS          ├─SHO_TITLE (Table) · Books By Title
                      │  └─UPD_BOOK (Form) · Book Record
                      ├─SHO_AUTHOR (Table) · Books By Author
                      │  └─UPD_BOOK (Form) · Book Record
                      ├─SHO_SUBJ (Table) · Books By Subject
                      │  └─UPD_BOOK (Form) · Book Record
                      ├─PRT_RPTS (ToDo)
                      └─RETURN




       Ins to Add              Enter to Change        Del to Delete
```

4-29. Application summary window

4-30. Report menu screen design

```
┌─────────────────────────────────────┐
│             Report Menu              │
├─────────────────────────────────────┤
│                                      │
│            Books By Title            │
│                                      │
│           Books By Author            │
│                                      │
│           Books By Subject           │
│                                      │
│               Return                 │
│                                      │
└─────────────────────────────────────┘
```

Create this menu as you did the Main Menu, by placing four menu items on the screen. The first item has the string of Books By Title and should call a procedure named TITLE_RPT. Likewise, Books By Author should call AUTHOR_RPT, Books By Subject should call SUBJECT_RPT, and, of course, Return should call RETURN. After completing the menu to look like Fig. 4-30, you should see the application summary window as shown in Fig. 4-31.

```
                          Application:BOOKS

        Files           Procedures

        MEMORY          START (Menu) - Bookstore Main Menu
        BOOKS           ├─SHO_TITLE (Table) - Books By Title
                        │ └─UPD_BOOK (Form) - Book Record
                        ├─SHO_AUTHOR (Table) - Books By Author
                        │ └─UPD_BOOK (Form) - Book Record
                        ├─SHO_SUBJ (Table) - Books By Subject
                        │ └─UPD_BOOK (Form) - Book Record
                        ├─PRT_RPTS (Menu) - Report Menu
                        │ ├─TITLE_RPT (ToDo)
                        │ ├─AUTHOR_RPT (ToDo)
                        │ ├─SUBJECT_RPT (ToDo)
                        │ └─RETURN
                        └─RETURN




        Ins to Add            Enter to Change          Del to Delete
```

4-21. Application summary window after report menu screen design

This sets the stage to describe the last type of procedure in the Bookstore example—the report procedure.

Reports

By placing the highlighted bar on the first ToDo procedure shown in Fig. 4-31, the TITLE_RPT procedure, and pressing the Enter key, you will see the procedure type selection window. Select the report type, and you will see the report window. A completed report window is shown in Fig. 4-32.

Report options

The first line of the report window is already filled out with the name of the procedure. The Procedure Title line asks you for the title of the report. What you type in here will appear on your report (which you can change

```
                              Report
        Procedure Name :TITLE_RPT
        Procedure Title:Books by Title
        Setup Procedure:
        Access Key     :BOO:TITLEKEY
        Record Selector:
        Record Filter  :
        Page Length    :   58
        Combine With   :BOOKS
        Model Procedure:
```

4-32. Report window

later) and also appears on the application summary window as a description of the report. Type Books by Title here and press Return.

The next line, with the Setup Procedure prompt, allows you to name a procedure to be called before the report starts printing. You can name a form or another menu procedure, or a procedure that is written in the language, called an Other procedure. (Other procedures will be discussed in Part 2, on the Clarion language. Since there is no setup required here, leave this line blank.

The next line is the Access Key line, which specifies the key that you have defined to retrieve records for printing. You must have a key defined to use a report procedure. Type BOO:TITLEKEY here so that the records in this report will appear in alphabetical order by title.

The next two lines, the Record Selector and Record Filter lines, allow you to specify printed records that match some kind of criteria. These two lines work like the Filter and Selector lines in the table window. Since this report will print information about all the books, leave these two lines blank.

The next line asks for a page length for the report. This determines the total number of lines that can be printed on the report, and is dependent on the size of the paper in your printer and the number of lines per inch your printer will print. A good starting number is 58 lines.

The Combine With Line has been discussed earlier, and you should take the default value supplied, BOOKS, by pressing Enter. The Model Procedure line has also been described; you should leave this line blank and press Enter, as well.

Report initialization

The next thing you will see is the report initialization window, as shown in Fig. 4-33. This window gives you one choice, asking you if you want to "populate" the report. Just as the form procedure would populate the form worksheet with all of the defined fields for the specified file, if you

```
┌─────────────────────────────────────┐
│        Report Initialization        │
│                                     │
│ Populate Report:Yes     Yes  No     │
└─────────────────────────────────────┘
```

4-33. Report initialization window

select yes here, the report will automatically be filled out with all the fields in the file. Since you want to put all of the information for each record in the report, and since it is easier to move them around the worksheet than add each one, select yes.

Report worksheet

The next thing you will see is the report worksheet with all of the fields, their field names, and the report title on the screen. This is shown in Fig. 4-34.

```
....:....1....:....2....:....3....:....4....:....5....:....6....:....7....:....8
══════════════════════════════════════Report Header════════════════════════════
══════════════════════════════════════Page    Header════════════════════════════
                                      Books by Title

TITLE           AUTHOR              SUBJECT            TYPE   PRICE PAGES QUA
══════════════════════════════════════Group   Header════════════════════════════
══════════════════════════════════════Body    Detail════════════════════════════
••••••••••••••••  ••••••••••••••••••••••  ••••••••••••••••••••• ••  $<<#.##  <<<#
══════════════════════════════════════Group   Footer════════════════════════════
══════════════════════════════════════Page    Footer════════════════════════════
══════════════════════════════════════Report  Footer════════════════════════════
....:....1....:....2....:....3....:....4....:....5....:....6....:....7....:....8
Body    Detail 1:1                                      LIN INS
```

4-34. Populated report

As you look at the report worksheet, you can see several design areas represented. These design areas are Report Header, Page Header, Group Header, Body Detail, Group Footer, Page Footer, and Report Footer. To explain these, it is important that you first understand the structure of Designer's reports.

Designer's reports allow you to have a report header and footer. A report header is most often used as a title page that simply names the report. It can also include the date the report was printed (by using a Computed field that calls the TODAY function), and can include many other fields. However, none of the records for the file will be processed in this part of the report—the records must appear in the main body of the report. Likewise, the report footer can contain similar fields, but is only printed once per report.

The page header is the area where you can specify what appears at the top of each page of the main body of the report. On the current worksheet, the title of the report appears, along with the names of all the fields in the file, which are used as column labels. Although the column labels appear to "go off the edge of the screen," they were put there by Designer for a wider report than the screen can display. This will be addressed shortly.

The Group Header area is where you can insert information about a particular group of records. For instance, if you had a file that listed books, keyed by publisher, each time the publisher field changed, a new group and information about the publisher could be placed here. Since this report will be a simple listing of all the books, however, this area should be left blank.

The next design area is the Body Detail. This is where the information about each record and its format is determined. Because this report was populated, all of the fields in the record are placed on this line so that they line up with their labels. Because one Body Detail area will be printed for each record, each of these fields will form a column down the page.

The next design area is the Group Footer, where additional information can be placed each time a designated group field changes. The page footer lets you specify information that will appear on the bottom of each page. A common use for the page footer is to place page numbers, dates, titles, etc. The report footer simply allows you to place fields on the last page of the report, like Totals or any other fields available when the report ends.

Assuming that the report must fit on paper that will only accommodate 80 columns, the first thing you need to do is move the fields around so that the information will not print off the page. Similar to the keys used in screen layout, you can move the cursor to the first field to be moved, the Price field, and press Ctrl–M. You should see the whole field highlighted. By pressing the Enter key, you will see another line appear in the Body Detail area. This means that for each record, there will be two lines printed on the report. After doing this, place the Price field on column 13, under the Title field. In a similar fashion, you should move the rest of the fields to the right of the Pages field so that they appear as they do in Fig. 4-35.

Note that the column labels in the page header also need to be moved to reflect the new position of the fields. By pointing to these labels and using Ctrl–M, you should be able to rearrange the report as shown in Fig. 4-35.

At this point, you have a report with no report header or footer, no

```
...:....1....:....2....:....3....:....4....:....5....:....6....:....7....:....8
═══════════════════════════════════════Report Header════════════════════════════
═══════════════════════════════════════Page    Header════════════════════════════
                              Books by Title

TITLE           AUTHOR           SUBJECT              TYPE
                PRICE PAGES QUANTITY PUBLISHED

═══════════════════════════════════════Group  Header════════════════════════════
═══════════════════════════════════════Body   Detail════════════════════════════
••••••••••••••••• •••••••••••••••••••• •••••••••••••••••• ••
        $<<#.##   <<<#      <<<#  mm/dd/yy
═══════════════════════════════════════Group  Footer════════════════════════════
═══════════════════════════════════════Page   Footer════════════════════════════
═══════════════════════════════════════Report Footer════════════════════════════
...:....1....:....2....:....3....:....4....:....5....:....6....:....7....:....8
Page    Header 2:1                                LIN OVR
```

4-35. Rearranged report

group information specified, a page header which forms a title and column headings, and two lines of record information printed for each
record. There are no group, page, or report footers. If you were to generate
and run the application, selecting this report would print the page with
the fields for each record printed down the page. If there are many
records, each time the page is "full" (depending on the page length specified in the Report window, for instance, 58 lines) a new header will print,
and records will continue to print down the page.

Now that the basic information is in the report, you can dress it up a
little. First, you can add a report header. Place the cursor on the Report
Header area, and press Enter a few times. This will add some blank lines
to the top of the report cover page. By typing Report of Books By Title and
centering this title on the screen, you will have a cover sheet for the
report.

You can also put page numbers at the bottom of the report. By placing
the cursor on the Page Footer area and pressing Enter twice, you have
ensured that two blank lines will appear at the bottom of each page. Place
the cursor near the center of the screen and type Page. Place the cursor
two spaces to the right and press Ctrl–V (This allows you to add new
variables to the report). You will then see the select field type window,
which allows you to specify a field as you did on forms, tables, and menus
(see Fig. 4-36).

```
┌────────────────────────────────┐
│     Select Field Type          │
│                                │
│  Field  Computed  Lookup       │
│                                │
│  Break  Control   Total        │
└────────────────────────────────┘
```

4-36. Report field type window

Select Field and you will be prompted for the name of the field. Here, you can specify any field that has been defined. By pressing Enter on this line, you will be shown a list of all those fields, as shown in Fig. 4-37.

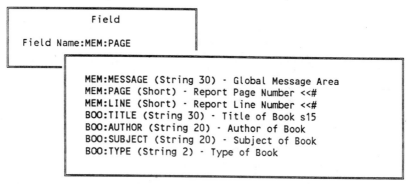

```
                      Field

        Field Name:MEM:PAGE



                 MEM:MESSAGE (String 30) - Global Message Area
                 MEM:PAGE (Short) - Report Page Number <<#
                 MEM:LINE (Short) - Report Line Number <<#
                 BOO:TITLE (String 30) - Title of Book s15
                 BOO:AUTHOR (String 20) - Author of Book
                 BOO:SUBJECT (String 20) - Subject of Book
                 BOO:TYPE (String 2) - Type of Book
```

4-37. Field selection window

Notice that there are three field names starting with the MEM: prefix, which were defined for you. When Designer applications print a report, a variable called MEM:PAGE is used to keep track of the current line being printed. By placing this variable after the page string in the footer, the current page number will be printed. Select MEM:PAGE, and your report should look like the one in Fig. 4-38.

```
=================================Report Header===================================



                          Report of Books by Title



=================================Page    Header=================================
                           Books by Title

TITLE            AUTHOR            SUBJECT              TYPE
                 PRICE PAGES QUANTITY PUBLISHED

=================================Group   Header=================================
=================================Body    Detail=================================
••••••••••••••• •••••••••••••••••••• •••••••••••••••••• ••
         $<<#.##  <<<#      <<<#  mm/dd/yy
=================================Group   Footer=================================
=================================Page    Footer=================================

                          Page <<#
=================================Report Footer==================================
....:....1....:....2....:....3....:....4....:....5....:....6....:....7....:....8
Report Header 0:30                              LIN INS
```

4-38. Completed report design

By using the same report format and changing the title and the Access Key field in the Report window to reflect the Books By Author and Books By Subject report procedures, you should have a complete example program, as shown in the application summary window of Fig. 4-39.

```
                      Application:BOOKS

    Files          Procedures

    MEMORY         START (Menu) - Bookstore Main Menu
    BOOKS          ├─SHO_TITLE (Table) - Books By Title
                   │ └─UPD_BOOK (Form) - Book Record
                   ├─SHO_AUTHOR (Table) - Books By Author
                   │ └─UPD_BOOK (Form) - Book Record
                   ├─SHO_SUBJ (Table) - Books By Subject
                   │ └─UPD_BOOK (Form) - Book Record
                   ├─PRT_RPTS (Menu) - Report Menu
                   │ ├─TITLE_RPT (Report) - Books By Title
                   │ ├─AUTHOR_RPT (Report) - Books By Author
                   │ ├─SUBJECT_RPT (Report) - Books By Subject
                   │ └─RETURN
                   └─RETURN




    Ins to Add            Enter to Change        Del to Delete
```

4-39. Completed application summary

Compiling and running the program

At this point (if curiosity hasn't gotten the better of you and you haven't already tried it), you should generate the code, compile, and run it. This is done by pressing Shift–F8 while in the application summary window. This causes Designer to generate the source program, invokes the compiler to compile your program, and starts the Processor executing your new application. Note that when your application first runs, and you select one of the table procedures to display the books, you are immediately placed into the form procedure. This is because there are no records in the book file, and your application can not really do anything until there are records to process.

Add some sample records and verify that the different tables present the records in the correct order. After you have added some records, try printing the reports. If you don't like the format of the screens, you can invoke the Designer, change the layout of the screens or reports, and press Shift–F8 to try them out.

Expanding the application

The Bookstore example shows only a small part of Designer's capabilities, so that you can get a feel for how you create procedures and how they relate to each other. Designer is capable of much more, however.

Although the example only uses one data file, Designer applications can use many files. For instance, you could add a field called BOO:PUBNUM to the BOOKS file that indicates the publisher. To do this you might assign an arbitrary publisher number, like 1 for publisher A, 2 for publisher B, and so on. You could also create a key for this field, called BOO:PUBKEY, which would tie each book to a publisher ID.

Now, to specify information about the publisher in only one place, you can create a new file—PUBS. In this file you can create fields that store the name, address, contact, telephone number, etc. in each record for every publisher. You can also include the publisher ID in this file, and create a key for it called PUB:PUBKEY.

You now have a file of books and a file of publishers. If the publishers need to be added or changed, you will need a table procedure to display them (maybe in PUB:NAME order, so you'll also need a PUB:NAMEKEY), and a form to update the publisher's records. You might also need a report that lists all of the publishers.

Relationships within each file can be more interesting—you can produce tables or reports that have Lookup fields, so that whenever a book record is displayed or printed, you can use the common field, PUBNUM, to place information about the publisher in the screen or report. For instance, you might want a report that lists the books by publisher. You could also specify PUBNUM as a Break field for group headers, displaying information about the publisher each time the publisher changes for each book.

Another important part of these file relationships is entering data. Instead of requiring the user to enter the publisher data each time a new book is added, you can specify a Lookup field for the Entry field type on a form. This can then display a table procedure of the publishers from which the user can select one of the publishers. If the one you need doesn't exist, pressing the Ins key will allow the user to add a new one.

In this way, quite complex applications can be built up from a combinations of menus, reports, tables, and forms, and all without writing a line of code!

Conclusion

This has been a brief tour of Designer (we still have the language to cover!) and there is so much more that it is capable of. To explore Designer further, the Clarion Professional Developer comes with several example applications that are worth your time to study and execute; many interesting techniques are presented and they will enrich your understanding of Designer and its capabilities.

PART TWO
The Clarion language

5

CHAPTER

Simple programs

This chapter, which presents the basic rules for writing Clarion source code, as well as some simple examples, begins Part 2 of *Working with Clarion*. This part of the book will teach you much more about the Clarion language, and you will learn how to write programs without a code generator (like Designer). The emphasis in this section will be on terms, principles, and solid programing advice.

Before looking at actual Clarion source code, however, a few simple terms must be defined.

A language consists of statements

The first basic idea to grasp is that all Clarion programs consist of statements. These statements are read by the compiler in order to generate the code that makes the program behave the way you want it to.

Statements in a Clarion program come in two varieties; they are either data declaration statements or they are executable statements.

A statement can consist of part of a line, a whole line, or several lines of source code. Statements end with either a Return or a semicolon. Normally, a semicolon is only used with multiple statements on one line. You can write a single statement that spans multiple lines by using Clarion's continuation character (shown as a pipe symbol, ¦, on the keyboard and screen, and a vertical bar, |, on laser print-outs) at the end of a line, which tell the compiler to continue the statement on the next line. Blank lines are ignored.

A statement can have a label. If a label appears on a data declaration statement, it is the name of the data being declared. If the label appears in the code section, it is the name of a function, procedure, routine, or the target of a GOTO statement. If a statement has a label, the label must begin in column 1. If the statement has no label, it cannot begin in column 1. Labels are case insensitive. For example, a label is the same, whether it is written as SHOWTITLE or showtitle.

Statements can have other statements within them. These compound statements are called structures and are terminated with either a period or an END statement.

Comments can be added with an exclamation mark. Anything after the exclamation mark will be ignored by the compiler to the end of the line.

A program example

Given these basic rules, let's look at a simple Clarion program. Although you won't be familiar with many of the language statements used in this example, just try to get a feel for the basic form for now. See Fig. 5-1.

The purpose of the program is simple — it uses a file that contains a record for every member of an organization. To be a member of this organization, you must pay your dues each year. Therefore, once per year each member's record must be updated to show that they now owe their dues. This means that you need to change each record by setting the Dues paid field to zero.

Notice that in this program, the first statement is the PROGRAM statement. This identifies to the compiler that this is the program procedure, and that this is the first part of the program that will run when this program is invoked. The program statement also serves another purpose; it names the program. The label on the program statement, ZERODUES, is the name of the program. When you create an .EXE version of this program, it will be called ZERODUES.EXE.

```
ZERODUES        PROGRAM

!               This program zeroes the dues paid for
!               each member in the membership file.
!               it should be run at the beginning of each
!               new year.

MEMBERS         FILE
MEMBERREC         RECORD
NAME                STRING(30)
ADDRESS             STRING(30)
CITY                STRING(20)
ZIPCODE             STRING(10)
TELEPHONE           STRING(13)
DUES                DECIMAL(9.2)
                  . .


!---------------------------------------------------------
CODE
!---------------------------------------------------------

SET(MEMBERS)                    ! Start at beginning of file
LOOP UNTIL EOF(MEMBERS)         ! Stop at end of the file
  NEXT(MEMBERS)                 ! Get record
    DUES = 0                    ! Zero out the dues paid
    PUT(MEMBERS)                ! Put back the record
  .
RETURN                          ! Return to DOS
```

5-1. Simple example program

As mentioned earlier, all of the lines that begin with an exclamation mark are comments—they are there for your benefit, and the compiler will ignore them.

The next area you see is the FILE structure. Immediately inside this structure is the RECORD structure, followed by the fields. Note that these fields are arranged like the fields in the Designer file. File declarations will be covered in more detail in Chapter 7.

Code and data

The third statement in the example program, CODE, separates the data declaration section of the program from the code section. Data types are declared before the CODE statement, and only executable statements follow the CODE statement.

Also, as stated in Chapter 2, everything you declare in the data declaration section of the program procedure is global—that is, all of the data before the CODE statement will be accessible by any procedure that is part of the program.

The code section contains executable statements that will manipulate the declared data. These statements are executed sequentially, starting with the first statement after the CODE statement. After the first statement completes, the next statement will execute, and so on.

In the example, you need to manipulate the records in the MEMBERS file. The first statement, SET(MEMBERS), opens the MEMBERS file, and sets up the file to begin accessing records at the start of the file. SET does not read any records from the file; it only positions the file to begin access.

The next statement, LOOP UNTIL EOF(MEMBERS) begins a LOOP structure that will repeat each statement in the LOOP until the EOF() function returns a true condition. Thus, this statement means "repeat the following statements in this structure until the last record in the MEMBERS file is reached." The structure ends with the last period.

Inside the LOOP, NEXT(MEMBERS) reads the first record (which was determined by the SET statement) into the RECORD area. The statement, DUES = 0, assigns the DUES variable (which is part of the record that was just read) to zero. The next statement, PUT(MEMBERS), returns the record back to the file.

When the period is reached, control is transferred back to the LOOP statement, which then checks the EOF() function. If it is not true (you haven't read the last record yet), you will continue to read, revise, and put records back into the file until you have revised every record.

At the end of the loop, you will RETURN back to wherever you were when you called the program. If the program was invoked from DOS, you will return to DOS.

There are also some more subtle aspects of this sample program. Notice how blank lines and comments are used to separate the main parts of the program. This helps make the program more "readable" so that someone else can easily understand it. Just about every book on programming recommends that you liberally comment your code and format the statements in a readable manner.

Also, notice how all statements inside a structure are indented two spaces. While the compiler doesn't care whether the statements are indented by 2, 4, or even no spaces at all, you can easily see which statements are inside the LOOP by following this coding practice. Also, the Editor provides an automatic indention feature that makes this a simple rule to follow.

You could continue to write more complex programs by simply adding more data declarations and more executable statements. However, you would quite likely end up with a monolithic program, several pages long, making it difficult to find where in the program a specific action occurred.

Another reason why writing a single long program is impractical is because in order to make any changes, you would have to recompile the entire program. If you can break up the program into smaller units, it becomes much easier to manage. That is where the process of writing your own procedures and functions comes in.

Procedures, functions, and routines

Programs can be broken up into procedures and functions. Creating your own procedures and functions is just like adding new statements to the language. To transfer execution to a procedure or function, you simply "call" it — that is, use its name in a statement. The procedure or function then "returns" to the caller when you use the RETURN statement.

You've already see some procedure and function calls — the SET, NEXT, and PUT statements in the ZERODUES example are procedures and the EOF() part of the LOOP statement is a function call. The difference between a procedure and a function is that a function returns a value; a procedure just returns to the caller.

The procedures and function calls in Fig. 5-1 are built-in; they are supplied with the package and the compiler already knows about them. You can call them at any time. Many of the built-in procedures and functions will be covered more fully in later chapters.

You can also create your own procedures and functions, but first you must tell the compiler where to find them. This is done by declaring a *map structure* in your PROGRAM procedure. The map structure contains the names of the modules and the procedures and/or functions they contain. For instance, if you have a program that has a main menu, a screen and report for vendors, and a screen and report for customers, you might have a map structure in the data declarations area of your PROGRAM procedure that looks like the following:

```
MAP
        PROC(VENDORS)
        PROC(LIST_VENDORS)
        PROC(CUSTOMERS)
        PROC(LIST_CUSTS)
```

The Main Menu for this program would follow in the CODE section of this program procedure. If you used some functions you've previously written, you would need to include them in the MAP structure, as well as:

```
MAP
        PROC(VENDORS)
        PROC(LIST_VENDORS)
        PROC(CUSTOMERS)
        PROC(LIST_CUSTS)
        FUNC(MONTHNAME),STRING
```

```
            FUNC(FULLNAME),STRING
            FUNC(CALCTAX),REAL
```

The functions MONTHNAME, FULLNAME, and CALCTAX can now be called by any of the procedures or functions in the program. This map structure tells the compiler that all of the procedures and functions are in the same source file.

If you wanted to put the procedures and functions in separate source files, or modules, you would use the module structure to tell the compiler in which modules the procedures and functions resided. Such a map might look like the following:

```
MAP
        MODULE('BUSINESS.CLA')
            PROC(VENDORS)
            PROC(LIST_VENDORS)
            PROC(CUSTOMERS)
            PROC(LIST_CUSTS)

        MODULE('FUNCTS.CLA')
            FUNC(MONTHNAME),STRING
            FUNC(FULLNAME),STRING
            FUNC(CALCTAX),REAL
```

Now the compiler will expect to find the source files BUSINESS.CLA and FUNCTS.CLA to include as part of the source for this program. These new source files must have a MEMBER statement that simply declares the name of the source file for the program procedure.

Putting these procedures and functions into separate files also allows you to change the source lines in either module without having to recompile the program. However, if you make changes to the program module, the whole application will need to be compiled because all the other modules are linked with the global memory in the program module. You can also overlap parts of your program in the map structure, but that will be covered in Chapter 13.

As mentioned earlier, both procedures and functions have their own data and code sections. In addition, you can pass parameters to procedures and functions by simply including them in the line that calls them. In the example program of Fig. 5-1, the statement SET(MEMBERS,5) passes the label of a file structure, MEMBERS, as a parameter and also the constant 5 to the SET procedure. Likewise, the statement MEMBERAGE = AGE(BIRTHDAY,THISDATE) calls the AGE function by passing the BIRTHDAY and THISDATE variables to it; AGE then returns a value that is assigned to the MEMBERAGE variable.

There is one more way to break up parts of a program, and that is by writing *routines*. Routines are simply a collection of executable statements, local to a procedure or function, that can be called with DO (see Fig. 5-2). For instance, the statement DO MYROUTINE transfers control to a set of named executable statements that are placed after the code section of the calling procedure. The first of these statements would have the label MYROUTINE. The statements would then execute until an EXIT statement is reached, and control would return to the line after the DO statement. Routines cannot contain data declarations, only executable statements. These statements operate like the command GOSUB in BASIC.

```
MYPROC        PROCEDURE

              ...data...            ! Local Data

              CODE

              ...executable statements...

              DO MYROUTINE

              ...more executale statements...

              RETURN
MYROUTINE     ROUTINE

              ...executable statements...

              EXIT
```

5-2. Example of using a routine

The important thing to keep in mind is that routines are local to the procedure or function that declares them. This means they cannot be called from other procedures or functions. You always RETURN from programs, procedures, or functions; you EXIT from routines. If you RETURN from a routine, you will return to the original caller of the previous procedure, not EXIT back into the current procedure.

Another difference between procedures and routines is that procedures must be declared in the map statement. Routines do not have to be mentioned anywhere but in the procedure where they are declared.

Declaring your data

As shown in Fig. 5-2, data is declared before the code section. All of the data types that were discussed in Chapter 3 (BYTE, SHORT, LONG,

REAL, DECIMAL, STRING, and GROUP) can be used here. Because these variables are explicitly declared, they are called explicit variables. There is also another type of variable, the implicit variable.

Implicit variables are variables that are not declared in the data section. When the compiler sees a reference to an implicit variable that does not exist, it automatically creates one. For example, the statement I# = 123 is recognized as an implicit numeric variable, because of the trailing # character. If I# does not already exist, it generates an implicit LONG numeric variable called I#. The compiler supports three different implicit types:

label#	implicit LONG
label$	implicit REAL
label"	implicit STRING(32)

Implicit variables should be used to create only simple variables that have no representative meaning, and should be used with care. Because they have no explicit declaration, their overuse can make it difficult for someone else to understand your code.

Each of the explicit data declarations described thus far can also have several attributes declared with them. These attributes are DIM, OVER, and PRE.

The DIM attribute

The DIM attribute creates an array of the declared type. An array of LONG data types is simply a way of declaring many data types that allows you to reference them by their position. For instance, suppose you need to store a budget amount for each month of the year. You could write the following code:

BUD_JAN	DECIMAL(8,2)
BUD_FEB	DECIMAL(8,2)
BUD_MAR	DECIMAL(8,2)
BUD_APR	DECIMAL(8,2)
BUD_MAY	DECIMAL(8,2)
BUD_JUN	DECIMAL(8,2)
BUD_JUL	DECIMAL(8,2)
BUD_AUG	DECIMAL(8,2)
BUD_SEP	DECIMAL(8,2)
BUD_OCT	DECIMAL(8,2)
BUD_NOV	DECIMAL(8,2)
BUD_DEC	DECIMAL(8,2)

Unfortunately, this means you have to use the name of each data type in the code to access them all. The statement

```
BUDGET      DECIMAL(8,2),DIM(12)
```

creates the same twelve DECIMAL data types, each with 8 digits and 2 decimal places.

However, you cannot simply reference BUDGET in your code, because you haven't specified which DECIMAL you mean. You do this by including a subscript with the label. Subscripts are enclosed in square brackets. In this case, the third DECIMAL would be referred to as BUDGET[3]. Reference to any single data type with the DIM attribute requires a subscript. To set the budget for March equal to 100, you would write

```
BUDGET[3] = 100
```

Note that this implies that the first number in the array is 1 (*not* zero). Arrays can have more than one dimension. For instance,

```
BUDGET      DECIMAL(8,2),DIM(12,5)
```

creates an array of 12 monthly budgets for 5 different departments (60 DECIMALS.) Now you need two numbers to access an item in the array — the number of the month and the number of the department. If the Sales department is department number four, the BUDGET[3,4] would be the budget for the Sales department in March.

Arrays can be used for any data type (including GROUP), up to four dimensions deep. The only restriction is that the total length of all the declared data must not exceed 65,536.

The OVER attribute

Another useful attribute you can place at the end of a data declaration is the OVER attribute. This creates a data item that uses the same area of memory as another data item. Consider the following two statements:

```
FULLNAME     STRING(40)

NAME_CHR     STRING(1),DIM(40),OVER(NAME)
```

The first declaration statement allocates a 40-byte string in memory to hold string values. The second statement, because of the OVER attribute, doesn't allocate any new memory to store data, but shares the memory with FULLNAME.

However, notice that the second statement declares a 1-byte string array of 40 bytes. This allows you to access the same memory as a single string, or you can access any byte in the string by referencing the array. For instance, if you want to specify the second byte in the string, you would refer to it as NAME_CHR[2].

Although you have two declarations, the same area of memory is used for both variables. Therefore, the OVER attribute lets you access the same area of memory as two different data types.

The OVER attribute can also initialize an array without writing any executable statements. Consider the following:

```
INITMBR        GROUP
                   STRING('Associate ')
                   STRING('Member   ')
                   STRING('Partner   ')
                   STRING('Lifetime  ')

MBRTYPE        STRING(10),DIM(4),OVER(INITMBR)
```

The dimensioned variable MBRTYPE[X] now has the names of the types of members in it, and you didn't have to write any code to populate the array with these names. Here, MBRTYPE[3] is equal to 'Partner'. Now you can store a simple number for a member type throughout the application, and if you want to display the name of the type on the screen or in a report, you can use that number as a subscript for the MBRTYPE array.

The PRE attribute

The PRE attribute places a prefix on the label of a declared variable that is part of a larger structure. PRE was mentioned briefly in the Designer chapter, because Designer requires these prefixes. They help you in the task of naming variables. PRE simply adds a one- to three-character prefix in all the variable names in a structure. Prefixes are separated from the declared name with a colon. Look at the PRE attribute in the following group example:

```
MBR_DATA       GROUP,PRE(MBR)
NAME               STRING(30)
ADDRESS            STRING(30)
CITY               STRING(30)
STATE              STRING(2)
ZIP                LONG
```

All the variables in the group are referenced with a prefix, so the names are now MBR:NAME, MBR:ADDRESS, etc.

Prefixes are useful because one of the biggest problems in writing programs is determining meaningful names. If the above structure is part of a membership program, there will probably be many places throughout the program (in screens, reports, and files to name a few) where NAME or CITY is the obvious choice for the variable name. Without the PRE, you would have to make each name unique. Prefixes are simply a way to help you keep variable names meaningful and unique.

Assignment statements and expressions

The code section of a Clarion program will now be discussed. As stated earlier, statements in the code section are executed at runtime.

The most common type of statement generally used in a program is the assignment statement. These statements are declared to set a variable to a value. They consist of two parts, separated by an equals sign. The source, the right-hand side of the statement, can be any expression. The destination, the left-hand side of the statement, must be a variable name. For example, $A = B$ takes whatever value is in variable B and puts it in A; it moves the source to the destination. The statement $A = (B*C)/(D + 1)$ is still an assignment statement, but its source is now an expression to be evaluated, with the result assigned to variable A. Expressions will be described in more detail in a moment.

An operating assignment statement is a type of assignment statement that also performs arithmetic on a variable. It is a "shorthand" way of writing a commonly used type of assignment statement. For example, the statement $A += 1$ takes A, adds 1 to it, and puts the result back in A. It is equivalent to the statement $A = A + 1$. Likewise,

$A -= 1$	is equivalent to	$A = A - 1$
$A *= 2$	is equivalent to	$A = A * 2$
$A /= 3$	is equivalent to	$A = A / 3$
$A \wedge = 2$	is equivalent to	$A = A \wedge 2$
$A \% = 7$	is equivalent to	$A = A \% 7$

The CLEAR statement is another type of assignment statement, because it clears variables. In the trivial case, CLEAR(A) is equivalent to $A = 0$ (if A is a numeric). However, CLEAR works on all data types. If A is a string, it will be set to blanks. If A is a dimensioned variable, CLEAR(A[]) will clear the entire array. If A is a GROUP,CLEAR it will set each numeric variable in the GROUP to a 0 and each string variable in the GROUP to a blank.

Before leaving assignment statements, there is one more to thing discuss. Consider the statement $A = B$. If B is declared as a SHORT and contains 10,000, and A is declared as a SHORT, then the value of 10,000 will be moved into A. However, what happens if A is declared as a BYTE?

Since a BYTE can only contain a number from 0–255, how will it fit? It can't.

Most languages require you to call functions that convert one data type to another. However, Clarion will automatically convert one type to another through the assignment statement. It does this with *conversion rules*.

Chapter 5-4 of the *Language Reference* manual provides an explanation of Clarion's conversion rules. The main thing to remember is that if the destination is smaller than the source, the value will be truncated. In the example above, A will end up a zero because the high-order bits in the SHORT will not be transferred. For strings, the source will be chopped off to fit what can be stored in the destination.

As long as you are using the same data types in a statement, and the data types are correctly chosen to hold the possible range of numbers you need, you don't have to worry about the conversion rules.

So far, you have only seen simple assignment statements. However, a statement can contain an expression. An expression is simply a formula that produces a value. Expressions consist of variables, constants, and function calls that are connected by operators. For instance, the simple expression 1 + 1 contains two constants and the addition operator that results in a value of 2.

Constants are either numerics, like 1, or a string literal, like 'This is a string constant'. Note that these numeric constants are normally expressed in a decimal format. However, they can also be expressed in octal, binary, or hexadecimal formats by placing an O, B, or H as the last character of the number.

Functions that can be used in expressions are either user-created functions (that you write, which returns a value), or built-in functions supplied by Clarion, like TODAY() and ABS().

An expression can be used as a parameter to a function, procedure, or subscript of a dimensioned variable. They can also be used as part of an assignment statement or in IF, CASE, EXECUTE, or LOOP statements, which will be covered in the next chapter.

These constants, variables, and functions can be manipulated with operators. There are three types of operators: *numeric*, *string*, and *logical*. The numeric operators are the following:

+	Addition
–	Subtraction
*	Multiplication
/	Division
^	Exponentiation
%	Modulus

Expressions are evaluated at execution time in a set order of precedence. The order of precedence is determined by the operator type and parentheses in the following order from highest precedence to lowest, as shown in Table 5-1.

Table 5-1. Order of precedence

Level	Symbol	Description
1	()	Parenthetical grouping
2	—	Unary minus
3		Function call
4	^	Exponentiation
5	* / %	Multiplication, division, modulus
6	+ —	Addition, subtraction
7	&	Concatenation

If you are writing a complex expression, like the following:

X = 1.25*COST / PRICE + 10

and you are in doubt about which arithmetic operator will take place first, look at the order of precedence to make sure. In this case, the multiplication and division will take place before the addition. If you are ever uncertain about this, so will the next person who looks at your code. A good rule of thumb is to use parentheses to make sure that the order in which you want the operations to occur is obvious.

The only string operator is the concatenation operator, (&), which concatenates (ties together) strings, like the following:

FULLNAME = 'Mr.'& FIRST &'' & LAST

Using this statement, if FIRST contains 'Tom' and LAST contains 'Jones', then FULLNAME will contain 'Mr. Tom Jones'.

Logical operators are used in logical expressions and always produce a true or false condition. They are used mostly in control statements, which will be described in the next chapter. They are as follows:

A = B	True if A is equal to B
A < B	True if A is less than B
A > B	True if A is greater than B
A<>B	True if A is not equal to B
A~=B	True if A is not equal to B

A NOT = B	True if A is not equal to B
A AND B	True if A and B are both true
A OR B	True if A or B or both is true
A XOR B	True if A or B but not both are true

Note that there are three different ways to specify the "not equal" operator.

Making the Compiler work for you

When you write source code, you are writing statements for the Compiler. There are several statements you can make directly to the Compiler to help you write your programs. These statements are called *compiler directives*. There are three compiler directives that are useful in the data section of a Clarion procedure: SIZE, EQUATE, and INCLUDE.

The SIZE directive

The SIZE directive returns the amount of memory required to hold a variable. Because it is a compiler directive, there is no code generated; it simply causes the Compiler to compute the size of a variable and substitute this value in place of the SIZE directive. Consider the following data declarations:

```
GROUP_NAME      GROUP
BYTE_NAME         BYTE
SHORT_NAME        SHORT
LONG_NAME         LONG
REAL_NAME         REAL
DECIMAL_NAME      DECIMAL(7,2)
STRING_NAME       STRING(10)
PICTURE_NAME      STRING (@P###-##-####P)
```

With this GROUP, you can use the following directives in your statements:

SIZE(BYTE_NAME)	returns 1
SIZE(SHORT_NAME)	returns 2
SIZE(LONG_NAME)	returns 4
SIZE(REAL_NAME)	returns 8
SIZE(DECIMAL_NAME)	returns 4
SIZE(STRING_NAME)	returns 10
SIZE(PICTURE_NAME)	returns 11
SIZE(GROUP_NAME)	returns 40

Why use SIZE when you can just count the size of things yourself? Using the above example, if you code 40 in a statement that represents the size of the GROUP, this would be equivalent to SIZE(GROUP_NAME). If you later add a new data type to the GROUP, you might forget to look in the code section to add this new length to 40. Using the SIZE directive lets the Compiler worry about this for you, and you can just add new data items to the group and recompile. This eliminates a common source of bugs that can be difficult to track down.

The EQUATE directive

The EQUATE directive tells the Compiler to substitute a label for another label, constant, picture, or even a keyword. For example,

```
PI      EQUATE(3.1416)
```

Tells the Compiler to substitute the constant 3.1416 whenever it sees the label PI. Other examples of the EQUATE statement are the following:

```
TRUE            EQUATE(1)
FALSE           EQUATE(0)
ENTER_MSG       EQUATE('Press Ctrl-Enter to Accept')
SOC_SEC_PIC     EQUATE (@P###-##-####P)
INIT_PROC       EQUATE(SET_UP_PROC)
```

These EQUATE statements are useful in order to standardize values that are used throughout your program. Perhaps you will use the message 'Press Ctrl-Enter to Accept' on all your screens to indicate when the user completes the screen. You would then code this string on every screen. By using EQUATE statement and referencing the label ENTER_MSG, however, you need to write this string in only one place in your code. To change this string throughout your program, you only have to change the one statement and recompile your modules. You cannot equate something to itself, use reserved words, or use any keyword that is already declared in the data section.

The INCLUDE directive

Another very useful directive is the INCLUDE directive. Its two general forms are the following:

```
INCLUDE('source filename'),LIST

INCLUDE('source filename',structure name),LIST
```

The INCLUDE directive tells the Compiler to look for the specified source file and substitute it for the INCLUDE statement at this point in the program. You can also specify that only a single structure out of the named source file will be included. The LIST attribute on this statement only determines if the included source will be included in the compiler listing.

The INCLUDE directive is useful to keep source code in only one place. For example, if you are writing several different programs that use the same data files, you might declare the file definitions in each program. However, if you need to change the file layout, you will need to change the code for each program. This is another common source of bugs if you forget one.

By placing the file definition in a separate file and using the INCLUDE statement throughout your program, you have to change the file definition only once, and recompile.

Every Clarion program should use the INCLUDE directive for key code definitions. For instance, the statements:

```
INCLUDE('C:\CLARION\STD_KEYS.CLA')
INCLUDE('C\CLARION\SHF_KEYS.CLA')
INCLUDE('C:\CLARION\ALT_KEYS.CLA')
INCLUDE('C:\CLARION\CTL_KEYS.CLA')
```

cause the Compiler to include only those pre-defined files that have many EQUATE statements in them. The EQUATE statements define the non-alphabetic keycodes for the PC keyboard, and allows you to reference the keys symbolically, like using F1_KEY instead of 2049.

Formatting directives

Formatting compiler directives are simply commands you issue to the compiler to manipulate your source file listing; they have no effect on program execution. They are the OMIT, TITLE, SUBTITLE, and EJECT statements.

The OMIT directive

The OMIT statement can be used to create a large area of comments in your code. You can always create comments by prefacing each line with an exclamation mark, but if you have many lines of comment, this can become tiresome. The OMIT directive has the following form:

OMIT('terminator')

This directive would cause the compiler to ignore anything in your source file until the 'terminator' string is reached. For example:

OMIT('*STOP*')

```
* * * * * * * * * * * * * * * * * * * * * * * * * * * * * * * * * * * * *
This is where you can include a description of the module or proce-
dure, your name, a copyright notice, or anything else you want.)

* * * * * * * * * * * * * * * * * * * * * * * * * * * * * * * * * * * * *
```

STOP

The TITLE directive

Another formatting compiler directive is the TITLE directive. This simply places a title at the header of each page in your listing. It has the following form:

TITLE('Title of Program or Module')

The quoted string is included on the first line of every page of the program listing, starting in column 1.

The SUBTITLE directive

Similarly, the SUBTITLE('String') directive puts a quoted string on the third line of the heading of your listings.

You might use the TITLE to specify the name of your program, and the SUBTITLE to specify the procedure of this program.

The EJECT directive

One last directive is the EJECT statement. It has the following two forms:

EJECT

EJECT('New subtitle goes here')

This simply causes the compiler to include a form feed at that point in the listing. This directive can also be used to reset the subtitle for the following pages.

Conclusion

You have now seen all of the basic rules that cover writing statements in Clarion. Basic program components, techniques to declare data, assignment statements and expressions, and compiler directives are all statements that you use each time you write a Clarion program. In Chapters 6 through 10, you'll see how you can use more powerful statements.

6
CHAPTER

Controlling program execution

In this chapter, you will learn about the various Clarion statements that allow you to modify the order in which your program statements are executed.

Beginning with the code section of a Clarion program, your statements are executed in the order in which they appear in your source file, one right after the other. You have already been shown how a procedure or function call transfers control to the called procedure or function, and then returns. Also, you have seen how a routine transfers control to another part of the code section and then return to the next line after the DO statement that called it.

There are other types of control statements besides DO. They are: GOTO, IF, CASE, EXECUTE, LOOP, RESTART, STOP, RUN, CALL and CHAIN.

The GOTO statement

The simplest and most famous (infamous?) control statement is the GOTO statement. It names the label (or location) of an executable statement, and transfers control to that statement when executed. Consider the following program statements:

```
            CODE
            (. . . some executable statements . . .)
TRYAGAIN  ASK
            (. . . more executable statements . . .)
            GOTO TRYAGAIN
```

Execution begins with the first statement after the CODE statement. Execution then continues through the ASK statement and the second set of statements until it reaches the GOTO statement. When the GOTO statement is reached, control is transferred back to the ASK statement with the label TRYAGAIN.

Note that all the statements from the ASK to the GOTO will execute forever unless you find some way out of this infinite cycle. You could put another GOTO inside the second set of executable statements with a target label somewhere outside the cycle.

Overuse of GOTO statements produces what is sometimes called "spaghetti code." Trying to follow the execution of the code becomes so tangled that it is very difficult to read or maintain, even for the author of the program. Although a GOTO statement can be the simplest way to get out of a deeply nested structure, you should use them very sparingly.

The IF statement

The IF statement forms a structure with at least one other statement inside of it. It executes the statements within the structure, depending on one or more logical expressions. Since this statement forms a structure, it is always terminated with a period. The simplest form of the IF statement is:

```
IF AMOUNT = 0 THEN EXIT.
```

In this example, AMOUNT = 0 is a logical expression that will either evaluate to true or false. In this case, if the variable AMOUNT has a value of zero, then the expression is true. If AMOUNT has any other value, the expression is false. If the expression is true, then the EXIT statement will be executed. Otherwise, execution will continue with the next statement after the period.

The THEN part of the IF statement is optional if the statement after the THEN is on a separate line, as in this example:

```
IF AMOUNT = 0
    EXIT
```

The IF statement is actually much richer than this. The full form of the IF statement can be:

```
IF (logical expression 1)
    (statement group 1)
ELSIF (logical expression 2)
    (statement group 2)
ELSE
    (statement group 3)
```

The logic of this IF statement can be described as "If the first logical expression is true, execute statement group 1, and continue after the period. If it is not true, evaluate the second logical expression. If this expression is true, execute statement group 2, and continue after the period. If the second expression is not true, then execute statement group 3."

Note that only one statement group will be executed and execution always resumes after the period. You can have as many ELSIF tests in the IF statement as you need!

The CASE statement

The CASE statement forms a structure and executes a group of statements, depending on the value of an expression. For example, if you have statements that you need to execute depending on the membership type in a club member's record, you might use the following:

```
CASE MEM_TYPE
    OF 'Associate'
        (statement group 1)
    OF 'Regular'
        (statement group 2)
    OF 'Partner'
        (statement group 3)
    OF 'Lifetime'
        (statement group 4)
    ELSE
        (statement group 5)
```

Here, statement group 1 is executed if the membership type (MEM_TYPE) is equal to the string 'Regular', and so on. Statement group 5 (after the ELSE) is executed if MEM_TYPE is not equal to 'Associate', 'Regular', 'Partner', or 'Lifetime'. Regardless of which statement group is executed, execution resumes after the period. You can have as many OF tests as you need.

You don't have to include an ELSE line in a CASE structure. Without the ELSE, none of the statement groups will be executed if there is no match with the CASE variable.

You can use an OROF in a CASE structure. Let's say that, in the above example, you want to process the member's data the same way, regardless of the type. The above code would still work if the statement groups 2 and 3 were the same. Instead of repeating the statement groups, however, you could use OROF, as follows:

```
CASE MEM_TYPE
    OF 'Associate'
        (statement group 1)
    OF 'Regular' OROF 'Partner'
        (statement group 2)
    OF 'Lifetime'
        (statement group 4)
    ELSE
        (statement group 5)
```

The EXECUTE statement

The EXECUTE statement also forms a structure and is used to execute one (and only one) of several statements, based on the integer value of an expression. It has the following form:

```
EXECUTE expression
    (statement 1)
    (statement 2)
    (statement 3)
    (statement 4)
    (statement 5)
```

Unlike the CASE statement, whose CASE variable can be any data type, the EXECUTE statement must specify an expression whose value will be an integer. If the expression evaluates to 1, then statement 1 will execute. If the expression evaluates to 2, then statement 2 will execute, and so on. Only the selected statement will execute; execution then resumes after the period.

The most common use for EXECUTE is to dispatch procedure calls.

Each statement in the above example would be a procedure call. Suppose you have a variable, DEPARTMENT, which has a department code in it. The department codes are 1 for sales, 2 for development, 3 for shipping, and 4 for marketing. If you need to call a particular procedure to update personnel in separate departments, you could write:

```
EXECUTE DEPARTMENT
    UPD_SALES
    UPD_DEVEL
    UPD_SHIPPING
    UPD_MARKET
    .
```

In this case, only one of the procedures would be called, and execution always resumes after the period.

The LOOP statement

The LOOP statement forms a structure that executes a group of statements repetitively. You can break out of a LOOP with a BREAK statement, and you can continue the next iteration of the loop with a CYCLE statement. The simplest form of the LOOP statement is:

```
LOOP
    statement group 1
    .
```

After executing the LOOP statement, statement group 1 is executed; when the period is reached, control is transferred back to the start of the LOOP. This form is called an unconditional loop; the only way out is with a BREAK, GOTO, or RETURN statement inside the statement group. You can also write:

```
LOOP expression TIMES
    statement group 1
    .
```

Here, the expression determines the number of times through the LOOP. The expression can be a constant, or it can be a variable that is modified by statement group 1. If the expression ever becomes zero or minus, you break out of the LOOP. You can also write:

```
LOOP UNTIL logical expression
    statement group 1
```

This causes statement group 1 to be executed UNTIL the expression evaluates to true. You saw an example of this in the simple program in Chapter 5. The code:

```
LOOP UNTIL EOF(MEMBERS)
        NEXT(MEMBERS)
```

was used to LOOP through the records of the MEMBERS file. When the EOF function became true (when the last record is read), you finally break out of the loop.

Likewise, the following form causes statement group 1 to executive repetitively while the expression evaluates to true:

```
LOOP WHILE logical expression
        statement group 1
```

The form of the LOOP statement that gives the most control is:

```
LOOP X = initial value TO limit BY step
        statement group 1
```

and

```
LOOP X = 1 to 10
        statement group 1
```

causes statement group 1 to execute 10 times. (This assumes that nothing in the statement group changes the value of X.) If the BY parameter is omitted, it is assumed to be 1. Likewise, both

```
LOOP X = 1 TO 10 BY 2
        statement group 1
```

and

```
LOOP X = 10 TO 1 BY −2
        statement group 1
```

will loop 5 times. There are also some higher level statements that can alter program execution. They are RESTART, STOP, and RUN.

The RESTART statement

The RESTART statement starts the execution of a program over again, at a specified procedure. This statement does not unload or reload the current program, or even reset the value of any of the current variables. It simply begins execution at a specified procedure. Parameters cannot be passed to the given procedure.

Remember that when you call a procedure, the location of the code to which you will return to is recorded. As you call more and more procedures without returning, more and more locations are recorded. As you become "deeply nested" in procedure calls, you will have to execute many returns to get back to your starting point. The RESTART statement will "unwind" all of these calls. For example,

```
RESTART(MAIN_MENU)
```

Puts you back to the beginning of the MAIN_MENU procedure. All of the variables, including the global variables, are as they were before the RESTART. If you execute a RETURN statement from the procedure specified by the RESTART, you will always return to DOS.

The STOP statement

The STOP statement changes control of execution temporarily, and is used to call the Debugger while running under the Processor. Placing the STOP statement at a particular location in the code is sometimes called "setting a breakpoint."

When a program (running under the Processor) executes a STOP, the Debugger is called. From it, you can display variables, examine system parameters, and even inspect the source code. You can optionally pass a string expression which will then be displayed in the debugger window. For example,

```
STOP('After get record')
```

You can also help determine error conditions with STOP. If you have a program that adds records to a file, but they don't seem to be written to disk, you could verify the ADD statement by placing the following code after it:

```
IF ERROR() THEN STOP('Error' = & ERROR()).
```

If there is an error, the ERROR function will evaluate to true, and the error message would then be displayed in the Debugger window.

While in the Debugger, you can return to program execution, or exit the program.

Since the runtime processor (CRUN) and translated .EXE programs do not have the Debugger present, a STOP statement in these programs will cause the program to end and a halt window to be displayed.

The RUN, CALL, and CHAIN statements

A very useful statement in Clarion is the RUN statement. RUN simply lets you execute an entirely separate DOS program, and then returns you to your Clarion program. It has the following form:

RUN(expression)

where the expression parameter is any command you would give to DOS to run the program. For instance, you could write the statement:

RUN('DIR')

and as soon as the statement executed, you would see the same thing on your screen had you typed DIR at a DOS prompt. Clarion accomplishes this by performing the following three steps:

1. It closes all open files and writes a memory image of the currently running program to a file called $TX.TMP in the current directory, where X is a uniquely assigned number.

2. It returns all but approximately 4K of the memory used by the Clarion program to the operating system.

3. The RUN statement then loads the current command line processor (usually COMMAND.COM) and executes the program specified by the expression. When the called program completes, the $TX.TMP file is reloaded and deleted, and execution begins after the RUN statement.

It is important to remember that any open files you might have been using are closed when the RUN command completes.

The CALL control statement is very much like the RUN statement, except that it is only used to call other Clarion programs. In programs running under the processor (CPRO) or the runtime processor (CRUN), the processor stays resident while the Clarion program itself (the .PRO files) is written to the $TX.TMP file. When the called program completes, the calling program is restored. This saves the load and restore time that is required for the processor. In translated programs, CALL and RUN are identical. For example,

```
CALL('BATCH')
```

would save the current program to a temporary file, and then load and execute the BATCH.PRO program. When BATCH.PRO completes, the calling program is restored and execution resumes after the CALL statement.

The CHAIN statement is like CALL, except that CHAIN terminates the current program and starts another Clarion program. No memory image of the current program is saved. For translated programs, the CHAIN.COM file must be invoked to start up a new Clarion program (see the *Language Reference* manual for details). However, for programs running under CPRO or CRUN, the processor stays resident, loads and initializes the new program, and then starts execution. For example,

```
CHAIN('LEDGER')
```

loads the LEDGER.PRO program and begin its execution.

Basic input/output statements

In this section, the simple, low-level types of statements that let you write characters to the screen and get characters from the keyboard will be discussed.

DOS receives keystrokes from the user by placing each keystroke into a buffer, often called the "typeahead" buffer. It get this name from the fact that when a keystroke occurs, the currently running program is interrupted long enough to place the keystroke in the buffer. This allows the user to type keystrokes while the program is doing other things, so the user can "type ahead" of where the program is executing.

Clarion retrieves its keystrokes from this buffer, as well, and places them in your data declarations when you call keyboard procedures.

The ASK statement

This statement has two basic forms. The simplest form simply waits until a keystroke is in the buffer. ASK does not return the keystroke, it only waits until one is present. To see the keystroke, you would have to follow the ASK statement with the KEYCODE function (see below). To use this form, simply type ASK with no other parameters.

The other form of the ASK statement is more powerful and retrieves the typed data from an entire field on the screen. It has the form:

```
ASK(row,column,variable,picture)
```

This allows the user of your program to enter a value according to a specified picture token, using all of the field editing keys available with that picture, and places that value in the named variable when the user presses Enter. For example, when the statement

```
ASK(5,10,NAME,@s20)
```

is executed, the program takes what is currently in the NAME variable, formats it according the name picture token, and displays it on the screen starting at 5,10, in reverse video. If the NAME variable is blank, the user starts with a blank field to enter.

The program then allows the user to enter keystrokes and complete the field (most commonly with an Enter). When the field is completed, the value of the string is then moved to the named variable. Note that the NAME variable in this example is most likely a string; however, it could be a numeric or any other data type.

It is important to remember that when you execute an ASK statement, of either form, control is transferred to the user. The user must then either press a key when using the simpler form of ASK, or press Enter when using the field entry form of ASK, in order for control to be returned to the next statement in your program.

The KEYCODE Function

As mentioned above, this function returns the last key pressed from an ASK statement (or an ACCEPT statement, which will be covered in Chapter 8). For example, you might want to execute some statements if the user presses the F5 key. You could write the following:

```
ASK
IF KEYCODE () = F5_KEY
      statements
```

The KEYBOARD function

This function returns a keycode for the first keystroke in the buffer (if any), or a zero if the buffer is empty. It does not remove the keystroke from the keyboard buffer, but simply returns the value of the last value placed in the buffer, or zero if empty. Because zero is a logical false value, and any other value is a logical true value, this function is often used in logical expressions.

The most common use of this function is to check to see if any keystroke has been made. If the KEYBOARD function is non-zero, the next ASK statement will immediately complete and remove the keystroke from the buffer. To clear all the keystrokes in the buffer, you need only write:

```
LOOP WHILE KEYBOARD()
   ASK
```

The keycodes returned from KEYCODE or KEYBOARD are all numeric values and can be of two basic types. Character keys are those normal "typewriter" keys that you test for as written characters. For example,

```
IF KEYCODE() = 'A'
```

will test true if the user typed an uppercase 'A', but not a lowercase 'a'. Because KEYCODE or KEYBOARD returns the ASCII value for these keystrokes, the value they return can be tested directly by using the ASCII character.

However, you might want to test for keycodes that are not simple ASCII characters. For instance, when the function key F3 is typed, the keycode that will be returned is the value 2051. Likewise, separate values are returned for a shift-, CTRL-, or ALT-F3.

Clarion provides several source files that have all the possible key-codes already symbolically defined for you. These files are fully documented in Appendix B of the *Language Reference* manual. You can use these files by using the INCLUDE directive. For example, in a module that would reference these keystrokes you would place the line:

```
INCLUDE('STD_KEYS.CLA')
```

so that you can write:

```
IF KEYCODE() = ENTER_KEY
```

rather than:

```
IF KEYCODE() = 257
```

It is strongly recommended that you use these INCLUDE files for key-stroke definitions! They make your program much more readable.

The ALIAS statement

You can also reassign keys with the ALIAS statement—it allows you to substitute one keystroke for another. Two examples are:

```
ALIAS(F10_KEY,F1_KEY)
ALIAS(F1_KEY,F10_KEY)
```

These statements swap the F1 key (default key for help) and the F10 key. In a similar fashion, you can substitute any of the keystrokes available to you. Once a keystroke is aliased, it remains that way for the life of the program, or until you execute an ALIAS to put it back.

Basic I/O to the screen

Before describing the Clarion statements that allow you to display data on the video monitor, it is important to review how monitors on PCs work. Every PC monitor (whether monochrome, CGA, EGA, VGA, etc.) continuously displays whatever is placed in a reserved area of the PC's main memory. This memory is called *video memory*. It can be both written to and read from a Clarion program.

Clarion programs run in text mode on these monitors. (A Graphics LEM is available to let you to run it in graphics mode, but that is another book.) The video memory is organized on a 25 × 80 array, allowing 2000 characters to be displayed. In addition to storing the one byte needed to display a single character, there is also a byte allocated in video memory for each character that contains information like color, blink, etc. This extra byte is called the *video* attribute. Therefore, the amount of memory needed to specify an entire screen is 4000 bytes, 2000 bytes for character data and 2000 bytes for video attribute data.

The BLANK statement

The BLANK statement clears the character data from the screen. It has the following form:

```
BLANK(start row,start column,rows down,columns across)
```

and the defaults for each parameter are 1, 1, 25, and 80, respectively. Examples of the BLANK statement, including explanatory "comments:"

```
BLANK               ! Blanks the entire screen
BLANK(1,41,12,40)   ! Blanks upper right quadrant
```

BLANK erases only character data. It leaves the video attributes as they were, unless there is an active attribute (for color, blink, etc.) set by an earlier SETHUE statement.

The SHOW statement

This statement displays a variable on the screen, and has the form:

    SHOW(row,column,expression,picture)

"Row" and "column" are the starting position where the value of the expression will be displayed. "Picture" is a picture token used to specify the format for the value. For example,

    SHOW(10,20,COMPANY,@S20)

    SHOW(2,2,CLOCK(),@T3)

The first example receives the value for the declared data named COMPANY and displays it in an @S20 picture, starting at row 10, column 20. The second example calls the CLOCK function, which returns the current time and displays it in an @T3 picture, starting at row 2, column 2.

Note that only character data is shown on the screen. SHOW uses the video attributes already in place to set color, blink, etc.

The LOOK statement

This statement is like the inverse of SHOW. It takes the character data from the screen and places in a variable. It has the form:

    LOOK(row,column,variable,picture)

LOOK takes data from the screen, starting at row and column, and expects the data to be in picture format. It then deformats the string on the screen and places the resulting value into the variable. The statement

    LOOK(2,2,DATE,@D3)

will get a character string, starting at row 2, column 2, for the length of a @D3 picture. It will then deformat the string and place the resulting value into the named variable.

The SCROLL statement

The scroll statement is a very powerful and fast way of moving whole blocks of characters on the screen — either up or down and by a specified amount. If you specify the SCROLL statement to scroll one line in an upward direction, the top line of the block will disappear, all other lines will move up, and a blank line will appear at the bottom of the block. If you specify a downward direction, the bottom line of the block will disappear and a blank line will appear at the top of the block. SCROLL has the form:

    SCROLL(start row,start column,rows down,columns across,count)

with the first four parameters specifying the block of screen to be moved. The count parameter is a signed integer that specifies how many lines to scroll. If the count is positive, it scrolls upward. If the count is negative, it scrolls downward.

The HELP statement

This statement simply declares the currently active help filename, and, optionally, the help window to be displayed. No help will be available in your program until the HELP statement has specified where to find the help screens. For example,

    HELP('ORDERS.HLP')

is all you have to do to include help in your programs. The helper utility does the rest by letting you design help windows, complete with menus, transparency, etc. To create context-sensitive help, you can tie help windows to specific help screens. You will see how to do this in Chapter 8.

A simple Clarion program

Now that you have covered some of the fundamental concepts of the Clarion language, examine the program in Fig. 6-1 to see if you can explain what the program does, and what the purpose of each line is.

Figure 6-1 is just an example of using low level input/output statements in a program, like you would in C or Pascal. There are, however, much more powerful and interesting statements to come.

```
            TITLE('Metric Length Conversion')
METERS      PROGRAM

METER       REAL
FEET        REAL

            CODE

            SETHUE(7,0,0)
            BLANK

            HELP('METER.HLP','METER')

            SHOW(4,20,'Enter Length in Feet:',@S32)
AGAIN       ASK(4,42,FEET,@N_8.3)

            METER = FEET/3.28

            SHOW(6,20,'Length in Meters:',@S26)
            SHOW(6,38,CENT,@N_8.3)

            SHOW(8,20,'Do you want to try again (Y/N)?',@S31)
            ASK
            IF KEYCODE() = 'Y' OR KEYCODE() = 'y'
              METER = 0
              FEET = 0
              GOTO AGAIN
              .

            RETURN
```

6-1. Simple Clarion program

Built-in statements

Clarion supplies many procedures and functions that you can use, without having to write them or include them in your map structure. They are called "built-in" functions and procedures, and can be separated into the categories of String, Time and Date, Math, Bitwise, and Miscellaneous statements. Not all of the statements will be covered in this book. For instance, the trigonometric and bitwise functions are very simple to use (if, of course, you already know trigonometry and binary—if not, there are many other sources for this information), and will therefore not be covered here.

String functions

The string functions use strings as parameters or as return values, or both. Remember that the maximum size of a string in Clarion is 255 bytes. If the result of a string calculation could result in a longer string, only the first 255 bytes will be returned. This is also true for intermediate calculations of strings. If a numeric expression is used as a string parameter, it will be automatically converted to a string. Also, remember that the only string operator you can use in string expressions is the concatenation operator (&).

CENTER A simple string function is the CENTER function, which has the following format:

```
CENTER(string,length)
```

CENTER is used to center a string. Leading and trailing spaces are removed from the string, which is then centered inside the return string. The string parameter is a string expression containing the string to be centered. The length parameter is an optional numeric expression containing the length of the return string. If length is omitted, the return string is the same length as the string parameter.

The following are examples of strings returned by the CENTER () function:

```
CENTER('ABC ') returns ' ABC '
CENTER('ABC',5) returns ' ABC '
```

Another common use for CENTER is to center messages on a screen or a report. For instance, the following statement will center an error message in a screen variable of any size (the screen variable name is ERRORMSG):

```
ERRORMSG = CENTER(ERROR(),SIZE(ERRORMSG))
```

LEFT The LEFT function has the following format:

```
LEFT(string,length)
```

and is used to left-justify a string. This is done by removing leading spaces in the string, which is then left-justified in a return string. The string parameter is any string expression containing the string to be left-justified. The length parameter is an optional numeric expression containing the length of the return string. If length is omitted, the return string is the same length as the string parameter. Here are two examples of strings returned by the LEFT function:

```
LEFT(' ABC') returns 'ABC '
LEFT(' ABC',3) returns 'ABC'
```

RIGHT The RIGHT function has the following format:

```
RIGHT(string, length)
```

and is used to right-justify a string. Trailing spaces are removed from the returned string, and the remaining characters are then right justified. The string parameter is a string expression containing the string to be right justified. The length parameter is an optional numeric expression containing the length of the return string. If length is omitted, the return string is the same length as the passed string parameter.

Examples of strings returned by the RIGHT () function are as follows:

```
RIGHT('ABC ') returns ' ABC'
RIGHT('ABC',5) returns ' ABC    '
```

CLIP The CLIP function has the following format:

```
CLIP(string)
```

CLIP simply removes trailing spaces from a string. The string parameter is a string expression that can contain trailing spaces. The return string will be a substring that has no trailing spaces. CLIP is frequently used with the concatenation operator.

For example, the following statement produces a name such as Doe, James R. from several variables:

```
NAME = CLIP(LAST) & ', ' & CLIP(FIRST) & '' & INIT & '.'
```

strings returned by the ALL() function:

```
LEN(string)
```

and returns the length of a string. The string parameter is a string expression. If the string expression consists of a single string variable (STRING, GROUP, RECORD, and so forth), LEN returns its declared length. Otherwise, this function evaluates the expression, converts from numeric if necessary, and returns the length of the final intermediate value.

Note that the blanks at the end of the string are included. If you want to find the length of a string without the blanks you would use CLIP(LEN(string)). The following are examples of lengths returned by the LEN() function:

```
LEN ('ABCDEFG')                returns 7
```

LEN(NAME)	returns declared length of NAME
LEN(−12 * 9.1)	returns 6
LEN('−109.2')	returns 6
LEN(CLIP(LEFT(' ABC')))	returns 3

ALL   The ALL function has the form:

ALL(string, length)

and returns a string containing repetitions of a character sequence. The string parameter is a string expression containing the character sequence to be repeated. The length parameter is an optional numeric expression containing the length of the return string. If length is omitted, the return string is 255 characters long. The following are examples of strings returned by the ALL() function:

ALL('*')	returns '********** . . .' (255 characters long)
ALL('12')	returns '1212121212 . . .' (255 characters long)
ALL('*',5)	returns '*****'

UPPER   The UPPER function has the following format:

UPPER(string)

UPPER converts lower-case letters to upper-case ones. The string parameter is a string expression that contains the string to be converted. The return value is a string with lower-case letters (a through z) replaced by their upper-case equivalent (A through Z). Examples of strings returned by UPPER are:

UPPER('ab-CD-ef')	returns 'AB-CD-EF'
UPPER('AB-CD-EF')	returns 'AB-CD-EF'
UPPER('ab-CD-ef')	returns 'AB-CD-EF'
UPPER('AB-CD-EF')	returns 'AB-CD-EF'

LOWER   Like UPPER, the LOWER function has the format:

LOWER(string)

and converts upper-case letters to lower-case ones. The string parameter contains the string to be converted. The return value is a string with upper-case letters (A through Z) replaced by their lower-case equivalent (a through z). The following are examples of strings returned by LOWER:

LOWER('AB-cd-EF')	returns 'ab-cd-ef'
LOWER('ab-cd-ef')	returns 'ab-cd-ef'

SUB   The SUB (substring) function has the following format:

SUB(string,position,length)

and is used to get part of a string out of another string. SUB is a function that returns the part you want (the substring) out of the string you name. The string parameter can be a string expression. The position parameter is a numeric expression that represents the starting point of the substring. Once the starting position has been established, the length parameter provides the length of the substring. The position parameter can be used in two different ways:

- If the value of the position parameter is positive, it represents the position of the first character of the substring, starting with the front of the string. For example, position 4 means the substring will start with the fourth character of the string.

- If the position is negative, its value represents the starting character of the substring, relative to the end of the string. For example, position "−3" means start the substring at the third to last character of the string.

Note that there is more than one way to specify the same position. In a five character string, both positions 2 and −3 refer to the second character and positions 3 and −2 refer to the third character. If you specify a position outside the length of the string, spaces will be supplied for those characters. For the string 'MONTY', the following are returned substrings:

```
SUB(NAME,1,2)      returns 'MO'
SUB(NAME,5,2)      returns 'Y '
SUB(NAME,-2,2)     returns 'TY'
SUB(NAME,-5,2)     returns 'MO'
SUB(NAME,3,5)      returns 'NTY '
SUB(NAME,10,3)     returns '  '
```

INSTRING   The INSTRING function has the format:

INSTRING(substring,string,step)

and determines if part of a string (a substring) exists within another string. If it does exist, you will be told the starting point of the substring. The function does this by stepping through a string and searching for the occurrence of a substring. Upon completion, it returns the successful step number (one is the first step), or zero if the substring was not found.

The substring parameter is a string expression that contains the search string. The string parameter is the string to be searched. The step parameter is a numeric expression containing the step length. A step length of one searches for the substring, starting at every character of the string; a step length of two starts at every second character, and so forth. If the step parameter is omitted, the step length is set to the length of the substring.

The INSTRING function returns a long integer, containing the step number of either the first successful match or zero. The INSTRING function is useful for parsing or editing, as illustrated by the following example:

```
IF NOT INSTRING(TYPE, 'ADDREVDEL',3)
    ERRMSG = 'ACTION MUST BE ADD, REV OR DEL'
```

In this example, assume that the TYPE variable is a field the user has entered, and that you need to check to see if TYPE is ADD, REV, or DEL. The INSTRING function is passed the substring, TYPE, to see if its value is in the string 'ADDREVDEL'. Since it should only match starting with every third character, it is given a step number of three. If TYPE does not contain one of these values, it will return zero (false) and the error message will be displayed. If TYPE is 'REV', however, the INSTRING function would return a 2 (true), indicating a match on the second step.

In another example, consider part numbers that consist of two numbers separated by a dash, such as 1234-56789. The numbers on either side of the dash have a variable number of digits. To obtain the second part of the number, you could write:

```
LASTPART = SUB(PARTNO, INSTRING('-',PARTNO,1)+1,255)
```

This statement first uses the INSTRING function to find out the position of the dash, and then adds one to it, which gives the position of the first character of the number. This position is then passed as a parameter to the SUB function, which returns the string, starting at this position to the end of the string. The length will automatically be truncated to the declared size of LASTPART.

NUMERIC   The NUMERIC function has the following format:

```
NUMERIC(string)
```

and is used to check for a valid numeric string. A valid numeric string contains only the following characters: the digits 0 through 9, optional leading spaces, an optional leading minus sign, and an optional decimal point. The string parameter is a string expression containing the numeric string. The return value is a long integer containing a one (true) if the numeric string parameter is valid, or a zero (false) if not. Examples of the values returned by the NUMERIC() function are:

```
NUMERIC('−53389.45')        returns 1 (true)
NUMERIC('−53,389.45')       returns 0 (false)
NUMERIC('53389.45−')        returns 0 (false)
```

FORMAT The FORMAT function is written in the following way:

```
FORMAT(value,picture)
```

and formats a value according to a picture code. The value parameter is an expression containing the value to be formatted. The picture parameter is an optional picture code or the label of a string statement that uses a picture token as a parameter. The return string is the value after it has been formatted by the picture. Examples of strings returned by the FORMAT function:

```
FORMAT(1234.59,@N8.2)                returns '1,234.59'
FORMAT(309539954,@P###-##-####P)     returns '309-53-9954'
FORMAT(349514427,SOC_SEC_NO)         returns '349-51-4427'
FORMAT(67350,@Ddd.mm.yy)             returns '22.05.85'
```

DEFORMAT The DEFORMAT function has the following format:

```
DEFORMAT(string,picture)
```

and removes formatting characters from a string. The string parameter is a string expression containing a string that is expected to be in the picture format. The picture parameter is a picture code or the label of a string statement that uses a picture code as its initialization parameter.

The numeric function NUMERIC(DEFORMAT(string)), is true for any string. In the following examples, DATA is a STRING (@D1) variable with a value of '5/22/85'.

```
DEFORMAT('1,234.59')              returns '1234.59'
DEFORMAT('309-53-9954')           returns '309539954'
DEFORMAT('40A1-7',@P##A1-#P)      returns '407'
DEFORMAT(DATE)                    returns '67350'
DEFORMAT(DATE,@P##/##/##P)        returns '052285'
```

CHR The CHR (ASCII character) function has the format:

```
CHR(code)
```

and converts a numeric code to its corresponding ASCII character. The code parameter is a numeric expression containing a numeric ASCII code. The return value is a one-byte string containing the corresponding ASCII character. The CHR function converts ASCII values to characters. Therefore, the expression CHR(VAL('A')) returns 'A'. Examples of ASCII characters returned by the CHR function are as follows:

CHR(65)	returns 'A'
CHR(122)	returns 'z'
CHR(38)	returns '&'

VAL The VAL function has the form:

VAL(character)

and converts a character to its corresponding numeric ASCII code. The character parameter is a one-byte string containing a character. The return value is a long integer containing its corresponding ASCII code. The VAL function converts characters to ASCII codes, therefore, the expression VAL(CHR(65)) returns 65. The following are examples of numeric ASCII codes returned by the VAL function:

VAL('A')	returns 65
VAL('z')	returns 122
VAL('&')	returns 38

Time and Date statements

Clarion stores both dates and times in a default internal format, called the "standard" format. This standard format for both times and dates uses a LONG variable. Remember, you don't have to use the standard format — you can always store a date as three separate numbers for day, month, and year if you like. However, using this standard format reduces storage requirements and simplifies the associated arithmetic. Also, there are a variety of picture codes that you can use that already assume a standard format.

Actually, dates have plagued computer programs for many years, because the calendar is a discontinuous number line. Every year has 365 days except for every 4th year, which has 366. Another problem is that for dates older than a few hundred years, a different system was used, depending on the country you're in. It can be difficult to write a routine to figure out what day of the week any given date represents.

In Clarion, a standard date is simply the number of days that have elapsed since December 28, 1800, covering the range of dates from January 1, 1801 to December 31, 2099. It is not important for you to remember those dates, but simply to be aware that any date is an integer number of days since a specific point in the past.

Storing dates this way has several advantages. To find the days of the week of a standard date, divide the standard date number by seven. If the remainder is zero, the day was a Sunday; a remainder of one is Monday, two is Tuesday, and so forth.

In a similar way, a standard time is the number of hundredths of a second since midnight, covering the range of one hundredth of a second past midnight (standard time 1) to midnight (standard time 8,640,000). Although expressed to the nearest hundredth of a second, the system clock is updated only 18.2 times per second.

Finding the elapsed time between two times is therefore simple arithmetic—just remember that the answer is in hundredths of a second. Similarly, finding how many days will elapse between two dates is simply a matter of subtracting them. Clarion also provides several functions to convert standard formats into other forms.

TODAY The TODAY function has the form:

```
TODAY()
```

and returns what DOS thinks is the current date. This function has no parameters; however, all function calls require parentheses. The return value is a long integer containing today's date in standard date format.

The FORMAT function can be used with the TODAY function to obtain a formatted version of today's date. For example,

```
FORMAT(TODAY(),@D1) returns 07/23/89
```

CLOCK The CLOCK function has the form:

```
CLOCK()
```

and returns the time of day from DOS. The return value is a long integer containing the current time in standard time format. The FORMAT function can be used with the CLOCK function to obtain a formatted version of the current time. For example,

```
FORMAT(CLOCK(),@T3) returns 10:46AM
```

You can also set the time and date.

SETTODAY The SETTODAY procedure has the form:

```
SETTODAY(date)
```

and sets what DOS thinks is the current date. The date parameter is a numeric expression containing a standard date to be used as today's date. For example, SETTODAY(67995) sets the DOS system date to 2/26/87. Note that this does not update any battery-driven clocks that you find on many PCs; it only emulates the DOS DATE command.

SETCLOCK The SETCLOCK procedure has the form:

SETCLOCK(time)

and sets the DOS system time of day. The time parameter is a numeric expression containing a standard time to be used as the current time.

DATE The DATE function has the form:

DATE(month,day,year)

and computes a standard date for a given year, month, and day. The month, day, and year parameters are numeric expressions containing the month, day, and year of the date you want to convert. The return value is a long integer containing a standard date.

The month and day values must be greater than zero. However, these values can also be outside of their normal range. A month of 13 means January of next year, and a day of 32 in January means the first of February. Consequently, DATE(12,32,87), DATE(13,1,87) and DATE(1,1,88) all produce the same result. Year must be in the range of 00 to 99, or in the range of 1801 through 2099. 1900 will automatically be added to the year value if it is less than 100.

There are also functions to retrieve the month, day or year of a standard date. They have the following names and forms:

MONTH(date)
DAY(date)
YEAR(date)

DAY returns the day of the month (1 to 31) for a given standard date. MONTH returns the month of the year (1 to 12) for a given standard date. YEAR computes the year (1801 to 2099) for a given standard date.

AGE The AGE function has the following form:

AGE(birthdate,base date)

and returns the age relative to a base date. The birthdate parameter is a numeric expression containing a birthdate. The base date parameter is a numeric expression containing a date, usually the current date, or TODAY. Both birthdate and base date are in standard date format.

The return value is a string containing the age associated with the difference between the two dates. If the base date is omitted, TODAY's date from DOS is used. The age is returned in the following format:

1 to 60 days	'nn DAYS'
61 days to 24 months	'nn MOS'
2 to 1?? years	'nnn YRS'

Miscellaneous statements

BEEP   The BEEP statement has the form:

```
BEEP(frequency,duration)
```

and simply causes the speaker on the PC (such as it is) to make a sound for a specified period of time. The frequency parameter is a numeric expression representing the frequency tone of the sound. If frequency is omitted, the default is 150 Hz.

The duration parameter is a numeric expression that represents the duration of the sound in hundredths of a second. If duration is omitted, the default is 16 (16/100 second).

A good use for the BEEP statement is to induce a delay in your program. Suppose you want to wait for one second before going on to the next statement. You would simply call BEEP with a duration of 100 and a frequency you can't hear, like 50. Frequencies under 100 Hz will make no sound from the speaker.

MEMORY   The MEMORY function has the form:

```
MEMORY()
```

and returns a LONG with the amount of free memory available (in bytes). Free memory is used, among other things, for memory tables, file buffers and caches.

IDLE   The IDLE statement has the form:

```
IDLE(procname,timeout)
```

and specifies a procedure to be called while the program is waiting for a keystroke during an ASK or ACCEPT statement. (ACCEPT will be discussed in Chapter 8.) Earlier, it was stated that control is transferred from your program to the runtime system when you execute an ASK. This is so the user can enter data using the editing keys. With IDLE, you can get control back if there is no keyboard activity within a specified time period.

After you declare an IDLE procedure with this statement, that procedure will be active until you clear it. From then on, during an ASK or ACCEPT, if a certain number of seconds elapses without a keystroke, then the named procedure will be called. If zero is used, the idle procedure will be called immediately. This is useful for causing a screen change while waiting for input. The following sample code demonstrates the idle statement:

```
         . . code . .
         IDLE(SHOTIME,2)
         ASK
         . . code . .
SHOTIME PROCEDURE
         SHOW(2,5,CLOCK(),@T1)
         RETURN
```

This procedure will cause the current time to be displayed every 2 seconds while waiting for keystrokes.

NOTE: You cannot call ASK or ACCEPT inside an IDLE procedure.

7
CHAPTER

Access
to data

In this chapter, you will learn about statements that can define and manipulate Clarion files and how to improve file performance. Clarion files are structured files that allow a variety of methods to access stored data.

As mentioned earlier, Clarion supports two kinds of files — DOS files and Clarion data files. Clarion allows you to read and write any file that you access with DOS. However, the kind of access that DOS gives you is relatively limited — you can only read or write a number of bytes, starting at a certain point in the file. While this access might be enough for some applications, you will often need to get at your data with more control.

In Fig. 3-2, it was shown how Clarion data files are stored on disk. Now it is important to consider how the files look from a programmer's point of view — how files are declared and manipulated in a Clarion program.

The basic unit of a Clarion file is the *record*. Much like group structures, the record is a fixed-length group of declared Clarion data types.

Records must be declared within a file structure, and from this structure, new records are added and existing records are searched and revised.

File declarations

Before I explain the file structure in detail, consider the following statements created by Designer for the sample application in Chapter 4.

```
BOOKFILE       FILE
                   RECORD
TITLE              STRING(30)
AUTHOR             STRING(30)
SUBJECT            STRING(20)
ISBN               STRING(12)
DEWEY              STRING(10)
PAGES              LONG
PUBLISHED          LONG
```

Because you have already covered the regular data types, the only new statements are FILE and RECORD. In this example, a file (which will be named BOOKFILE.DAT) is assumed to be in the current directory when the program runs.

The record is formed by all of the data types declared within the record structure. Each field in the record is stored on disk in the order they are declared. The length of the record is the sum of the lengths of all the fields.

Reading and writing records using this structure is simple. When you add a new record to the file, all the values of the variables that are currently inside the record structure are written to the file. Similarly, when you read a particular record, all the variables in the record structure are set to the values that are stored in that record on disk. Also, to revise a particular record, you read that record into the record structure, assign the variables in the record structure to their new values, and simply put the record back to disk. To delete a particular record, mark that record in memory as deleted. It now cannot be retrieved.

So, with this basic understanding, take a closer look at the format of the FILE and RECORD statements.

The FILE statement

As explained above, the FILE statement forms a structure. For Clarion files, it has the following form:

```
(label)     FILE,NAME('filename'),CREATE,RECLAIM,PRE(xxx)
```

The NAME, CREATE, and RECLAIM attributes are optional. Prefixes (discussed earlier) are not only allowed on files but are quite useful. They are required by the Designer, but not by the Compiler. Let's look at these attributes more closely.

NAME The NAME attribute declares the name of the file that will be found in the DOS file directory. If omitted, the label of the structure will be used. The extension for the file will default to .DAT if it is not specified.

Note that the NAME attribute can also contain a directory path to explicitly declare a location for this file. If the directory is not specified, it defaults to the current directory when the program is run.

CREATE This attribute tells the compiler to include all the information needed to create an empty Clarion file in the running program. You might want to leave off the CREATE attribute, however, because the amount of memory the compiler needs to include can be quite large for a complex file. You can make your programs smaller by not using this attribute, if you know that the file already exists when your program runs.

RECLAIM As you delete records in a Clarion file, you leave "holes" where the old record was positioned. If you have an application where you need to add and delete records frequently, you should use the RECLAIM attribute. This tells the Clarion file system to reuse deleted records by writing new records over the holes left by the deleted records. This keeps files as compact as possible, but leaves the records in an indeterminate physical order.

The only reason you might not want to RECLAIM records is if you want to keep the records in the order in which you add them.

The RECORD statement

This statement is required in a file structure; it forms a sub-structure within it. Both a label and a prefix are optional. If a label is specified and used in an assignment statement, the record is treated exactly like a group structure.

You can also have a prefix on the RECORD statement, as well as on the FILE statement. If there is a prefix on both statements, the RECORD prefix applies to the field names, and the FILE prefix applies only to those statements with labels between the FILE and RECORD statements.

Within the RECORD structure, variables can be declared as arrays, or dimensioned. Variables can also consist of groups. Groups can have groups within groups, and any of these can also be dimensioned!

Given the above basic structure, you can also declare statements to determine how to retrieve data. There are several basic ways to access data:

- *Sequential access* means reading records one after the other. In this mode, you typically start at the beginning of the file and read each record until you reach the end.
- *Direct access* means you read a record by specifying which record you want, like "get record number 5." This is sometimes called *random access.*
- The above two forms of access are limited to the actual order in which the records appear in the file. A much more interesting and useful access method is one that allows you to determine the order that the records are accessed. This method is called *keyed* or *indexed access.*

Keyed access requires a separate index to maintain a list of the records in the order you specify. This order is similar to books in a library—they are usually stored in some physical arrangement (like Dewey or ISBN order). The most useful order is usually alphabetically by subject, author, or title. Instead of looking at every book until you find one you want, you only need to go to the card catalog (index). You use this index by finding the key value for the book, like subject, author, or title, which then tells you the location of the book. This lets you go directly to the book without having to search among thousands of books.

This library analogy can be extended further; if you add a new book to the library, you must also add an entry to the card catalog (index). You must also delete index entries when a book is removed.

Clarion makes this indexed or keyed access very simple. Consider the following statements:

```
BOOKFILE        FILE
SUBJKEY             KEY(SUBJECT,AUTHOR)
AUTHORKEY           KEY(AUTHOR)
TITLEKEY            KEY(TITLE)
                RECORD
TITLE               STRING(30)
AUTHOR              STRING(30)
SUBJECT             STRING(20)
ISBN                STRING(12)
DEWEY               STRING(10)
PAGES               SHORT
PUBLISHED           LONG
```

Note that there are three new statements. These statements declare a new ordering that lets you look at the file in ascending alphabetical order—by subject, author, and title.

The KEY statement

The form for this statement is the following:

(label)   KEY(variable1,variable2, . . .),DUP,OPT,NOCASE

The KEY statement declares an order in which you can access a file. This statement can declare any number of any of the fields declared in the record structure that follows. It must appear before the RECORD statement and follow a FILE statement.

Specifying more than one variable as part of the key lets you order records that, for instance, have duplicates for variable1 to be in further order by variable2, and so on. You might use KEY(SUBJECT,AUTHOR) as a KEY statement. This would order records by subject, and then duplicate subject records by author. For example, books on Science would then be in alphabetical order by author.

You can construct as many components in a key as you wish, as long as the total length of the key components does not exceed 245 bytes. Note, however, that it is best to keep keys as small as possible for performance and disk space reasons.

A KEY statement also causes a separate file to be made when the file is created. This file holds the keys and location of the records. The name of the key file is BOOKFILE.K01 for the first key named, BOOKFILE.K02 for the second, etc.

The attributes NOCASE, OPT, and DUP are all optional and can appear in any order:

NOCASE   In a KEY statement, this attribute specifies that you do not care whether the key component fields appear in upper- or lower-case. It specifies that STRING variables are all upper-case, and does not effect numeric variables.

OPT   With the OPT attribute, records whose key components contain null values are not placed in the key file. Here, *null* means all spaces for STRINGS, and zero for numeric fields.

DUP   The DUP attribute allows you to key records that have duplicate keys. Normally, if you add a record to a file that already has a record with the same key value, you get a "creates duplicate key" error. Since the default is to not allow duplicates, this means that the extra step of determining if there are duplicates present must be taken.

If you do not care if there are duplicate keys for the records, or if you already know that duplicates will not be present, you can eliminate considerable disk activity by using the DUP attribute, which specifies that duplicates are not checked when the record is added or changed.

The INDEX statement

This statement creates a key (just like the KEY statement does), except an INDEX is not updated automatically upon adding, revising, or deleting records. An INDEX must be built on demand by the program. This statement has the same form as the KEY statement, except the DUP attribute is unnecessary because indexes are never updated.

Why use an index? If you have a file with several keys, there is overhead involved in keeping the keys current each time you add, revise, or delete a record. If you need to process the records in a certain order, but only need to do it once in a while (for a year-end or month-end report, for instance) you can specify the order using an index. An index imposes no overhead during normal operation, and is built only when it comes time to print that report. For the example file structure, you might write:

```
BOOKFILE        FILE
SUBJKEY             KEY(SUBJECT,AUTHOR)
AUTHORKEY           KEY(AUTHOR)
TITLEKEY            KEY(TITLE)
DEWEYINDX           INDEX(DEWEY)
                    RECORD
TITLE                   STRING(30)
AUTHOR                  STRING(30)
SUBJECT                 STRING(20)
ISBN                    STRING(12)
DEWEY                   STRING(10)
PAGES                   SHORT
PUBLISHED               LONG
                    .   .
```

This INDEX statement allows a file to be built under the control of your program, which you can then use to access records like any other key file. The DEWEYINDX file, in this case, will have the name BOOKFILE.I04, while the other keys will have the names BOOKFILE.K01, BOOK-FILE.K02, and BOOKFILE.K03.

The MEMO statement

There is yet another file that can exist in concert with the main data file—a memo file. This file can contain variable length text fields associated with each record. Using our example, you might insert the statement:

```
COMMENTS        MEMO(1000)
```

as the last line of the file structure preceding the RECORD statement. The

MEMO statement adds another field for each record that consists of a variable length block of text whose maximum size is 1,000 bytes. Whenever a record is read, the associated memo field is also placed into the COMMENTS field.

The memo file must have the name of BOOKFILE.MEM. Only records that have a non-blank memo field have anything stored in the memo file. Memo fields are stored in 252 byte blocks, so that only those records that have large amounts of data in them will take up that much room in the memo file. When a record is read that has a blank memo, the COMMENTS field is blanked. Deleted memo blocks are always reused when new memos are added.

The MEMO statement must occur between the FILE and RECORD statements. Only one MEMO field is allowed per file. Memos are frequently specified as USE variables in TEXT fields, providing a word processor-like editing capability (Text fields are covered in the next chapter, Screens and Windows).

The OWNER statement

This is the last statement that can go between the FILE and RECORD statements. You can use the OWNER statement to encrypt the file header and records from anyone who runs the program without using the correct password.

The password parameter is used to encrypt the file header. It can be a variable (possibly prompted from the program user), or a literal string constant that is present in the source program. However, if you use a variable for the password when the file is created, the password is not stored anywhere. If you forget the password, the file is no longer accessible!

ENCRYPT The ENCRYPT attribute in the OWNER statement is optional and tells the file system to not only encrypt the header, but also to encrypt the records in the file as well. Reading and writing records with the ENCRYPT attribute requires very little overhead while your program is running.

These statements and attributes can declare Clarion files. Many Clarion files can be declared and used in your programs at once, as long as the total number of open files does not exceed the number you have specified to the DOS CONFIG.SYS file, up to a possible 252 files.

File procedures

Now that you know how to declare Clarion files, there are a variety of statements with which you can manipulate them.

The OPEN statement

Before Clarion files can be accessed, they must first be opened. Many of the file operations automatically (implicitly) open files for you (e.g., SET, GET, ADD). However, these statements can cause a halt at runtime if an error occurs (like "file not found"). However, if an error occurs with the OPEN statement, it is posted, and you can check it with the ERROR function. Any associated key or memo files are also opened when a file is opened, except for index files. Each key file uses 512 bytes of free memory when they are opened. The format of the OPEN statement is:

```
OPEN(file-label)
```

where "file-label" is the label of the file structure for the file you want to open. This statement is most commonly used to check for the existence of a file, as shown in the following example:

```
OPEN(BOOKFILE)
IF ERROR() = 'FILE NOT FOUND'
CREATE(BOOKFILE)
```

Note that, in this example, the FILE statement must include the CREATE attribute to allow the file to be created. In Designer, when you are prompted for the creation of the file, Designer places the CREATE attribute in the file structure, and generates the statements shown above for each file you have specified.

The COPY statement

The COPY Statement has the following form:

```
COPY(file-label,'filename')
```

and simply copies a Clarion file and all its associated files to another name and/or directory. Note that the first parameter is the label of a file structure, not a string expression. The filename parameter is a string expression which can include a different directory path name.

The RENAME statement

The RENAME statement has the same form as COPY:

```
RENAME(file-label,'filename')
```

and simply renames the file specified by the label to a new 'filename', including all the key and memo files.

The REMOVE Statement

The REMOVE statement has the form:

REMOVE(file-label)

and, like the DOS DELETE command, REMOVE deletes the data file and its associated files. The file, however, must be closed before you can remove it. Be careful when using this, because the REMOVE statement is executed immediately, regardless of the kind of records in your file.

The CREATE statement

The CREATE statement has the form:

CREATE(file-label)

and creates a file on demand. The CREATE attribute in the FILE statement must be specified in order to use this statement. All associated files except index files are also created, and the file is left open.

WARNING! The CREATE statement is executed immediately. If the file you specify already exists, it will be deleted and replaced with a new empty file!

The EMPTY statement

The EMPTY statement has the form:

EMPTY(file-label)

and removes all records from a file, clearing away any key or memo files. Obviously, you should also use this statement with caution. If the file is closed, EMPTY will open it and leave it open.

The CLOSE statement

The CLOSE statement has the form:

CLOSE(file-label)

Since all files are closed whenever you properly end a Clarion program, the CLOSE statement is not required. If you exit your program with a normal RETURN, or through the Debugger, or any other way than simply turning off the machine, your files will be closed.

However, you might want to use CLOSE because it will free up any memory that may have been allocated by the file. This is especially true for files with keys.

The BUILD statement

The BUILD statement has the form:

```
BUILD(label)
```

and rebuilds key or index files. If the label is that of a KEY statement, that particular key file will be rebuilt. If it is the label of an INDEX, that index file will be rebuilt. If it is the label of a FILE statement, all key files (but not index files) will be rebuilt. BUILD can be time-consuming for large files, and should be used only at an appropriate time.

The PACK statement

The PACK statement has the form:

```
PACK(file-label)
```

and reads through the entire data file, making a new copy of the file without the deleted records and deleting the original file when finished. All key and memo files are rebuilt. If the file is closed when PACK is called, PACK will open it and leave it open. Like BUILD, PACK can be time-consuming for large files, and should be used only at an appropriate time.

Record procedures

The process of using records in Clarion files is very simple. Let's start by looking at the simplest procedures: ADD, PUT, DELETE, and APPEND.

The ADD statement

The ADD statement has the form:

ADD(file-label)

and takes whatever values have been placed in the variables declared in the record structure and MEMO statement (if any) and adds them to the data file as a new record. If there are any key files declared, they will also be updated.

Two error conditions can result from ADD. These conditions can be checked by calling the ERROR function, which will return a string if an error has occurred. "Access denied" is the error message returned from DOS if there is no room on the disk, or if Clarion is unable to write to the file. "Creates duplicate key" is the error string returned by ERROR if the new record would have caused a duplicate key entry for any key that does not allow duplicates.

The PUT statement

The PUT statement has the form:

PUT(file-label)

and allows you to change the values for the fields stored in a record. The PUT statement requires that a record has been previously retrieved, using GET, NEXT, or PREVIOUS. You can then assign new values to any of the fields in the record or in the memo field, and call PUT. This will replace the old field values with the new ones.

If any of the changed variables cause a change in key components, the appropriate key will be updated. Because of this, you can get the "creates duplicate key" error from PUT if you change a key value to one that already exists in the file. If there is not already a record in memory (from GET, NEXT, PREVIOUS, ADD, or APPEND), you will get a "record not available" error.

The DELETE statement

The DELETE statement has the form:

DELETE(file-label)

Like PUT, DELETE requires that a record already be retrieved from the file with GET, NEXT, and PREVIOUS. DELETE marks the current record in the file as deleted, and adds it to the reusable chain if RECLAIM is specified. It also marks all memo blocks (if any) as reusable. It then removes any keys (if any). You can get the "record not available" error from ERROR if no record is currently in memory. Deleted records cannot be "undeleted."

The APPEND statement

This statement has the same form as and works exactly like the ADD statement, except that no key files are updated when the record is added to the file.

Why would you use APPEND? If you are adding many records to a file as a single operation, sometimes called a *batch* operation, remember that there is overhead in updating each key file for each record you add. It can be faster to append all the records first, and then build the keys. For example, if you have a file with two keys declared, a simple test shows that when adding 50 or more records, it is faster to append each record and build the key files than it is to add each record. However, if you do use the APPEND statement, make sure you build the key files.

Clarion provides several different ways of reading records from a file, so each of the following GET, SET, NEXT, and PREVIOUS statements have several forms.

The GET statement

The GET statement reads a record either by record number or by key value into the record structure. It has the form:

    GET(order,record)

where "order" specifies the order to retrieve the records, and "record" specifies which record to get. "Order" must be the label of either a file or a key statement. "Record" must be an expression or the label of a KEY statement.

For example, the simplest form is GET(BOOKFILE,5). This reads record #5 from BOOKFILE into memory. However, this will be the fifth record according to whatever order happens to occur in the file.

You can also specify a keyed order. If you write GET(TITLEKEY,5), you would also get the fifth record from BOOKFILE, but it would be the fifth record according to the alphabetical order of TITLEKEY. Using this form of the GET statement requires that key entries be counted, so it will take longer to execute for larger files.

Both of these forms use a numeric value to specify the record to retrieve. However, you can also read a record based on its key (or index) value. Using the example BOOKFILE structure, you might write the following statements:

```
TITLE = 'Stranger in a Strange Land'
GET(BOOKFILE,TITLEKEY)
```

In this case, the GET procedure will construct a key based on the values in the fields of the record structure. It then looks through the specified key file, searching for a match. If a match is found, it then reads that record into memory. If an exact match is not found, it posts the error "record not available." Therefore, this GET statement will either read the record with "Stranger in a Strange Land" in the TITLE field, or the error will be returned.

The most powerful way of reading statements uses a combination of the SET, NEXT, and PREVIOUS statements.

The SET statement

The SET statement usually sets up the conditions to read records sequentially. SET does not read any records; it only sets up the initial conditions. The logical form of the SET statement is:

```
SET(order, starting point)
```

and, like the GET statement, the order parameter in a SET statement specifies the order in which records are retrieved. It must be the label of either a FILE, KEY, or INDEX statement. If it is a FILE label, then the NEXT or PREVIOUS procedures will read records in file order. If it is a KEY or INDEX statement, the NEXT or PREVIOUS procedures will read records in the order defined by the specified key or index.

The starting point parameter tells the following NEXT or PREVIOUS statement where to begin reading. This parameter is optional. If it is omitted, the beginning of the file is assumed. Otherwise, the starting point can be the label of a KEY statement or a record number value. For instance, SET(BOOKFILE,5) sets up the following NEXT or PREVIOUS statements to read the fifth record, according to file order. After reading the fifth record with NEXT, another NEXT statement reads the sixth record, and so on. If you call a PREVIOUS statement after the SET, you will still get the fifth record, but another PREVIOUS will retrieve the fourth record, and so on.

SET(BOOKFILE) does the same thing that SET(BOOKFILE,5) does, except that the following NEXT or PREVIOUS statement starts at the beginning of the file and then reads records in file order. That is, if after SET(BOOK-FILE) you execute a NEXT procedure, the first record (in file order) will be read. A following NEXT statement will read the second record, and so on. However, if you execute a PREVIOUS after the SET(BOOKFILE) statement, it will read the last record from the file. A following PREVIOUS will read the next to last record, and so on.

This SET, NEXT, PREVIOUS combination allows you to process records in a file by going in a forward or backward direction. Likewise, SET(TITLEKEY) sets up the NEXT procedure to start at the first record (as defined by the key) and then reads records in key order. SET(TITLEKEY,5) does the same thing, except that it starts with the 5th record in key order.

There are two more forms of the SET statement that handle the problem of starting at a particular key value. For instance, if you want to start viewing authors named Zelazny, you might write:

```
AUTHOR = 'Zelazny'
SET(AUTHORKEY,AUTHORKEY)
```

This would access records alphabetically by author, starting with 'Zelazny'.

There are two functions that are useful with SET, NEXT, and PRE-VIOUS. They are the EOF and BOF functions.

- EOF(file) returns a TRUE condition, if the current record in memory is the last one in the file (in an order defined by the SET).

- BOF(file) returns a TRUE condition, if the current record in memory is the first record in the file.

Consider this example, which uses the above statements:

```
SET(AUTHORKEY)
LOOP UNTIL EOF(BOOKFILE)
     NEXT(BOOKFILE)
     DO PRINTBOOK
```

These statements will read every record in the file alphabetically by author's name, and will call a routine to print some information about the book. The following statements:

```
AUTHOR = 'Niven'
SET(AUTHORKEY,AUTHORKEY)
LOOP UNTIL EOF(BOOKFILE)
     NEXT(BOOKFILE)
     IF AUTHOR<> 'Niven' THEN BREAK.
     DO PRINTBOOK
```

will read all records in the file alphabetically by author's name, starting with the author 'Niven', and call a print routine for each record. When the author's name is no longer 'Niven', no more records are printed. Therefore, only those records with the author's name of Niven are printed.

A very important thing to remember is that the "pointers" used by SET, NEXT, and PREVIOUS are not affected by other GET, ADD, PUT, or DELETE statements. It is also important to remember that reading records in keyed order using SET, NEXT, and PREVIOUS is much more efficient than using keyed GET statements.

The POINTER function

The POINTER function has two forms. POINTER(file-label) returns a LONG integer that contains the record number of the current record in memory, by the order in which the records appear in the file. POINTER(key-label) or POINTER(index-label) returns the record number of the current record in keyed order.

Note that the forms POINTER(key-label) or POINTER(index-label) count each keyed entry in the key or index file. This can be time consuming for large files.

The most common use for POINTER is to save the location of a particular record, so that you can restore it at a later time.

The RECORDS function

The RECORDS(file-label) forms of the RECORDS function returns a LONG integer that tells you how many records are in the file. This number does not include any deleted records.

You can also use the form RECORDS(key-label) or RECORDS(index-label). These two forms return the number of records that are keyed in the specified key or index file. Because of the OPT attribute and the APPEND statement, the number RECORDS(file-label) returns might be more than the number RECORDS(key-label) or RECORDS(index-label) returns.

The PATH function

The PATH function simply returns a string that is the current drive and directory path, like C:\CLARION\EXAMPLE.

The NAME function

The NAME(file-label) function simply returns what is currently known about the name of the file. If the file is open, NAME will return the full file specification, including drive, directory path, name, and extension. If the file is not open, it will return whatever information is provided by either the NAME attribute, or the default name given by the label of the file statement.

With these simple statements, you can create very complex applications involving many files and relationships. Because each file maintains its own pointers, you could read a record by key from one file, use a field in that record to do a keyed GET into another file, and so on. In just a few statements, you can easily build up quite complex data retrieval procedures.

Improving file performance

There are many functions and procedures that Clarion provides to help you increase the speed with which you can process Clarion data files.

The STREAM and FLUSH statements

When any DOS program writes data to a file, it asks DOS to write the data to the disk. If there are buffers set up (with the BUFFERS = command in CONFIG.SYS), it also updates the buffers. When the file is extended enough, the file allocation table is also updated. Also, the directory must also be updated to reflect the fact that the file has increased in size. However, the directory is only updated when the file is closed. This is why a DOS file can become corrupted during a power failure if it has been writing to the disk without ensuring that the directory is current.

Using Clarion files will alleviate this problem by forcing DOS to update the file directory on every write to the disk. This mode of operation is called flushing the directory to disk, and can be controlled by two procedures: FLUSH and STREAM. FLUSH makes sure the directory is updated on every file extension, but it takes more time to add records with FLUSH than with STREAM.

When you open a Clarion data file, either explicitly or implicitly, the mode defaults to FLUSH. From then on, the records will be safe on disk. For many applications, the safety of the records which have been added is more important than speed. For instance, suppose you bring up your application every day at 9:00 AM and then add records continuously during the day. If there is a power failure at 1:00 PM, you want to make sure that all of that morning's records are safe on file.

However, there are "batch" oriented procedures where you might need to add many records at once. Using the STREAM procedure can speed up your file changes dramatically. Note that STREAM and FLUSH only affect the ADD or PUT procedures that extend the data, key, or memo files; they do not apply to those file operations that only read records.

Besides making sure that your application does not access the disk any more than necessary, you can further improve your file performance by using your system resources intelligently. The primary system resource that can be used to speed up file operations is free memory. The general principle used here is that it is much faster to read a large amount of data once than it is to read a small amount of data many times. Therefore, using free memory to store large amounts of data that you will need at a later time is more efficient than reading only the data you need at the moment.

When your application runs, there is usually some amount of free memory left over. Clarion gives you two commands to use free memory that can make a dramatic difference in file performance: the BUFFER and CACHE statements.

The BUFFER statement

The BUFFER statement has the form:

```
BUFFER(file-label,memory-amount)
```

and allows you to specify an amount of free memory as a record buffer for a particular file. You can have a separate BUFFER for any file in your application.

When this command is executed, it allocates the specified amount of memory. Nothing else happens until the first record is read with a GET or NEXT or PREVIOUS statement. When that request is executed, instead of reading one record, it fills the buffer with records in sequential file order. (This assumes a forward direction for GET or NEXT; a backward direction for PREVIOUS.)

From then on, if the required record is in memory, no disk input/output will be performed to read the record. As soon as a record is read that is not in the buffer, the buffer will load the requested record into memory. The memory amount parameter allocates memory for the buffer according to the following rules:

- If the value of the memory amount is greater than zero, but less than or equal to one, this fraction specifies the percent of free memory to use.

- If the memory amount is greater than 1, but less than 1000, it specifies the number of records to buffer.

- If the memory amount is greater than 1000, it specifies the amount of memory in bytes to allocate for the buffer.
- If the memory amount specifies more than the amount of available free memory, then all the free memory will be allocated.

The amount of memory allocated is always rounded off to the number of whole records that will fit. If the memory amount specifies more memory than is necessary to place the file in the buffer, only the amount necessary to place all of the records will be allocated.

The records kept in the buffer are *write through*; that is, when a record in the buffer is changed, it is updated in memory as well as written to the disk.

There is a very important rule to remember about the BUFFER statement: Do not use it with random, keyed, or indexed access. When doing these kinds of record access, the order of the record numbers to be read is unpredictable, and each time a record is read outside the buffer, the entire buffer is replaced. In the worst case, the BUFFER statement will actually slow down your record access.

However, you should use BUFFER when you are reading sequentially through a file in record order (or when the order doesn't matter). This is the fastest way to read records from a Clarion file.

Buffers are freed when the file is closed, when another BUFFER statement is issued, or when the FREE statement is used.

The CACHE statement

The CACHE statement has three forms:

CACHE(file-label,memory-amount)

CACHE(key-label,memory-amount)

CACHE(index-label,memory-amount)

and is similar to the BUFFER statement in that it allocates memory to a particular file to speed up input/output. However, because accessing Clarion files can mean reading both the data file and a key or index file, you can use CACHE to improve access to the key and index files, as well as the records.

The CACHE statement is executed immediately. Unlike the BUFFER statement, when a CACHE statement is executed, the memory amount is allocated, and the records or keys are read into the CACHE. You can have more than one cache allocated for different files at once.

The first form of the CACHE statement allocates a fixed number of records (depending on the memory value), and, starting with the first one, reads them into memory. From then on, if the record in is memory, no input or output will be necessary to read the record. If the requested record is not in the cache, it will be read from the file normally. Unlike buffers, a cache is not automatically replenished.

The first form of the CACHE statement is used to cache records, and the memory-amount value uses the following rules:

- If the memory amount is greater than zero, and less than or equal to one, it specifies the percent of free memory to use.
- If the memory amount value is greater than 1 and less than 1000, it specifies the number of records to read into the CACHE.
- If the memory amount value is greater than 1000, it specifies the amount of memory to allocate in bytes.

Using CACHE for records is useful if you have a small but frequently accessed file that will fit into memory. For example, a file that contains the names of the states with their abbreviations will only have fifty records. Instead of reading them from disk each time you need the records, you can place all fifty records into a cache. This effectively places the data file into a RAM disk in your computer.

CACHE will only allocate what it has room for, and in whole multiples of record sizes. Memory for a cache is freed when the file is closed, by issuing another CACHE statement to the same file, or by using the FREE procedure.

The second and third forms of the CACHE statement read parts (or all) of a key or index into memory. Depending on the size of the key and the number of records in the file, there can be several disk accesses to the key or index file before the record is retrieved. For instance, when using a keyed GET statement with a file that has a 20-byte key and 5000 records, there might be three disk accesses needed from the key file for each record you want to read. Therefore, it is a much more efficient use of memory to place the key file in a cache before you put the records in a cache.

When using the second and third forms of cache, the following rules apply to the memory amount value:

- If the memory amount is greater than zero, but less than or equal to one, it specifies the percent of free memory to use.
- If the memory amount is greater than one, but less than 1000, it specifies the number of accesses to save by placing the amount of the key or index into memory.

- If the memory amount is greater than 1000, it specifies the amount of memory to allocate, in bytes.

A key or index cache is allocated in 512-byte blocks. The cache is allocated immediately. If more blocks are requested to be cached than will fit into memory, only those that fit will be read. If more memory is specified than is necessary to cache the entire key, only the amount of memory needed is allocated. Memory for the cache is freed when the file is closed, by issuing another CACHE statement, or by using the FREE procedure.

The best part of the BUFFER and CACHE statements is that they are single statements; their effect can be measured simply by placing them into the code and running the program to see if they make a difference. Remember to always free buffers and caches when done with them.

Also, remember that there are higher priority uses for free memory. While your program runs, free memory might be needed to store windows and memory table entries. If you have allocated all free memory for a cache or buffer, Clarion will need to deallocate some of this memory if you are also opening and closing windows or adding items to a memory table.

Transaction processing

Clarion provides the higher level procedures normally found on mainframe or minicomputers to support transaction processing. The need for these functions is typically found in applications that require several files to be updated when a particular event occurs. These multiple updates are referred to as a *transaction*.

For example, say you have a program that allows the user to enter an order for widgets. Furthermore, suppose that the order is from a new customer and that the order should automatically remove the ordered items from inventory, update a sales file, remove the items from inventory, and generate a shipping notice. All of these actions can be treated as a single event, and this event is called a transaction.

With the statements defined so far, you can write all of the ADD, PUT, and DELETE statements that are required. However, what if the power goes out in the middle of processing this transaction? You could end up with items removed from inventory but not shipped, a customer order without all of the ordered items, or worse. You could end up with a partial, or "dangling" transaction!

By carefully thinking about the sequence of file operations, you can avoid some of these problems, but not all of them. You should always place your file statements together so that the time period in which a power failure can affect a transaction is as small as possible.

To solve these potential problems, Clarion provides three statements: LOGOUT, ROLLBACK, and COMMIT. These statements are used to "frame" a transaction (define its boundaries), and make sure that if the entire transaction is not completed, none of it is applied.

The LOGOUT statement starts a transaction. It tells the file system to maintain a log of all of the changes made to *any* Clarion data file and its associated key or memo files. These changes can occur with the ADD, APPEND, PUT, or DELETE statements.

The COMMIT statement completes a transaction. It tells the file system that the transaction is done, in order to clear the log and stop logging changes.

The ROLLBACK statement restores a partial transaction. It tells the file system to restore all the affected files to their state when the LOGOUT statement was issued.

The LOGOUT statement

The LOGOUT statement has the form:

```
LOGOUT(log-list)
```

and tells the file system to create the log-list file and begin logging file changes. The log-list file contains the name of all the files affected during the transaction. When a new file is affected, the name of that file is added to the log-list file, and another file is created with the name of the data file with a .LOG extension to hold the state of the file before any changes.

Recording the state of the file before the change is applied is referred to as *pre-imaging.*

The COMMIT statement

The COMMIT statement completes a transaction. It has no parameters and simply turns off logging and deletes the log and pre-imaging files. A LOGOUT statement must have been issued prior to this statement.

The ROLLBACK statement

The ROLLBACK statement has the form:

```
ROLLBACK(log-list)
```

and restores all the affected files. If a LOGOUT statement is currently active, the log-file parameter is not needed. When the rollback occurs, it looks for the log-list file. If one is not found, then rollback immediately completes. If it finds a log-list file, it reads any filenames it contains, and opens the pre-image file to begin restoring the files. All keys and memos are also restored. It does this until all files listed in the log-list file have been restored. The ROLLBACK statement is used in two ways:

- To restore files if any error condition is returned during a transaction.
- To rollback a partial transaction. If a power failure occurs, you can use ROLLBACK(log-file) as one of the first statements in your program. This tells the file system that if any file exists with the log-list filename, it exists only because a transaction did not complete, so ROLLBACK removes the partial transaction.

Remember that there is extra disk activity involved with using LOGOUT. Extra disk input/output must be performed to log all the changes, so transactions will slow down. However, because only those bytes in a file that have changed are logged, it is fairly efficient.

The program shown in Fig. 7-1 illustrates the ROLLBACK, LOGOUT, and COMMIT statements.

```
        PROGRAM

        [global data]

        CODE

        [setup code]

        ROLLBACK('BOOKFILE.TRN')      ! If not present,
                                      ! nothing happens
                                      ! Otherwise, remove any
                                      ! partial transactions

        [application code]

        RETURN

TRANS   PROCEDURE

        LOGOUT('BOOKFILE.LOG')        ! Start Logging

        [add, put or delete statements]

        IF ERROR()
           ROLLBACK                   ! Restore everything
           SHOW_ERROR                 ! Handle condition
           RETURN                     ! Go Back
           .
        COMMIT                        ! Turn Off Logging
        RETURN
```

7-1. Program illustrating ROLLBACK, LOGOUT, and COMMIT statements

8
CHAPTER

Screens
and
windows

The Clarion language provides structures that you can use to create screens and windows. You create these structures with the screen formatter and process them with language statements.

Using the Designer demonstrates some of the power and possibilities of the Clarion applications developer. Designer, however, only permits the development of three types of screens for use in your application: The basic menu, table, and form. Although these screens will meet the needs of many of the programs that you write, occasionally you will want to reach beyond Designer and create your own screens.

Screen development in most traditional languages is one of the most difficult portions of a program to write and maintain. Difficulties arise when you have to rely upon trial and error to arrange the components of a screen via a series of display commands. Remember, the traditional approach of program development involves writing code, compiling the source, linking, and then testing. This can become a long, drawn-out process when designing a difficult screen.

Clarion, as you have already seen in the chapter on the Designer, takes a different approach to screen development. You can use statements to make your own screens in Clarion just as you would in any other language, but this is usually not necessary. Clarion screens can be defined with structures that designate the position of all the elements that are contained within them. This unique approach is what allows Clarion to offer the sophisticated screen painters that are found in both the Designer, and the screen formatter of the Editor. Although you will rely upon the screen formatter to write your screen structures, it is important to understand some of the statements it generates.

The screen structure

The beginning of a screen's definition is designated by the SCREEN statement. The syntax of this statement is:

```
label      SCREEN,WINDOW(rows, columns),AT(row,column), |
                 HUE(foreground,background,border),TRN, |
                 HLP(id),PRE(xxx)
```

Notice that the SCREEN structure has a label, by which it must be referenced. Remember that Clarion labels must begin in column 1. A screen is a structure, and all Clarion structures are terminated with a period. Each element of the screen will be defined between the SCREEN statement and the ending period. The WINDOW, AT, HUE, TRN, HLP, and PRE attributes are optional. Although not required, each attribute offers important control of the screen.

The WINDOW attribute

Without this attribute, Clarion assumes that you intend to create a screen that fills the entire display. The WINDOW attribute limits a screen to a certain number of rows and columns. Also, when this attribute is used, the information covered by the window is saved so that the display is restored when the window is removed. If you want what is sometimes called a "popup" window, use this attribute.

It is important to remember that the display will be saved only if the WINDOW attribute is used. If you open a screen that does not have this attribute, the original screen will not be restored when the second screen is closed. If you want to have your window cover the entire display, use a WINDOW(25,80) attribute in the second screen's definition.

Note: The term "window" will be used in the remainder of this book to refer to a screen structure that has a WINDOW attribute declared.

Another important thing to remember is that each open window requires memory to store the portion of the display it covers. The memory is freed when the window is closed, but it is possible to run out of memory by opening too many windows at one time. Each time a SCREEN structure is opened without the WINDOW attribute, however, all the memory used by any previously opened windows is released.

The AT attribute

This attribute is only meaningful if the WINDOW attribute has been used. AT forces a window to appear in a fixed position. The row and column parameters specify where the top left-hand corner of the window will appear relative to the top left-hand corner of the display. For example, if you want a window to always appear in the top left column of the display, then you might use a definition like this:

```
label      SCREEN,WINDOW(10,40),AT(1,1) .
```

Likewise, using AT(12,20) will cause a window to open on the twelfth row of the screen beginning at column twenty.

The parameters of the AT attribute can be constants. If you specify constants that cause the screen to be placed off the screen, you are notified by the compiler that the window will not fit.

However, the row and column parameters of the AT attribute can be variables. This allows your program to control where the window will appear when the program runs. The variables must be set prior to using the window. When using variables, the compiler cannot predict if the parameters will be correct. If the specified location requested by the variable parameters is not valid when the open occurs, the window will simply be centered on the display.

If the AT attribute is not used, the window will float around the last accessed position of the previous screen or window. The position, therefore, is determined by the last SHOW statement or field ACCEPT statement. The program also attempts to not cover the active area of the screen. Clarion's screen processing assumes that the last accessed area, usually a field being accepted, is related to the window being opened.

A window first attempts to open below the last accessed area. If it will not fit, the window will attempt to open above the area. If the window cannot open without covering the field, it is simply centered on the screen.

The HUE attribute

Parameters of this attribute are used to define the default colors for the screen (or window). When a screen opens, the specified foreground and background color first clears the area that the screen will cover. The elements of the screen are then placed in their positions. Any element that does not specify its own HUE will accept the color attribute already displayed on the screen.

The border color is an optional parameter. If a border color is included, the display's border is changed to the specified color when the screen opens. It is permissible to omit both the foreground and background parameters if you merely want to set a border color. For example, HUE(,,2) specifies that the border is set to green when the screen opens. Some color display devices do not show a border, but specifying one will not cause any problems.

The TRN attribute

It is best to specify a foreground and background color, unless you are using the TRN attribute. The TRN attribute stands for transparent. When the TRN attribute is used, two things will occur. First, if a HUE attribute was not specified in the SCREEN statement, the color attributes from the display under the window will show through. The elements of the screen that do not specify a HUE will accept the color from the underlying screen. The second effect is that all space characters (that do not have their own HUE attribute) will be replaced with the character from the underlying display. This second feature of the TRN attribute will occur whether or not a HUE is specified in the SCREEN structure.

TRN can design windows that point to (or highlight, using a HUE) an area of a screen that has already been displayed. When a window that has specified the TRN attribute is closed, the display is restored just as it is with other windows. Probably the best demonstration of transparency can be found by visiting the Director utility. While using the Clarion Director, press F1 and examine how the various help screens are displayed.

The HLP attribute

It is possible to identify the help window you want to associate with this screen, using the HLP attribute. When you do this, any fields on this screen that do not have a HLP attribute defined will default to the one declared in the screen structure. Usually, the HLP attribute of the SCREEN statement is used to designate a global help screen for the entire window.

The PRE attribute

Prefixes have been discussed before. The PRE attribute defines the prefix by which your program will identify the screen's variables.

Other screen components

Understanding the SCREEN statement's construction can help you to visualize the basic skeleton of a screen or window. The elements in the structure definition rely upon the first statement, the SCREEN statement, for absolute positioning and other information not specified by the statements themselves.

Figure 8-1 is an example screen structure that was designed with the screen formatter in the Clarion Editor. Examine the SCREEN statement. ADDRBOOK is the name of the structure, and it is a window that takes up 12 rows and 58 columns. Since it does not have an AT attribute, the window will float. A prefix of SCR has been defined and a default HUE of 7 (white) on 1 (blue) has been designated. The remainder of the screen structure contains the elements that comprise the window.

```
ADDRBOOK     SCREEN       WINDOW(12,58),PRE(SCR),HUE(7,1)
             ROW(2,58)    PAINT(10,1),HUE(7,0)
             ROW(12,2)    PAINT(1,57),HUE(7,0)
             ROW(1,58)    PAINT(1,1),TRN
             ROW(12,1)    PAINT(1,1),TRN
             ROW(1,1)     STRING('<201,205{55},187>'),ENH
             ROW(2,1)     REPEAT(9);STRING('<186,0{55},186>'),ENH .
             ROW(11,1)    STRING('<200,205{55},188>'),ENH
             ROW(2,20)    STRING('LITTLE ADDRESS BOOK'),HUE(14,1)
             ROW(4,13)    MENU(@S4),USE(FIL:TITLE),SEL(0,7),REQ
               COL(18)       STRING('Mr.'),SEL(0,7)
               COL(22)       STRING('Mrs.'),SEL(0,7)
               COL(27)       STRING('Ms.'),SEL(0,7)
               COL(31)       STRING('Dr.'),SEL(0,7)
                           .
             ROW(5,7)     STRING('Name:'),HUE(14,1)
               COL(13)    ENTRY(@S20),USE(FIL:NAME),LFT
             ROW(6,4)     STRING('Address:'),HUE(14,1)
               COL(13)    ENTRY(@S25),USE(FIL:ADDRESS_1),SEL(0,7),REQ,LFT
             ROW(7,13)    ENTRY(@S25),USE(FIL:ADDRESS_2),SEL(0,7),LFT
             ROW(8,7)     STRING('City:'),HUE(14,1)
               COL(13)    ENTRY(@S20),USE(FIL:CITY),SEL(0,7),REQ,LFT
               COL(34)    STRING('State:'),HUE(14,1)
               COL(41)    ENTRY(@S2),USE(FIL:STATE),SEL(0,7),REQ,LFT,UPR
               COL(44)    STRING('Zip:'),HUE(14,1)
               COL(49)    ENTRY(@p#####p),USE(FIL:ZIP),SEL(0,7),REQ,NUM
             ROW(10,19)   PAUSE('Press Enter to Accept'),USE(?PAUSE_FIELD) |
                          HUE(14,4)
```

8-1. Example screen definition generated by the formatter

Elements can be placed in specific locations by using the ROW and/or COL statements. Note that the positions indicated by ROW and COL are always relative to the top left-hand position of the screen structure. If the WINDOW attribute is omitted, the positioning commands also represents the absolute screen positions for the items. In windows, you do not have to be concerned about the absolute position of an item. Since the positioning is relative to the structure definition, you only have to designate where an item should occur relative to the top-left hand corner of the window.

An internal row and column position is maintained while a screen is generated. This position is where the next display item in a screen structure will begin. Before the first screen structure command is executed, the internal counters are set to row 1, column 1. This internal position is changed as items are displayed and when a ROW or COL command is encountered. If no ROW or COL commands are encountered in a structure, then the elements of the screen simply appear one right after the other on the same line.

In order of elements in a screen structure can affect how the screen looks and operates. Components of a screen structure are displayed (or executed) in sequential order from top to bottom. If two screen elements are specified for the same position, the latter will overwrite the former once the screen has been completed. For example, if a screen is displayed that has these two statements:

```
ROW(2,1) STRING('987654321')
ROW(2,1) STRING('12345')
```

the actual characters displayed on row 2, beginning at column 1, will be '123454321'. This potential error is not usually a problem if you use the screen formatter to generate your source, because you get to see the screen while you design it.

Elements of a screen structure generated by the screen formatter will be ordered similar to those shown in Fig. 8-1. PAINT statements occur first. Painting is a way to designate colored areas of the screen without interfering with the characters that are displayed there. Next, the STRING and REPEAT statements that represent any tracking characters are included. The remaining statements are the string variables an characters displayed on the screen, as well as all data entry fields (menus, entrys, pause, text, etc.).

The screen formatter

The Screen Formatter is accessed through the Editor. Once a filename has been accepted on the Editor's basepage, the edit worksheet displays the text of the file. As discussed in Chapter 2, there are actually two format utilities available in the Editor (the other one is the report formatter). Each formatter is accessed by pressing the key combination, Ctrl−F, while in the Editor's worksheet. The specific formatter that is loaded depends upon whether you are creating something new or modifying a structure that already exists.

An important feature of the Editor is that it contains a portion of the Clarion Compiler. This enables it to read and modify the source of existing structures with the special formatters. Several other applications developers offer screen formatters but very few, if any, can read and write code directly into (and while editing) your source files.

To edit an existing screen structure, you must first move the Editor's cursor to any line within the screen structure. When you press Ctrl−F, the Editor's compiler begins examining the source from the first line in the file until the cursor's line has been reached. Compiling must always begin with the first line to ensure that you are, or are not, inside an existing screen structure. As mentioned earlier in this chapter, a screen structure has a label (that begins in column 1) followed by the remainder of the SCREEN statement, and ends with a closing period. If the cursor is found to be within the structure, then the remainder of the screen is compiled and the information is sent directly to the screen formatter.

If the cursor is not within a screen (or report) structure then the Editor will let you decide which formatter to load. Figure 8-2 shows the window that lets you decide which formatter to load. Selecting Screen will cause the screen formatter to be loaded.

8-2. Formatter selection window

```
Format New Structure

Type:Screen   Screen   Report
```

When creating a new screen, the screen formatter's worksheet is completely blank. An existing screen, however, would appear almost exactly as if your application was executing. The example in Fig. 8-1, when displayed by the screen formatter, looks like Fig. 8-3. "What you see is what you get," or WYSIWYG, is the objective of the screen formatter. Allowing you to design screens in this fashion is a distinct advantage of Clarion over traditional programming languages.

To create a sample window, begin by editing a new source file. Since there are no existing structures, Ctrl−F will bring up the window displayed in Fig. 8-2. Select Screen and press Enter to load the screen formatter. The screen formatter makes very few assumptions about the

8-3. Display of an existing structure in the screen formatter

screen you are about to make. Pressing Ctrl–S brings up the Summary window shown in Fig. 8-4.

The Summary window can be called at any time you are using the screen formatter, and contains the information currently known about the screen structure: the various fields (entry, point, pause, menu, and text); repeat statements; and strings that are used by menu fields or that have defined labels. All other information, the paints and all other characters, is derived from what is displayed on the worksheet. If the screen is saved at this time, the formatter will simply generate the SCREEN statement and a closing period since there is no information about the screen to be generated.

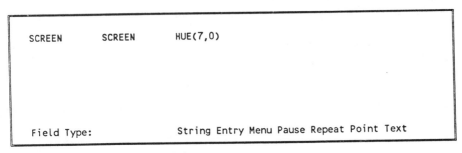

8-4. Screen formatter's summary window

The Summary window is a very important part of the screen formatter. It is through this window that the SCREEN statement can be tailored and all fields are entered. Items that the window displays can be modified by moving the selection bar over the item and pressing Enter. For example, to edit the SCREEN statement for this window, press Enter. (No positioning is required since this is the only item displayed.)

The screen definition window

An example of the screen definition window is shown in Fig. 8-5. Your screen currently has the uninspired name of SCREEN. This is the default name given to all new screens. When making your own screens, you will probably want to give each a unique name. This adds readability to the code and helps to identify the function the screen will perform. Edit your window so it matches the one in Fig. 8-5.

```
                              Screen

    Label     :ADDRBOOK                 Comment   :No    Yes  No
    Help      :                         Prefix    :SCR
    Attribute :White On Blue
    Border    :No Border
    Window    :No         No  Float  Fix
    Fix at Row:
    Fix at Col:
    ADDRBOOK      SCREEN      PRE(SCR),HUE(7,1)
```

8-5.   Screen definition window

Refer back to the attributes of the SCREEN statement presented at the beginning of the chapter. Most of the prompts in this window have a one-to-one correspondence with those attributes. As you follow the example presented in Fig. 8-5, notice that the source code that would be generated by the current settings is updated at the bottom of the window.

A response to the Help prompt would be placed in the HLP attribute. The parameter can be a string constant or a variable name.

The color attribute that you can identify will be placed in the HUE statement. Selecting a color attribute is done in the color selection window, just as it was described in Chapter 2. You will notice that after selecting a hue, it is applied immediately. An important fact to remember is that if you change the hue here, all paints that were previously entered on the worksheet will be overwritten. It is assumed that if you change the screen's hue during your design, you probably intend to remove (or redo) your painted areas. Also, if you ever paint the entire worksheet area a new color, that color will be used as the HUE attribute in the structure definition.

Notice in the Attribute prompt how you can select an attribute and also indicate that you want transparency by pressing the letter T. As explained earlier in this chapter, a "transparent hue" will assign your chosen color but also allow the characters from the overlaid screen to be seen. If you select the word "Transparent" from the bottom of the window, this indicates that you want both attributes and characters to be seen from the window under this one.

"No Border" has been defined in this example. Selecting a border is done in much the same manner as the HUE attributes. Using no border means that the current border (if any) will not be changed. As you move the selection box through the possible colors, each is displayed by the worksheet to give you an idea of how it looks.

The Window prompt has 3 possible answers. If the screen that you are designing is not going to be a window, then No is the choice to make. The other two choices, Float and Fix, will define whether the window should float around the last accessed screen position or whether the window should have the AT attribute assigned to fix the location. If you answer No or Float, the next two fields will be skipped. Although Float is the appropriate answer for this window, select No for this example.

Fix at Row and Fix at Col are how you designate the position, or the variables containing the position, that are the parameters to the AT attribute. The screen formatter will default the values to the current window location on the worksheet. You can override the defaults, but the formatter will validate whether the window can fit the described location if constants are used. Additionally, if constants are used, the formatter will move the entire window to the designated location if it is not already at that position.

Answering yes or no to the Comment question will not alter the screen's definition. This prompt does not relate to any screen attribute, but does provide a valuable feature. If you answer yes, a comment block (using the OMIT statement) will be generated in your source file that is the text representation of your screen. Figure 8-6 shows how this feature would appear if used on the example screen from Fig. 8-3. You can see how this helps to document your program at the source level.

The last prompt is where the Prefix for the SCREEN statement is designated. Only after you accept this line, have you accepted the entire screen definition. Always remember: If you need help to complete any line, press F1.

At this point, the screen formatter's worksheet is restored. If you examine the summary window (Ctrl–S) shown in Fig. 8-7, you will see the screen's definition as currently established. Notice that since no was selected at the Window prompt, the WINDOW attribute is not part of the

```
ADDRBOOK       SCREEN        WINDOW(12,58),PRE(SCR),HUE(7,1)
     OMIT('**-END-**')            Rows 7 thru 17
```

```
┌──────────────────────────────────────────────────┐
│                LITTLE ADDRESS BOOK                 │
│                                                    │
│              •••• Mr. Mrs. Ms. Dr.                 │
│        Name: ••••••••••••••••••                    │
│     Address: ••••••••••••••••••••••••              │
│              ••••••••••••••••••••••••              │
│        City: •••••••••••••••••• State: •• Zip: #####│
│                                                    │
│                Press Enter to Accept               │
└──────────────────────────────────────────────────┘
```

```
**-END-**

          ROW(2,58)  PAINT(10,1),HUE(7,0)
          ROW(12,2)  PAINT(1,57),HUE(7,0)
```

8-6. Partial screen definition, with comment

```
┌────────────────────────────────────────────────────────┐
│                                                         │
│   ADDRBOOK       SCREEN        PRE(SCR),HUE(7,1)         │
│                                                         │
│                                                         │
│                                                         │
│                                                         │
│   Field Type:              String Entry Menu Pause Repeat Point Text │
└────────────────────────────────────────────────────────┘
```

8-7. Summary window, after modifying the screen structure

statement. Since this window will not use the entire display, the WIN-DOW attribute is implied once the window is reduced to the proper size.

Sizing the window

Dimensioning (Ctrl–D) sizes windows. To ensure that you only design within the regions designated for the window, the screen formatter lets you move the borders of the worksheet. After pressing Ctrl–D, one side of your window will contain a reversed area. This area tells you which border is currently being manipulated. You can choose which border you want to move by pressing Home for the left border, End for the right border, PgUp for the top border, and PgDn for the bottom border.

When in the top or bottom border mode, the up and down arrow keys will adjust the border. When in the left or right border mode, the left and right arrow keys will move the border. Notice that as you move the border in, the outer area of the display is filled with special characters to help delineate the window. Also notice that a partial ruler is displayed to help you determine the exact size of the window as you dimension.

Figure 8-8 demonstrates the correct size of the window for this example. Once you have sized your window like the one shown in Fig. 8-8, press Enter to return to the worksheet. Now press Ctrl–S to see the summary window again. Figure 8-9 is what it should look like.

8-8. Dimensioning feature's ruler and border display

```
ADDRBOOK      SCREEN       WINDOW(12,58),PRE(SCR),HUE(7,1)




Field Type:              String Entry Menu Pause Repeat Point Text
```

8-9. Summary window, after dimensioning the window

The SCREEN statement has been modified to be a window. Your answer of no to the Window prompt on the definition was changed as soon as the screen formatter determined that you did not intend to use the entire screen.

Dimensioning can be done at any time during the editing process. If you decide later that more room (or less) is required by the window, press Ctrl–D and resize the window accordingly.

Track and border characters

Drawing border characters is simple in the screen formatter. Move the cursor to the top left-hand corner of your window and then press Ctrl–T. This popup is called the track type window and is the entry point to the tracking feature in the formatter. Five pre-defined track types are available at the top of the screen, and the menu is shown in Fig. 8-10.

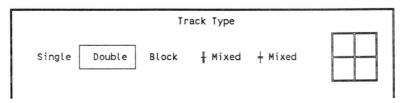

8-10. Predefined track types available in the screen formatter

Use the left and right arrow keys to move the selection box over each type. Notice that a sample representation of that type is displayed in the top right side of the window. The lower region of the window is filled with all the other available characters, so you can design your own borders. Examples of how characters appear are also displayed in the top corner. Select Double and then press Enter.

Although it will appear that you have returned to the worksheet, notice that the cursor shape has changed. This is an indication that you are in the track function. Start moving the cursor to the right to produce the track character. When you reach the right corner, press the down arrow. Notice that the Formatter determined that you needed a corner character. This is the advantage of selecting one of the pre-defined Track types—all intersections are calculated for best fit.

If you make a mistake in turning a corner or when making an intersection, use the backspace key to remove the track characters, one at a time. This only applies to your current track session. Previous sessions are not remembered once the Tracking function has been completed. If you want to remove all the characters that were made during a tracking session, press Ctrl–Backspace.

From this position, press PgDn. Notice that the entire right side of the window has been tracked. Press Home and then PgUp and you will have completed the entire border. Press Enter to complete the tracking function. Figure 8-11 illustrates how the screen should appear now.

If at any time during tracking, you want to change track types, press Ctrl–T again and the track type window will reappear. This is how you can design your own borders using multiple characters or a combination of the pre-defined border types. Additionally, it is important to note that

8-11. Worksheet display, after tracking the window

the characters that you have placed on the screen are not any different from any that you might type in at the keyboard.

Tracking is merely a convenient way of drawing lines. The formatter does attempt to treat the line characters differently in certain situations, like centering and inserting, but it cannot distinguish line characters drawn with tracking and those that you might input using the keyboard.

With the cursor on the top left corner, press Ctrl–T again. Select Double as you did before and press Enter. Now suppose you want to designate a particular color for your track characters. You can press Ctrl–V (for video attribute) to bring up the track attribute window, shown in Fig. 8-12.

This window looks like many of the other attribute windows that have been discussed, especially those found in Designer. The words on the left side of the popup screen reflect variations of the default screen colors. Default screen colors are determined by the HUE attribute of the SCREEN statement, and any paints that have been made. The area on the right side of the attribute window demonstrates all the available color combination from which you can select. Select Enhanced and press Enter.

Now press End, PgDn, Home, PgUp, and Enter. This new tracking character has replaced the previous character, using the selected attribute. Press Ctrl–Enter and return to the Editor's worksheet. Figure 8-13

```
                  Track Attribute
                     Enhanced

    Normal      · · · · · · · · · · · · · · · · ·

    Reversed    · · · · · · · · · · · · · · · · ·

   ┌─────────┐
   │ Enhanced│  · · · · · · · · · · · · · · · · ·
   └─────────┘
    Rev+Enh     · · · · · · · · · · · · · · · · ·

    Blink       · · · · · · · · · · · · · · · · ·

    Rev+Blk     · · · · · · · · · · · · · · · · ·

    Blk+Enh     · · · · · · · · · · · · · · · · ·

 Rev+Blk+Enh    · · · · · · · · · · · · · · · · ·

                  Press B to toggle Blink
```

8-12.   Track attribute window with Enhanced mode selected

shows the source code required to draw the screen the way it currently
exists.

The screen formatter was able to optimize the code tremendously.
Each STRING statement takes advantage of the character repeat by using
the curly braces, {}, to indicate a count. This enables the statement to
contain a character once and follow it with the total count required. The
second STRING if further optimized by using a repeat structure. Since the
side characters are the same for each line other than the top and bottom,
the REPEAT statement specifies to duplicate this string 10 times. And
since you drew the tracks using the ENHANCED attribute, each STRING
statement also uses the ENH hue indicator.

```
ADDRBOOK     SCREEN      WINDOW(12,58),PRE(SCR),HUE(7,1)
             ROW(1,1)    STRING('<201,205{56},187>'),ENH
             ROW(2,1)    REPEAT(10);STRING('<186,0{56},186>'),ENH .
             ROW(12,1)   STRING('<200,205{56},188>'),ENH
                 .
```

8-13.   Source generated for the track border of a window

Notice that the second STRING uses the character repeat for zero.
Zero is a special character that has no display value. It will not alter any
character that it is displayed onto. For example, suppose a structure
contained these statements:

```
ROW(2,1) STRING('AAAAAAAAAA')
ROW(2,1) STRING ('B<0{8}>B')
```

The resulting display would be: 'BAAAAAAAAB' because the zero characters will not replace the characters that were already on the display. This is a convenient method to indicate space without redefining how the space is used.

Painting and shadowing

Reenter the screen formatter by pressing Ctrl–F. The example window shown in Fig. 8-3 uses a shadow. This is decorative effect that simulates the appearance of floating above the previous screen.

To draw a shadow, you will first have to move the borders of the window. This example places the shadow on the lower and right sides of the window. By using Ctrl–M, you can move the characters one side at a time. Move the right side in by one position and move the lower side up by one position. The screen should now look like the one displayed in Fig. 8-14.

8-14. Worksheet display, after moving the tracks

The shadow effect is made by painting the outside area of the screen. A more pronounced effect can be made by using a transparent paint in the outside corners of the shadow. Place the cursor in the lower left corner of the window. Press Ctrl–P to call the paint function. This function begins by letting you select the color of the paint. Select White on

Black (the top left attribute) and press Enter. Now you are ready to designate the area to paint. Move the cursor to the right until you reach the corner.

Painting is a block function, unlike tracking, which is a character function — which means that you cannot turn corners without increasing the area that will be included in the block. Before accepting the paint, however, make note that if you want to change the attribute at this time, you can, by pressing Ctrl – V (video attribute) to recall the paint attribute window. Each time you select a new color, the area that you currently have marked will change to the new attribute. This is a good way to try color combinations until you find one you like. This example depends upon the dark color for the shadow effect, so just press Enter to complete the paint function.

Press Ctrl – P again, press Enter, and then PgUp. This marks the right side of the window for the shadow effect. Press Enter to complete the paint.

Making the transparent corners is done like any other kind of painting. Your cursor should be in the upper right corner at this time, so press Ctrl – P. At the bottom of the paint attribute window, is the word "Transparent" (see Fig. 8-15). Move the selection box over the word. As mentioned in the discussion of the HUE attribute in SCREEN statements, it is also possible to paint an area with a transparent color. Doing this causes the area to have the indicated attribute, but all information shows through from the lower levels. This example, however, uses the transparent without a hue, allowing both color and character to be seen from the underlying window. Press Enter after selecting Transparent.

Because you want only the one space to be transparent on this side, press Enter again to complete the paint function. Notice that a special character has been displayed on the transparent area. This is done to help you visualize where characters and attributes are going to show through. If you had selected a hue as well, these characters would reflect the attribute that you choose. Follow the same steps to make the transparent area in the lower left corner.

At this point, press Ctrl – Enter to produce the source code again. The source produced in the Editor will look like that shown in Fig. 8-16.

The PAINT statements are generated following the SCREEN statement. These statements have row indicators, which designate where the paint should be placed. The parameters of the PAINT statement are the number of rows and columns that are to be affected. Two statements reflect the two transparent corners. You can recognize these because the PAINT statement does not have a HUE attribute indicated, and the TRN attribute is attached. The remaining paints do have hues indicated.

One thing that you might not have noticed, however, is that the screen formatter optimizes the PAINT statements. Remember, you

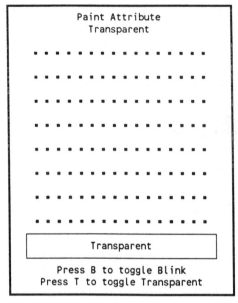

```
                Paint Attribute
                Transparent

        . . . . . . . . . . . . . . .

        . . . . . . . . . . . . . . .

        . . . . . . . . . . . . . . .

        . . . . . . . . . . . . . . .

        . . . . . . . . . . . . . . .

        . . . . . . . . . . . . . . .

        . . . . . . . . . . . . . . .

        . . . . . . . . . . . . . . .

        ┌─────────────────────────┐
        │        Transparent       │
        └─────────────────────────┘
         Press B to toggle Blink
         Press T to toggle Transparent
```

8-15. Paint attribute window with Transparent mode selected

painted the entire side areas with the white on black attribute and then painted only the corners with the transparent attribute. The formatter determined that the previous paints were clipped and optimized them. Likewise, the lower right corner was included in both paints but was optimized to appear only in one statement.

```
ADDRBOOK      SCREEN      WINDOW(12,58),PRE(SCR),HUE(7,1)
              ROW(2,58)   PAINT(10,1),HUE(7,0)
              ROW(12,2)   PAINT(1,57),HUE(7,0)
              ROW(1,58)   PAINT(1,1),TRN
              ROW(12,1)   PAINT(1,1),TRN
              ROW(1,1)    STRING('<201,205{55},187>'),ENH
              ROW(2,1)    REPEAT(9);STRING('<186,0{55},186>'),ENH .
              ROW(11,1)   STRING('<200,205{55},188>'),ENH
```

8-16. Source generated, after completing the shadow paints

Titles, prompts, and centering

Enter the screen formatter again. Move the cursor to the second line, inside the borders, and type LITTLE ADDRESS BOOK. This will serve as the title for the window. Normally, it would be tedious for you to determine how to center the text in the window, so Clarion has provided a function to do this. Press the key combination Ctrl – ^. The centering function searches from the cursor in both directions for two things: 1) The borders or track characters on either side of the text, and 2) the first and last non-blank characters that fall within the first criteria. The characters are centered within the area. This feature removes all the guesswork about centering.

You can spruce up the screen using different colors for the prompts and title. When you want to change the current attribute for typed characters, press Ctrl – V. This calls the key-in attribute window. You should be familiar by now with making selections from these type windows. This example uses Yellow on Blue for the key-in attribute. More information about general screen design considerations will be covered in Chapter 12.

You have already typed the title of the screen using a different attribute. Rather than retyping it again, use the change attribute function by pressing Ctrl – A with the cursor placed at the beginning of the title. This does not alter the character where the cursor is located, but does apply the currently selected key-in attribute.

Fields

The specific fields required for any screen are determined by the procedure you are creating. If you intend for the user to input the fields found in a file structure, then you will want a corresponding entry field for each item. If the window is merely for display purposes, then entry fields might not be required, but strings with labels defined might be. Of course you might require some combination of all fields types. Unlike Designer, which can make certain assumptions about the fields allowed on a screen, the screen formatter allows you to make all the rules. For this exercise, assume that you are in the process of completing the following file structure:

```
ADDRESS FILE,PRE(FIL)
                RECORD
    TITLE           STRING(4)
    NAME            STRING(20)
    ADDRESS_1       STRING(25)
    ADDRESS_2       STRING(25)
    CITY            STRING(20)
    STATE           STRING(2)
    ZIP             LONG
```

Completing the record means that you must have a field for each item. When designing with the screen formatter, you can place fields on the screen and move them around until you have a satisfactory combination of look and feel. To aide you in this example, use the ruler (Ctrl—R). Move the cursor to the position indicated in Fig. 8-17, row 11 and column 18. Type the prompt Name: and then move one space beyond the colon.

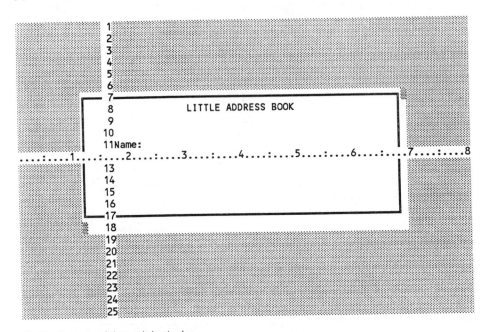

8-17. Example of the worksheet ruler

You are now ready to place a field on the screen. All fields are entered through the summary window. Press Ctrl—S to display it. The selection bar will be on the SCREEN statement. Press the Ins key to insert a field, and the summary window will appear, like the one shown in Fig. 8-18. Notice that the ROW statement has defaulted to the current cursor position, and the field type defaults to STRING when the menu at the bottom of the window becomes active.

```
 ADDRBOOK      SCREEN      WINDOW(12,58),PRE(SCR),HUE(7,1)
                ROW(5,13)   STRING




 Field Type:String         String Entry Menu Pause Repeat Point Text
```

8-18. Summary window, after pressing Ins to add a new field

The type of field that you choose depends upon what is required. Here is a brief explanation of each type:

String This type of field displays a string literal on the screen. This literal can be typed as a string constant or contained in a variable. Strings also designate the available responses to a MENU statement.

Entry This is the standard field statement that allows users to input data. The format of the input is controlled by the picture associated with the field.

Menu This field type also accepts user input, but the choices are limited to the strings that are defined within the menu structure.

Pause This statement usually establishes checkpoints for the user. A string literal or label is required as a parameter. This string is not displayed until the field is ready to be accepted. It is a convenient way to stop a process and ask the user whether information is correct or if everything is completed.

Repeat This is a structure for placing multiple items on the screen. Any field can be contained within a repeat except another repeat. Generally, this statement might be used if dimensioned variables are required, or when the POINT statement is used.

Point This is an input statement that allows the user to "point" to a particular area of the screen, and allows you to determine which area was pointed to by the user. It is similar to a menu statement, but makes no assumptions about the information that can be pointed to and can span multiple lines. Usually, a repeat structure is required if several items are displayed on the screen. For example, the selection bar in the scrolling table procedures is generated by the Designer using point fields.

Text This field allows a user to input free-form text that can span multiple lines. Memo fields in files are normally input via a text field, but other field types can be the destination of a text field, if desired.

In the example, the Name field will require the user to type the name, so an Entry field is needed. Move the menu selection until Entry is selected and then press Enter. This will display the Entry field definition window. An example definition for the field appears in Fig. 8-19.

This window has a number of questions that correspond to the parameters and attributes that an entry field can contain. Most of these are the same attributes that the Designer asks about when creating screens and files. A detailed definition for each item can be found in the Clarion *Language Reference* manual and the *Utilities Guide*.

The important thing to remember is that the screen formatter contains its own field definitions. The way Designer knows about the format of fields on a screen is through its file definitions. Because of this, Designer limits what you can do with your fields in a specific situation.

```
┌─────────────────────────────────────────────────────────────────────┐
│  Row: 5 Col:13                        Entry                          │
│                                                                       │
│  Picture    :@s20              Type Mode :AsIs  Ins  Ovr   AsIs       │
│  Use        :FIL:NAME          Required  :No    Yes  No               │
│  Help       :                  Immediate :No    Yes  No               │
│  Escape to  :                  Num Lock  :No    Yes  No               │
│  Attribute :Normal             Left Just :Yes   Yes  No               │
│       Select :Reversed         Upper Case:No    Yes  No               │
│                 ROW(5,13)  ENTRY(@s20),USE(FIL:NAME),LFT              │
└─────────────────────────────────────────────────────────────────────┘
```

8-19. Entry field definition window

For example, Designer requires you to designate whether or not a field is required in the file definition. Any time it appears on a Designer-generated screen, it will use the definition you specified for the field in your data file. In the screen formatter, however, you can have the same field on two screens defined in entirely different fashions: One required, one not; one upper, the other not; one immediate, the other not; etc.

When the field pop-ups are called from the summary window, the first two fields are usually skipped. These are the row and column questions. Normally, the current cursor location is assumed to be where you want the field placed. When this is not the case, press Escape to reach the Column prompt and Escape again to reach the Row prompt. Then enter the proper placement that you require.

This example uses the optional select attribute (SEL) of black on white for each entry field. Users have to be able to readily identify which field is active on your screens. Without the SEL attribute, the active field will simply be reversed. Although this is usually sufficient to identify which field is active, the effect can be maximized by choosing a specific color for your active fields. When the field is no longer active, it will return to its former color.

Notice that, like the screen definition window, a source line is continuously updated at the bottom of the display. This is done to help you become familiar with how your definition would look in the source code and to help you identify the field in the summary window.

The following fields should be entered in the same fashion as the FIL:NAME field. Using the summary window, create these fields:

```
ROW(6,13)     ENTRY(@S25),USE(FIL:ADDRESS_1),SEL(0,7),REQ,LFT
ROW(7,13)     ENTRY(@S25),USE(FIL:ADDRESS_2),SEL(0,7),LFT
ROW(8,13)     ENTRY(@S20),USE(FIL:CITY),SEL(0,7),REQ,LFT
ROW(8,41)     ENTRY(@S2),USE(FIL:STATE),SEL(0,7),REQ,LFT,UPR
ROW(8,49)     ENTRY(@P#####P),USE(FIL:ZIP),SEL(0,7),REQ,LFT
ROW(4,13)     ENTRY(@S4),USE(FIL:TITLE),SEL(0,7),REQ,LFT
```

Position the prompts for your fields like those shown in Fig. 8-3. The text at the bottom of the window is a pause field. This field can be entered with a method similar to that used for the entry fields. Figure 8-20 shows how this field is defined.

```
Row:10 Col:19                              Pause

Parameter :'Press Enter to Accept'
Use        :?PAUSE_FIELD
Help       :
Escape to  :
Attribute :Yellow On Red
             ROW(10,19) PAUSE('Press Enter to Accept'),USE(?PAUSE_FIELD),H
```

8-20. Pause field definition window

Notice that the answer to the Use question for a pause field is not a variable destination, as those defined for entry fields. The answer here defines a field equate label by which this field can be referenced. Field equates will be discussed in more detail in a later section of this chapter, entitled Screen and field processing.

Make note that although the field is displayed on the screen formatter's worksheet continuously, the pause is only displayed by your program while it is the active field. The screen formatter displays it so that you are aware of where it is located.

Field order

Now you have created a screen structure that allows the user to complete all the fields found in the file definition, and prompts the user to verify that the screen should be accepted. You could write the source and go test it right now, but don't leave yet. The screen formatter is going demonstrate the sequential processing order of the fields by using the browse function (Ctrl–B).

When you press Ctrl–B, the fields are first removed from the screen, and then processed the way a user will view them when the program runs. Naturally, the screen formatter will not look for input, so it will merely display the fields in the selected colors, and display the appropriate picture. Press any key to continue the browse until all the fields have been displayed.

Did the fields appear in the order that you intended? If you followed the instructions presented here, they probably did not and this was intentional. It was done first, in this manner, to demonstrate just how important the browse feature can be and, second, to demonstrate the importance of field order.

You might remember that early in the chapter it was pointed out that screens are processed sequentially. This is an important point to grasp. By examining the summary window, you can see the default order in which your fields will be processed. It is from top to bottom.

Fortunately, the summary window has an additional feature that will help you rearrange the fields. The addition and subtraction keys found on the cursor keypad can move the currently selected item up or down in the field list. Examine your summary window and order your fields in the following order:

```
FIL:TITLE
FIL:NAME
FIL:ADDRESS_1
FIL:ADDRESS_2
FIL:CITY
FIL:STATE
FIL:ZIP
PAUSE
```

Now exit the summary window using Escape (changes to the order of the fields are not lost if Escape is pressed). Try the browse feature again and verify that the fields are referenced in the proper order.

This last bit of explanation of the order of field processing raises an important point when: using the screen formatter, there is no relationship between the position of the fields on the screen and the order in which they are processed. However, Designer will always process fields in a left-to-right, top-to-bottom order. Although this might be proper for many applications, you might want to process fields in a different order and perhaps skip some fields altogether.

The screen formatter even lets you stack fields on top of each other (using the same location). This can be a useful feature if the field that you want the user to enter depends upon how a previous field was entered. The program is not confused because it merely references the fields in the order that you establish them.

By now, you are probably wondering why the example screen has a menu field and the exercise doesn't. This too was done to demonstrate another feature of the summary window. You could check each time the title field is entered, in order to verify that the data is one of the four designated titles (Mr., Mrs., Ms., or Dr.). A menu, on the other hand, forces the user to make a valid selection without requiring you to write code to verify the response.

A menu field is a good choice when there are a limited number of responses that can be easily displayed on the screen. In this example, Title is an excellent candidate. Bring up the summary window and move the selection bar over the entry field for FIL:TITLE. Rather than deleting the field and remaking it, the summary window will allow you to change the field type. Currently, the menu choice is Entry. Move it over to the Menu selection. As you move through the choices, notice how the field is adapted to each type. To make the new choice permanent, press Enter and then accept the definition screen for the new type. Figure 8-21 shows the menu definition screen.

```
Row: 4 Col:13                          Menu

Picture   :aS4
Use       :FIL:TITLE                    Required  :Yes  Yes  No
Help      :                             Immediate :No   Yes  No
Escape to :
Attribute :Normal
   Select :Black On White
           ROW(4,13)  MENU(aS4),USE(FIL:TITLE),SEL(0,7),REQ,LFT
```

8-21. Menu field definition window

All the information is already correct, so all you have to do is press Ctrl–Enter to accept the entire window. Make note, however, that a menu does not have to designate a picture code or a use variable. The picture code is necessary only if you intend to display the current selection as it is being made. And the use variable is necessary only if you intend to retain the selected information. Whether a picture or use variable is attached, you can always check which response the user made by using the CHOICE function. This function returns the item number that was selected. Now you are ready to define the menu's choices.

From the summary window, move the selection bar over the menu definition. Press Insert just as you did when entering the other field types. String is the only field type that can occur within a menu structure. A string inside a menu structure, however, has a few different characteristics than a normal STRING statement.

The parameter is still required to be a string literal or a picture. If you use a picture, then it will be important to use a label so that information can be placed in the proper location when the time comes. You are not required to have a label, but it makes the task much easier. If a menu item is blank when the MENU statement activates, that choice cannot be selected by the user. Naturally, this can be a useful feature if the application has security levels that provide some options to some users, but not all.

The Description is where you can designate something different to be displayed in the menu's picture. The best use for this is to have a series of one-word choices, each displaying a different descriptive sentence in the menu's picture. The Clarion Main Menu is an example of how the description field can be used.

Individual menu items can have their own help window names. This can be beneficial if the explanation of each item requires more information than can be conveniently placed in one help window. Menu items that do not identify their own help windows will use the help window identified by the MENU statement.

Finally, notice Key, the last prompt. This attribute allows you to define an alternate key that will activate this menu choice. Normally, the first letter of each menu item can be used to quickly move to a particular item. In some instances, however, you might want to designate a different letter than the first one. For example, perhaps you want a menu item named exit to use the letter X for the shortcut.

To complete the example window, enter these strings for the menu, and remember that order is important in the summary window:

```
ROW(4,18)      STRING('Mr.'),SEL(0,7)
ROW(4,22)      STRING('Mrs.'),SEL(0,7)
ROW(4,27)      STRING('Ms.'),SEL(0,7)
ROW(4,31)      STRING('Dr.'),SEL(0,7)
```

Before generating the source, check with the browse feature to ensure that all the fields will be handled in the order that you intend. If you are satisfied, exit the screen formatter and then compare your source to that shown in Fig. 8-1.

Screen formatting techniques

It would be impossible to cover everything that can be done with the screen formatter. There are, however, a few important techniques that should be discussed.

Paint versus other attributes

Sometimes confusion occurs over whether to use paint, or associate explicit attributes with variables and characters. Naturally, what you use depends upon what you are doing. Paint is always in a base color, while an attribute belongs to some kind of character data. An example might be a room in your house. You can paint the wall but it will not affect the pictures and posters that you attach to it. Those items have their own color attributes. You can move the picture and its attributes, but you can't move the paint from the wall. The only way to remove a paint on your screen is to paint over it with another color.

The screen formatter allows something that you probably do not have to worry about at home, however. Variables and characters can accept (or modify) the background color on which they are placed. Any character that does not have an explicit hue attached will use the painted color in some manner. Think of these items as having a chameleon quality. The chameleon can move, or be moved, from room to room, yet it will adapt to the color scheme no matter where it is placed.

Tracking and window sizing

If you have drawn a track around your window and you need to resize it, you are in luck. The dimensioning feature recognizes the special track characters and tries its best to size them along with the window borders. If you do not want to modify the tracks during dimensioning, however, you are out of luck. Your only option is to move the tracks (Ctrl−M) to their proper location once the sizing is completed.

Moving the entire window

Occasionally, you will want to move the entire window. This could be because you want to extend the borders in a direction where you have already reached the display limits (this is assuming the other side of the window has not reached the display limit). Or you might want to place a window in a particular location when using the AT attribute. There are two ways to tell the screen formatter that you want to move the entire window. With the first way, you can mark the entire window during the block move or copy function. Secondly, you can press Ctrl—M again after initiating the move function (Ctrl−M, Ctrl−M). When the screen formatter recognizes that you intend to move the entire display, any borders that you have established are removed and you can move the window to a different location. When you accept the location, the borders will return.

Multiple copies

Once you have marked a block for the copy function, you can make several copies of the block by moving to a destination and pressing Ctrl−C instead of Enter. This keeps the block marked so that you can move it to another destination. Be careful, however, if a field or string containing a label is covered by the copied block. Field and strings entered via the summary window will simply go into the background if you move or copy something over them. If you intend to remove the field, then delete it first, or you will have to delete it from the summary window later.

Screen and field processing

Now that you have seen how to create screen structures, the way in which screens are used in the code of your program section must be described.

Only one statement, OPEN, is required to display a screen or window. The OPEN statement, in turn, requires the label of the screen structure to be displayed. Any variables defined in the screen structure can be displayed by assigning a value to them before the window is opened. Fields that have Use variables assigned will display what is contained in those variables. What could be simpler?

When a screen is opened, an internal table is created for each of your defined fields. This table is used to keep track of which field is currently being processed, and which field will be processed next. Fields are processed via the ACCEPT statement. Unless you change the order in the code section, the order in which the fields are processed will be the order in which they are defined in the screen structure. You can change this order with the SELECT statement. This statement has the following syntax:

```
SELECT(field number)
```

The field number parameter must correspond to the sequential number of the field's definition. For example, refer to the screen structure code shown in Fig. 8-22.

Examining Fig. 8-22 reveals that the menu field will be number 1 because it is the first field defined. The entry for the field FIL:NAME is number 2 and so on. The pause field, which is the last field, is number 8. You could process all the fields on this screen with code like that in Fig. 8-23.

This code would allow a user to enter something in each field, but all the SELECT statements are unnecessary since the fields are being processed in sequential order. Remember that the order of acceptance defaults to the order of the fields in the screen structure. With this information, the code could be redone in a fashion like the following:

```
OPEN(ADDRBOOK)      ! OPEN THE WINDOW
ACCEPT              ! ACCEPT THE TITLE
ACCEPT              ! ACCEPT THE NAME
ACCEPT              ! ACCEPT ADDRESS_1
ACCEPT              ! ACCEPT ADDRESS_2
ACCEPT              ! ACCEPT THE CITY
ACCEPT              ! ACCEPT THE STATE
ACCEPT              ! ACCEPT THE ZIP CODE
ACCEPT              ! ACCEPT THE PAUSE
```

```
ADDRBOOK     SCREEN        WINDOW(12,58),PRE(SCR),HUE(7,1)
             ROW(2,58)     PAINT(10,1),HUE(7,0)
             ROW(12,2)     PAINT(1,57),HUE(7,0)
             ROW(1,58)     PAINT(1,1),TRN
             ROW(12,1)     PAINT(1,1),TRN
             ROW(1,1)      STRING('<201,205{55},187>'),ENH
             ROW(2,1)      REPEAT(9);STRING('<186,0{55},186>'),ENH .
             ROW(11,1)     STRING('<200,205{55},188>'),ENH
             ROW(2,20)     STRING('LITTLE ADDRESS BOOK'),HUE(14,1)
             ROW(4,13)     MENU(@S4),USE(FIL:TITLE),SEL(0,7),REQ
                COL(18)       STRING('Mr.'),SEL(0,7)
                COL(22)       STRING('Mrs.'),SEL(0,7)
                COL(27)       STRING('Ms.'),SEL(0,7)
                COL(31)       STRING('Dr.'),SEL(0,7)
                              .
             ROW(5,7)      STRING('Name:'),HUE(14,1)
                COL(13)     ENTRY(@S20),USE(FIL:NAME),LFT
             ROW(6,4)      STRING('Address:'),HUE(14,1)
                COL(13)     ENTRY(@S25),USE(FIL:ADDRESS_1),SEL(0,7),REQ,LFT
             ROW(7,13)     ENTRY(@S25),USE(FIL:ADDRESS_2),SEL(0,7),LFT
             ROW(8,7)      STRING('City:'),HUE(14,1)
                COL(13)     ENTRY(@S20),USE(FIL:CITY),SEL(0,7),REQ,LFT
                COL(34)     STRING('State:'),HUE(14,1)
                COL(41)     ENTRY(@S2),USE(FIL:STATE),SEL(0,7),REQ,LFT,UPR
                COL(44)     STRING('Zip:'),HUE(14,1)
                COL(49)     ENTRY(@p#####p),USE(FIL:ZIP),SEL(0,7),REQ,NUM
             ROW(10,19)    PAUSE('Press Enter to Accept'),USE(?PAUSE_FIELD)   |
                              HUE(14,4)
```

8-22.   Source generated by the screen formatter

```
OPEN(ADDRBOOK)          ! OPEN THE WINDOW
SELECT(1)                   ! SELECT THE MENU FIELD
ACCEPT                  ! ACCEPT THE TITLE
SELECT(2)                   ! SELECT THE NAME FIELD
ACCEPT                  ! ACCEPT THE NAME
SELECT(3)                   ! SELECT THE FIRST ADDRESS LINE
ACCEPT                  ! ACCEPT ADDRESS_1
SELECT(4)                   ! SELECT THE SECOND ADDRESS LINE
ACCEPT                  ! ACCEPT ADDRESS_2
SELECT(5)                   ! SELECT THE CITY FIELD
ACCEPT                  ! ACCEPT THE CITY
SELECT(6)                   ! SELECT THE STATE FIELD
ACCEPT                  ! ACCEPT THE STATE
SELECT(7)                   ! SELECT THE ZIP CODE FIELD
ACCEPT                  ! ACCEPT THE ZIP CODE
SELECT(8)                   ! SELECT THE PAUSE FIELD
ACCEPT                  ! ACCEPT THE PAUSE
```

8-23.   Example of code that processes fields

This method significantly reduces the amount of code required to process the fields, but it still has a few problems. First, one of the more powerful features of Clarion field processing is that the user can backup and reenter a prior field by pressing the Escape key. That method does not work in this situation. The best way to ensure that the fields can be processed in any order is to use a LOOP statement like this:

```
OPEN(ADDRBOOK)              ! OPEN THE WINDOW
LOOP                        ! PROCESS ALL FIELDS
    ACCEPT                  ! ACCEPT THE CURRENT FIELD
    IF FIELD() = 8 THEN BREAK.
```

Source like this will handle the fields in the order that the user processes them. Here, the ACCEPT statement will automatically select the next sequential field to be used. When the last field has been entered (the pause field) then the IF statement terminates the loop.

Although this code will accomplish the current task, referencing fields by number can make the code difficult to maintain. Any time a new field is added to, or an existing field is removed from, the screen, you will have to remember to change the numbers to match the new sequence. To eliminate this problem, the Clarion Compiler defines *field equate labels*.

When the source is compiled, a field equate label will be defined for each field in the screen structure. The name of the equate for each field will be the field's Use variable name prefixed with a question mark. For example, the menu field can be selected by either of the following statements:

```
SELECT(1)
SELECT(?FIL:TITLE)
```

Fields that do not require a Use variable, like the pause field, can declare their own field equate label. The pause field in Fig. 8-22 defines the field equate ?PAUSE_FIELD. When your screen is compiled, this equate will be assigned the value of 8, because this is the eighth field defined in the screen structure.

Field equate labels are valuable. When used properly, it is possible to write code that does not have to be modified every time a field is added or removed. Consider the following segment of code:

```
OPEN(ADDRBOOK)          ! OPEN THE WINDOW
LOOP                    ! PROCESS ALL THE FIELDS
    ACCEPT              ! ACCEPT A FIELD
    IF FIELD() = ?PAUSE_FIELD THEN BREAK.
```

This code has the distinct advantage that it will not need to be modified if you add new fields or delete existing fields, as long as the pause field is the last field in the window.

You can reference a field by its number. However, I strongly recommend that you use the field equate labels (which are still only numbers) that the compiler generates for you.

Field-level editing

What if you need to examine the data that the user enters in a field? Perhaps you need to verify that it is within a certain range, or check to see if it exists in another file, or even open another pop-up window. Examining the entered data immediately after the data is entered is called *field-level editing.*

Fields can be defined with attributes that do some of the editing, i.e., LFT for left justification, UPR for upper case, REQ for non-blank field, etc. Attributes are not, however, available for all the editorial possibilities that you will require. For specific field editing, you will need to write your own code.

Since fields can be processed in any order, it will be necessary to first determine which field the user has just accepted. This can be done with a series of IF statements like the one that determines when to terminate a loop. A better solution, in most instances, is to use a CASE statement. Example code that might be used to process this screen is presented in Fig. 8-24.

```
OPEN(ADDRBOOK)                     ! OPEN THE WINDOW
LOOP                               ! PROCESS ALL THE FIELDS
  ACCEPT                           ! ACCEPT A FIELD
  CASE FIELD()                     ! DETERMINE WHICH FIELD TO EDIT
  OF ?FIL:NAME                     ! THE NAME FIELD
    IF FIL:NAME = ''               ! AN ERROR HAS BEEN DETECTED

        [inform user that a name is required]

      SELECT(?FIL:NAME)            ! RESELECT THE FIELD
    .

  OF ?FIL:ZIP                      ! EDIT ZIP CODE FIELD
    IF FIL:ZIP <> 30301            ! NOT IN PROPER AREA

        [inform user that the zip is in error]

      SELECT(?FIL:ZIP)             ! RESELECT THE FIELD
    .

  OF ?FIL:ADDRESS_2                ! EDIT ADDRESS SECOND LINE
    IF FIL:ADDRESS_2 = ''          ! IF BLANK
      FIL:ADDRESS_2 = '*******'    ! ASSIGN STARS
        DISPLAY(?FIL:ADDRESS_2)    ! RE-DISPLAY FIELD
    . .

  IF FIELD() = ?PAUSE_FIELD THEN BREAK.
```

8-24. Example of field editing using a CASE statement

The code in Fig. 8-24 demonstrates how the CASE structure can handle specific field editing. It also demonstrates that the order a user inputs the fields does not affect the order that field editing occur in the CASE structure. As long as a SELECT statement is not encountered, the fields will occur in the order defined in the screen structure, not the order used in the CASE structure.

Several other notes about the sample code in Fig. 8-24. First, the next field to be entered can be forced with a SELECT statement. The code demonstrates this in the error conditions for the FIL:NAME and FIL:ZIP field edits. This does not mean that the next field, ACCEPT, will be that field, however. Remember, the user can backup to prior fields, using the Escape key, and reenter those fields again. The DISPLAY statement used in the example, can force a field that has a Use variable to display the current contents of that field. When a screen or window is opened, an implied DISPLAY statement is executed. If Use variables are changed by the program (such as reading new data into a record structure) then a DISPLAY statement should refresh the screen with the values in the Use variables.

A statement named UPDATE is available and is almost the opposite of the DISPLAY statement. Rather than updating the display with the value in the Use variable, the USE variable is updated with the information from the screen. This is a useful statement, especially if you have defined alert keys that might force the ACCEPT statement to complete. When a field is completed with an alerted key, the Use variable is not updated, but the data the user typed is on the screen. You would use the UPDATE procedure to take the data from the screen and place it in the Use variable.

Processing a point field

The examples presented thus far do not make use of point fields. Point fields must, in many occasions, be handled in a different manner to other fields because of the variety of things they offer. If you have examined the source that Designer generates, you will have noticed that all table functions use the point field.

Figure 8-25 displays the source of a screen structure that can use a point field. Assume that you want a point field to allow a user to select one of the strings presented on this screen. A point field does not care about the information that it covers. Usually, any discussion of point fields must also include a discussion of the repeat structure.

The point field requires a length and width. If several items will be "pointed to," then a repeat structure will be required to enable the point field to move between items.

Examining the window with the screen formatter's ruler (shown in

```
        PROGRAM
        INCLUDE('STD_KEYS.CLA')
SAMPLE       SCREEN       WINDOW(15,27),HUE(7,1,0)
    OMIT('**-END-**')
```

```
                    ┌─────────────────────────┐
                    │   SAMPLE POINT MENU      │
                    ├─────────────────────────┤
                    │      Chapter 1           │
                    │      Chapter 2           │
                    │      Chapter 3           │
                    │      Chapter 4           │
                    │                          │
                    │      Appendix A          │
                    │      Appendix B          │
                    │      Appendix C          │
                    │      Appendix D          │
                    ├─────────────────────────┤
                    │   LAST SELECTED: <#      │
                    └─────────────────────────┘
```

```
**-END-**

        ROW(1,1)    STRING('<201,205{25},187>')
        ROW(2,1)    REPEAT(2),EVERY(12);STRING('<186,0{25},186>') .
        ROW(3,1)    REPEAT(2),EVERY(10);STRING('<199,196{25},182>') .
        ROW(4,1)    REPEAT(9);STRING('<186,0{25},186>') .
        ROW(15,1)   STRING('<200,205{25},188>')
        ROW(2,6)    STRING('SAMPLE POINT MENU')
        ROW(4,10)   STRING('Chapter 1')
        ROW(5,10)   STRING('Chapter 2')
        ROW(6,10)   STRING('Chapter 3')
        ROW(7,10)   STRING('Chapter 4')
        ROW(9,10)   STRING('Appendix A')
        ROW(10,10)  STRING('Appendix B')
        ROW(11,10)  STRING('Appendix C')
        ROW(12,10)  STRING('Appendix D')
        ROW(14,6)   STRING('LAST SELECTED:')
SELNO       COL(21)    STRING(@N2)
```

8-25. Beginning of a sample program using point

Fig. 8-26), you can determine that nine items are to be contained in the selection area (include the blank line), in a single column. Each item is one line long. If a space is left on each side, next to the track characters, the width of the point field should be 23 characters. This is all the information you need at this time.

Through the summary window, it is possible to add the point field. When the point definition window appears, complete the window, using Fig. 8-27 as an example. The number of rows and columns that this point should have has already been established. While you answer the prompts, a sample display of the point is made on the worksheet. This is useful to verify that you have chosen the correct sizes for the field.

A point's Use variable is similar to the pause field's. It serves as the field equate label by which the field can be referenced. The Required

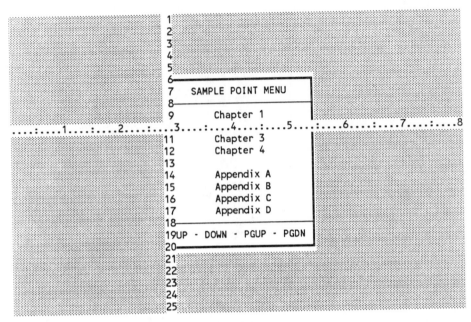

8-26. Using the ruler to determine point and repeat sizes

```
Row: 4 Col: 3                        Point

Rows      : 1
Columns   :23                        Required  :Yes  Yes  No
Use       :?POINT_FIELD
Help      :
Escape to :
    Select :Reversed
             ROW(4,3)    POINT(1,23),USE(?POINT_FIELD)
```

8-27. Point field definition window

attribute will cause the selection bar to move to the top if the user hits the down arrow at the very bottom of the screen and if the user hits the up arrow at the top, the selection bar will reappear at the bottom. If you intend to scroll information in the window, you will not want to use the Required attribute. This will, then, allow you to see if a scroll up or down is required by checking the last keystroke pressed.

If you press Ctrl−B (browse) at this time, it will demonstrate the area covered by this single point. To cover all the individual items will require a repeat structure. Repeat structures are entered through the summary window, like other fields. The repeat definition window is shown in Fig. 8-28.

The parameters of the REPEAT statement are the number of rows

```
                                    ┌──────────────────────────────┐
                                    │      Repeat Structure        │
                                    │                              │
                                    │        Rows    Columns       │
                                    │  Repeat: 9           1       │
   8-28.   Repeat field definition  │  Every : 1           1       │
           window                   │                              │
                                    │  Index :NDX                  │
                                    │  Prefix:                     │
                                    │                              │
                                    └──────────────────────────────┘
```

and the number of columns used to repeat the item. Rows are the number of times to repeat the item. In this case, you will need nine to cover all the items. Cols represents the number of columns of items. In this example, there is only one column of items.

The second series of questions determines how much room exists between items. Since these items occur on each line, the points should be one line apart. There is only one column of data, so the distance between columns will be ignored. If you had a second column of data, you would have to establish the distance, in character columns, to begin the repeat for that column.

When fields are involved in a repeat structure, it is necessary to have an Index variable. This is equivalent to the Use variables for other fields. The Index variable will be updated with the selected item number when the field completes. By setting this variable, you can also identify which item you want to be active the next time the field is referenced.

The Repeat structure is permitted to have a prefix. This example does not require a prefix because no variables are declared within it.

Once you have completed this pop-up screen, you will still be in the summary window. The point field and repeat structure will be displayed, but you are not finished. For the point to work correctly, it must be a part of the repeat structure. Use the appropriate addition or subtraction keypad keys to move the point field inside the repeat structure. When your summary window appears like the one shown in Fig. 8-29, then you can exit the window.

```
┌────────────────────────────────────────────────────────────────┐
│   SAMPLE      SCREEN       WINDOW(15,27),HUE(7,1,0)              │
│   SELNO       ROW(14,21) STRING(@N2)                            │
│                            REPEAT(9),INDEX(NDX)                 │
│               ROW(4,3)       POINT(1,23),USE(?POINT_FIELD),REQ  │
│                                  .                               │
│                                                                  │
│                                                                  │
│   Field Type:Repeat         String Entry Menu Pause Repeat Point Text │
└────────────────────────────────────────────────────────────────┘
```

8-29.   Summary window, containing a point field in a repeat

Generate the source by returning to the Editor's worksheet. Processing the point field will be similar to the processing proposed for other field types; you will simply have to handle more situations.

First, the Index variable should be defined locally, if it is not defined in a global module. Next, the field editing code that you will insert into the CASE statement will have to handle all the situations that you require. For example, Fig. 8-30 contains some code that might be used to process the point field in this situation.

```
NDX  SHORT
     CODE
     OPEN(SAMPLE)
     ALERT(ESC_KEY)
     LOOP
       ACCEPT
       CASE FIELD()
       OF ?POINT_FIELD
         CASE KEYCODE()
         OF PGUP_KEY
            NDX = 1
         OF PGDN_KEY
            NDX = 9
         OF ENTER_KEY
            SELNO = NDX
         OF ESC_KEY
            RETURN
         .
         SELECT(?POINT_FIELD)
         CYCLE
     . .
```

8-30. Sample source, demonstrating point field processing

Notice that the keys that complete the point field must be established first. This source example only handles the PgUp, PgDown, Enter, and Escape keys. If this were a scrolling table of information, the required attribute would be omitted from the point definition and then the up and down arrows would have to be processed, as well. It is possible to watch for, and process, any key that you want the user to be able to press during a point field. If it is not a key that automatically completes the point field, then alert it just as the Escape key is alerted in the Fig. 8-30 example.

An important feature of the point field is demonstrated by this example. If an area that a point is supposed to cover is completely blank, the point will skip that item. This helps to ensure that the user doesn't make invalid choices.

Conclusion

In this chapter, I have presented the structures used to create screens and windows in Clarion, along with statements and examples of how to process them. The screen formatter in the Editor will allow you to design virtually any type of screen that you can imagine. One of the best features of the screen formatter is that it gives you the luxury to experiment. Also, the Clarion language has many useful statements to help process the information obtained by the screens and windows that you design.

9
CHAPTER

Report processing

In this chapter, you will see report structures and how they are generated using the report formatter portion of the Editor. I will also discuss a variety of report formatting topics, including a simple report processing example and processing with group breaks.

Designer's report formatter outlines the basic flow of many of the reports that you are likely to process. Designer, however, only permits the development of a specific report layout consisting of a title page, a page header and footer, group breaks, and a report footer. Although this type of report might meet the needs of many programs, you will most likely want to reach beyond Designer's capabilities and create your own reports.

Report development in most traditional languages is very much like screen development—tedious. When using the traditional approach, a great deal of trial and error is needed to place fields, page breaks, and group breaks in their proper place using a series of print commands. In addition, this type of program development involves writing the program, compiling the source, linking, and, finally, testing. Designing reports in this manner is a tiring process.

With the PRINT statement, you can print any string constant or variable you have declared. In this way, you can always create any possible report by using the traditional approach.

However, Clarion takes a different approach to report development. You can use statements to print reports in Clarion, just as you would in any other language, but it is not necessary. Clarion reports are defined with structures that designate the position of all the elements in the report. The report structure can also contain other structures that define the portions of a report page. Some of these structures will operate automatically for you.

Using report structures is what allows Clarion to offer the sophisticated *WYSIWYG* (what you see is what you get) report formatter found in both the Designer and the Editor. Although you will rely upon the report formatter in the Editor to write your report structures, it is important to understand the statements that they can contain.

The report structure

The report structure has the following syntax:

```
label       REPORT, LENGTH(printed lines), |
                    WIDTH(columns), |
                    PAGE(page counter), LINE(line counter) |
                    PRE(prefix),DEVICE(device)
```

Notice that the attributes follow the REPORT statement and are separated by commas. The | character indicates a line continuation.

The report attributes LENGTH, WIDTH, PAGE, LINE, PRE, and DEVICE are optional, yet they offer important control over how a report works.

Most reports have three parts: A header (which prints at the top of each page), a detail area (the specific report information), and a footer (which prints at the bottom of each page). As you print your report, you will first print a header, and then print detail lines. As you reach the bottom of the page, a footer will be automatically printed, followed by a new header, and then more detail lines will be printed. When the point is reached when the footer needs to be printed, it is called a "page overflow." The report structure's attributes provide information about how these parts of the report are used.

The LENGTH attribute

The LENGTH attribute specifies the maximum number of lines that can be printed on a page. The parameter must be a numeric constant, not a variable. LENGTH determines when a page overflow will occur and can cause the footer to be printed. LENGTH includes the number of lines necessary for any header and footer. The footer will print at that line on every page when no more lines can be printed. After the footer is printed, a new header will be printed, and detail printing resumes.

Note that page overflow does not issue a form feed. If you need a form feed to be sent to the printer device, you can simply specify one in your FOOTER (or HEADER) structure.

The WIDTH attribute

The WIDTH attribute specifies how wide the report layout is. The parameter must be a numeric constant (not a variable) in the range of 1 through 255. This width is also used by the report formatter to draw and center guidelines. The formatter's screen scrolls horizontally to allow you to create a report with lines that are longer than the display's width.

The PAGE attribute

The page counter variable is the label of a numeric variable, which contains the number of the page being printed. This variable can be placed in the report header or footer to print the current page number, and is updated automatically each time a page overflow occurs.

The LINE attribute

The LINE attribute is similar to PAGE. The line counter parameter is the label of a numeric variable, and is updated each time a structure is printed. It is reset to 1 each time a page HEADER is printed. The LINE attribute is best used when you are handling your own page overflow conditions. However, changing the line counter value has no effect on the automatic page overflow, because another copy of this value is kept internally.

The PRE attribute

The PRE attribute is like those discussed in preceding chapters, and allows you to uniquely identify variables as part of a particular report. It is a good idea to use the PRE to distinguish a report's variables from those that might be in other structures.

The DEVICE attribute

The DEVICE attribute is a variable or string constant that contains a DOS device name or file specification. Without a DEVICE attribute, a report is automatically sent to the standard print device (LPT1). However, the DEVICE attribute makes it possible to send a report to a disk file, a different printer, or any available device. Since a variable can contain the device name, it is also possible to write your code so that the user can decide where to send the report.

If you specify a variable to contain the device name, make sure that the variable is set with the device name before the report is opened. If the device fails to open, the report will default to the standard printer device (LPT1). The common DOS devices are the following:

CON	Console Monitor
LPT1, PRN	First Parallel Port
LPT2	Second Parallel Port
LPT3	Third Parallel Port
COM1, AUX	First Serial Port
COM2	Second Serial Port
NUL	Null Device

The beginning of a report's definition is designated by the report statement. A HEADER, a FOOTER, and any number of DETAIL statements can reside within a report structure. Figure 9-1 is an example of an empty report in the Editor's report formatter.

```
....:....1....:....2....:....3....:....4....:....5....:....6....:....7....:....8
━━━━━━━━━━━━━━━━━━━━━━━━━━━━━━━━━Header━━━━━━━━━━━━━━━━━━━━━━━━━━━━━
━━━━━━━━━━━━━━━━━━━━━━━━━━━━━━━━━Detail━━━━━━━━━━━━━━━━━━━━━━━━━━━━━
━━━━━━━━━━━━━━━━━━━━━━━━━━━━━━━━━Footer━━━━━━━━━━━━━━━━━━━━━━━━━━━━━
....:....1....:....2....:....3....:....4....:....5....:....6....:....7....:....8
```

9-1. Report formatter's display of a new report structure

To use the report formatter, Press Ctrl−F with the cursor in the data area of a program you are writing with the Editor. You will see a report worksheet immediately if the cursor is located within a report structure. If the cursor is not within a report or screen structure, you will see the format new structure window, and you can choose the report option to see the blank structure worksheet shown in Fig. 9-1.

The information that you see on the worksheet can be represented in source statements like this:

```
REPORT      REPORT
label_hdr       HEADER
                  .
label_dt1       DETAIL
                  .
label_ftr       FOOTER
          .     .
```

Notice that the REPORT, HEADER, DETAIL, and FOOTER statements can have labels, by which they are referenced, and are terminated by a period. HEADER and FOOTER statements are optional, and numerous DETAIL statements can be defined within the same report structure. At least one DETAIL is required per report.

The header structure

The header structure declares the lines to be printed at the top of each page of a report. It includes the HEADER statement and the statements following it, until the structure is terminated by a period. This structure can be used as a group variable in assignment statements, expressions, or parameter lists.

The header is automatically printed when you open a report structure. You can also print the header at any time, with the PRINT statement.

The detail structure

The detail structure declares the lines to be printed in the body of a report. It includes the DETAIL statement and the statements following it, until the structure is terminated by a period. This structure, too, can be used as a group variable in assignment statements, expressions, or parameter lists. Detail structures are only printed by the PRINT statement and will never print automatically.

Some detail structures might contain name, address, city, and state variables on the same line, or they might be placed on multiple lines, as in the case of mailing labels. Other detail structures might print running totals or information from different files. Since there can be as many detail structures in your report as you want, you can have a wide range of formats and data within the same report.

If a LENGTH attribute is defined for the report structure and the lines contained in the detail structure will not fit within the page length boundary, PRINT automatically prints the report footer for this page and the next page's header before printing the detail structure.

The footer structure

A footer structure declares the lines to be printed at the bottom of each page of a report. It includes the FOOTER statement and the statements following it, until the structure is terminated by a period. Like the other structures, this structure can be used as a group variable in assignment statements, expressions, or parameter lists.

A footer structure is automatically printed when you close a report structure or when a page overflow occurs. You can also print the footer with the PRINT command any time you wish. As mentioned before, page overflow will occur only if a valid LENGTH attribute is used in the report structure.

The report formatter

You will probably rely upon the report formatter to generate the code for your structures. The statements generated in the report's structures are similar to those generated in the screen structures presented in Chapter 8. The best way to learn about these statements is to discover how (and why) they are used in the report formatter.

You might have noticed, from using Designer, that the report formatter is line-oriented, just like the Editor. Many of the same functions possible in the Editor are allowed in the report formatter (line/block copy, move, delete, etc.). Other features of the report formatter are similar to those found in the screen formatter. This "familiar" functionality should make it very simple for you to learn how to make reports quickly.

The report structure attributes, like PAGE, LENGTH, and WIDTH, can be set in the Editor's report formatter by pressing Ctrl–V when the cursor is on a header, detail, or footer structure line. Figure 9-2 illustrates this window.

The Structure window shown in Fig. 9-2 has two parts. The top portion of the window applies to the master report structure, while the lower portion applies to the specific structure that was indicated by the cursor.

To change any portion of the report structure definition, you will have to first press Esc. The label identifies the report structure, while the remaining prompts correspond to the individual attributes that can be declared. Enter the values for the fields, as shown in Fig. 9-2, into the window.

```
                         Structure

            Report Label :MYREPORT
            Report Width : 80
            Report Length: 60
            Report Line  :
            Report Page  :PAGENUM
            Report Prefix:RPT
            Report Device:

            Detail Label :MYDETAIL
            Detail Prefix:
```

9-2. Structure definition window for a detail record

You must use a label for the structure if you intend to reference it in the code. The label that should be used for the detail structure is shown in Fig. 9-2.

Notice that after you identify a label for the detail structure, a new detail structure appears in your report. This is done automatically by the report formatter to make sure that, at any time, you can define another detail structure. If nothing is added to the empty detail structure (including a label name) then the report formatter knows that it is not going to be referenced and does not generate any code for it.

Like the screen formatter, the report formatter has a summary window that is displayed when Ctrl–S is pressed. Figure 9-3 displays how the summary window appears. The screen formatter, however, requires all fields and structures to be selected from this window. The report formatter does not have to make this requirement. Remember, screens can have several different types of fields—the fields can overlay each other and order is very important. Reports, on the other hand, have a limited number of options, which permits direct control-key access through the keyboard. The summary window can select an item if you wish to change it.

```
  MYREPORT      REPORT        LENGTH(60),WIDTH(80),PAGE(PAGENUM),PRE(RPT)
  MYDETAIL                    DETAIL
                .             .
```

9-3. Report formatter's summary window

Figure 9-4 is how your report should look after you name the header and footer structures. Use the names presented in this example to change your report.

```
....:....1....:....2....:....3....:....4....:....5....:....6....:....7....:....8
MYHEADER━━━━━━━━━━━━━━━━━━━━━━━━━━━━━━Header━━━━━━━━━━━━━━━━━━━━━━━━━━━━━━
MYDETAIL━━━━━━━━━━━━━━━━━━━━━━━━━━━━━━Detail━━━━━━━━━━━━━━━━━━━━━━━━━━━━━━
━━━━━━━━━━━━━━━━━━━━━━━━━━━━━━━━━━━━━━Detail━━━━━━━━━━━━━━━━━━━━━━━━━━━━━━
MYFOOTER━━━━━━━━━━━━━━━━━━━━━━━━━━━━━━Footer━━━━━━━━━━━━━━━━━━━━━━━━━━━━━━
....:....1....:....2....:....3....:....4....:....5....:....6....:....7....:....8
```

9-4. Worksheet display, after naming each structure

Now that you see the skeleton of the sample report, assume that this report will process the records found in an employee file that has this file definition:

```
EMPLOYEE      FILE,PRE(EMP)
NAMEKEY       KEY(EMP:NAME),NOCASE
DEPTKEY       KEY(EMP:DEPT),DUP
              RECORD
NAME              STRING(20)
DEPT              SHORT
```

After reading a record from this file, possibly in keyed-in order, the name of an employee will be found in the EMP:NAME variable, while the employee's department number will be in EMP:DEPT. Instead of just printing the department number, however, the report should include the appropriate department name. The department numbers are fixed and correspond to the following names:

DEPT NO.	DEPT NAME
1	Accounts
2	Billing
3	Sales
4	Service

To begin designing the report, move the cursor to the detail structure named MYDETAIL. Press Enter to insert a blank line into this detail structure. Now press Ctrl–V while the cursor is on this blank line. The variable window will appear. An example of how to complete this window is shown in Fig. 9-5.

206

```
┌─────────────────────────────────────────────────────────────────────┐
│                              Variable                                 │
│                                                                       │
│  Control Before :              Label:            Use:                 │
│  Parameter      :@S20          Label:            Use:EMP:NAME          │
│  Control After  :              Label:            Use:                 │
│                                                                       │
│  Formfeed Before:No      Yes  No                                      │
│  Formfeed After :No      Yes  No                                      │
│  Overprint Next :No      Yes  No                                      │
│                                                                       │
└─────────────────────────────────────────────────────────────────────┘
```

9-5. Variable definition window, with Use variable defined

This window is divided into two parts. The upper section can define a report variable and/or printer control sequence. The lower section applies to the entire line.

Printer controls, Control Before and Control After, send information to the printer device. This information is included in the line but does not occupy space like a variable does. Controls are discussed in greater detail later in the chapter.

The Parameter field must be completed if you are defining a report variable. A Clarion picture or a string constant can respond to this field. This example defines a string picture which has a length of 20 and is the size of the EMP:NAME field in the employee file.

Because the name can be taken directly from the employee record, a label is not required for this variable. If you wanted to reference this variable in the report processing statements, you would identify the label you wanted to use after the label prompt.

The Use field is where you indicate the name of the variable that contains the information you want to print. Use variables in reports are similar to those that fields in screen structures define. A report field with a Use variable will simply print what is found in the variable after formatting it into the picture declared in the parameter field. This example will take the employee's name directly from the EMP:NAME variable.

As mentioned earlier, the lower section of the variable window asks questions relating to the entire line. These are normally called line controls.

Formfeed Before and Formfeed After determine whether the form feed character (12) should be sent to the device before printing a line and/or after printing a line. This example does not require this feature. Form feed options are allowed because some printers do not automatically eject to a new page once the form length has been reached. Indeed, you can intentionally design a report that has a LENGTH attribute less than an actual printer page. In these instances, you will have to indicate the line (usually in a footer) where you wish the form feed to occur.

The Overprint Next choice lets you print a line without sending a line feed to the printer device. This option can be used to perform special formatting, where all the information for a given line cannot occur on the same line. An example might be to stimulate a boldface option (assuming the printer does not support one) by over-striking the information again with the next line of the report. Naturally this means that one line will be specified by two lines of text.

Once you accept the last field, you also accept the entire window. The field that you have defined is represented on the screen by a line of box characters, showing you how much room that variable takes up on the line.

While in the worksheet, skip two spaces following the name and press Ctrl–V again. This time, define the string variable that will hold the department name. A string picture of a length of 10 will be sufficient to hold the name. Since an employee's record only contains the department number, you will have to assign a label for this variable so you can insert the appropriate department name. Label this variable DEPT.

Now you have two variables declares within the mydetail structure. Center the variables, using Ctrl–6, and compare your results to those shown in the detail area of Fig. 9-6. At the top of each page, you will want headings over each column. Move the cursor to the header structure and insert new lines containing the text, also displayed in Fig. 9-6.

```
....:....1....:....2....:....3....:....4....:....5....:....6....:....7....:....8
MYHEADER━━━━━━━━━━━━━━━━━━━━━━━━Header━━━
                    Employee Name        Department
                    ....................  ..........
MYDETAIL━━━━━━━━━━━━━━━━━━━━━Detail━━━━━━━━
                    ████████████████████  ██████████
                                    Detail━━
MYFOOTER━━━━━━━━━━━━━━━━━━━━Footer━━━
....:....1....:....2....:....3....:....4....:....5....:....6....:....7....:....8
```

9-6. Worksheet display, after adding variables and headings

Finally, a page number should be printed at the bottom of each page. To do this, insert a variable in the footer structure that has a Use variable that matches the report Page attribute shown in Fig. 9-1. The variable window shown in Fig. 9-7 provides the proper definition.

Notice, in Fig. 9-7, that the Formfeed After prompt has been answered with yes, and that the LENGTH variable is set to 60 lines per page. Since the normal printed page contains 66 lines, this will leave a margin at the bottom of each page. Unless the printer automatically sets to the top of the form after printing 60 lines, the formfeed is necessary to force the new page.

```
                                Variable

    Control Before :              Label:          Use:
    Parameter      :@n3           Label:          Use:PAGENUM
    Control After  :              Label:          Use:

    Formfeed Before:No      Yes  No
    Formfeed After :Yes     Yes  No
    Overprint Next :No      Yes  No
```

9-7. Variable definition, with line control set for Formfeed After

Type the word Page in front of the number variable and then center the line using Ctrl−^. Your Report worksheet should now look like the one in Fig. 9-8. When a line control has been defined, the first position of the line is reversed on the worksheet. This indicates that a line control exists on that line. The reversed character position can be treated like any other—you can type into it or define a field in it.

```
....:....1....:....2....:....3....:....4....:....5....:....6....:....7....:....8
MYHEADER────────────────────────Header──────────────────────────────────────
                   Employee Name          Department
                   -------------------    ----------
MYDETAIL───────────────────────Detail──────────────────────────────────────
                   ■■■■■■■■■■■■■■■■■■■   ■■■■■■■■■■
                                Detail──────────────────────────────────────
MYFOOTER───────────────────────Footer──────────────────────────────────────
                        Page <<#
....:....1....:....2....:....3....:....4....:....5....:....6....:....7....:....8
```

9-8. Worksheet display of the complete report

As described in Chapter 8, the screen formatter offers a browse function, which can verify how the screen will operate. This is a useful feature that can help you catch operation problems without having to compile and run the program. The report formatter offers a similar feature with Ctrl−L, for "list."

Ctrl−L can print a test listing of the report that you have currently defined, printed using the definitions and requirements that you have designated, including the header and footer.

Of course, the report formatter doesn't know how you intend to process the report, or any values for the variables contained within it. The listing simply demonstrates positioning, control sequences, and general page description. If you were laying out a report that used pre-printed forms, this feature could save you lots of time by giving you instant feedback on whether fields have the proper position and size.

Press Ctrl−Enter to generate the source for your report. The Editor's worksheet will appear with the structure that you have just defined. Now that you know what is contained in the report, it should be easier to understand the statements contained in the structure. The code generated by the Report Formatter should resemble that in Fig. 9-9.

```
MYREPORT    REPORT          LENGTH(60),WIDTH(80),PAGE(PAGENUM),PRE(RPT)
MYHEADER                    HEADER
            COL(25)           STRING('Employee Name {9}Department')
            ROW(+1,25)        STRING('-{20}  -{10}') CTL(@LF)
                              .
MYDETAIL                    DETAIL
            COL(25)           STRING(20),USE(EMP:NAME)
DEPT        COL(47)           STRING(10) CTL(@LF)
                              .
MYFOOTER                    FOOTER
            COL(37)           STRING('Page')
            COL(42)           STRING(@n3),USE(PAGENUM) CTL(@LF)
                              CTL(@FF)
        .               .
```

9-9. Report formatter source for a report structure

STRING statements

Strings declared within a report can take several forms. The statement in a report structure declares a string literal or variable located one character past the last string statement, or at the position specified by the ROW and COL attributes. Report strings can be used like any other string, whether or not their report structure is open.

The example shown in Fig. 9-9 has an example of using STRING statements for the literals typed into the header section of the report. Additionally, string variables have been declared in the detail section. One of these relies on a Use variable (EMP:NAME), and the other has been given a label (DEPT), which will allow you to assign its value.

Position attributes

ROW, COL, and CTL are position attributes used in report structures. They are attributes of the structure itself. Although the example in Fig. 9-9 does not contain explicit ROW instructions for each line, they are still important.

ROW and COL attributes operate in a similar fashion in reports as they do in screens. They specify the row and column position of strings within a report layout. ROW statements can optionally contain column positions, and when the row does not require modification, the COL statement can be used.

Unlike screens, a report is always defined sequentially. This means that explicit row positioning is not always required and the ROW statement can merely indicate the number of rows to increment. For example, ROW(+3) indicates that the internal row counter should be incremented 3 lines. This would cause enough line feeds and carriage returns to be issued in order to position the report properly.

Explicit row and column positioning can be done at any time. If a ROW statement that has a lower value than the current one is encountered, however, the program will assume that the item following the ROW statement should begin on the next page.

The COL statement operates in much the same manner as the ROW statement. It can designate an explicit column position, or designate the number of column positions to increment. If a COL statement sets a column that is less than the current column position, a Return is issued and the statement following the COL will overprint the previous line, beginning at the column parameter location.

The CTL statement specifies a print control sequence between strings. These control sequences control printer variables such as special fonts, character spacing, and tab stops. As a general rule, control characters will not generate printable characters, but rather modify the current row and column positions.

The sequence parameter of the CTL statement is a string constant or a printer control token defined by Clarion. The available printer control tokens and their definitions are:

@FFn	Form feed (ASCII 12) n times, then carriage return.
@LFn	Line feed (ASCII 10) n times, then carriage return.
@CRn	Carriage return (ASCII 13) n times.
@Bn	Insert n blank characters.

Each line in the example structure has a CTL(@LF) following it. This causes the printer to issue a line feed so that the next item will print on a new line. At the end of the footer structure, a CTL(@FF) also occurs. This is the result of the Formfeed After prompt in the variable/line control window.

The CONTROL statement

Controls are the final item that can be defined with a report structure. This statement has the following types of syntax:

Form 1	CONTROL(length)
Form 2	CONTROL(string constant)
Form 3	CONTROL(picture token)

Each form declares an area to be used as a printer control sequence.

CONTROL statements are similar to STRING statements, but will not use or affect the ROW and COL position attributes. It is assumed that a CONTROL will communicate with the printer device and not actually print characters on the page; therefore, they will not take up character positions in the report formatter.

The variable definition window, shown in Fig. 9-10, illustrates how control statements can be defined in a report. Figure 9-10 defines two CONTROL statements. The report formatter lets you define control sequences that occur before and after printing a variable.

```
                            Variable

   Control Before :'<27>E'      Label:         Use:
   Parameter      :@S10         Label:VAR      Use:
   Control After  :'<27>F'      Label:         Use:

   Formfeed Before:No    Yes  No
   Formfeed After :No    Yes  No
   Overprint Next :No    Yes  No
```

9-10.   Control definitions, using string literals

You do not have to include an After sequence if you have a Before sequence, or vice versa. Additionally, if you merely want to send the printer a control sequence, you can use either of the control definitions and not include a variable parameter.

Since a string literal is defined for each CONTROL statement in Fig. 9-10, Form 2 of the statement will be generated by the report formatter for each.

A literal, defined in this format, is normally called an *escape sequence*. This name is used because most printers require that an Escape character (ASCII 27) occur first in the string to indicate that control information follows, rather than printable characters.

The Escape character, or any other non-printable character, can be defined in Clarion by enclosing the ASCII code in angle brackets within a string. The strings in Fig. 9-10 actually represent two characters each. The <27> is interpreted to be one ASCII character.

Assume that the sequences in Fig. 9-10 are those required to turn on bold printing (Esc–E) and then turn it off (Esc–F) for a particular printer. Now you can see how the variable placed in VAR will be printed in boldface on the report page.

A sequence defined in this fashion cannot be changed after the program has been compiled. Occasionally, you might want to alter controls so that your program can support more than one printer type. To do this, you will need to define a label so that you can assign your sequences or rely upon a Use variable.

Figure 9-11 demonstrates how the previous example would look if you had chosen to declare a Use variable for the boldface-on sequence, named BOLDON, and a label for the boldface-off sequence, named BOL-DOFF. Of course, you would probably not mix your definitions in this manner; this merely demonstrates both methods.

```
                               Variable

     Control Before :@S2         Label:              Use:BOLDON
     Parameter      :@S10        Label:VAR           Use:
     Control After  :@S2         Label:BOLDOFF       Use:

     Formfeed Before:No     Yes  No
     Formfeed After :No     Yes  No
     Overprint Next :No     Yes  No
```

9-11. Control definitions, using Label and Use

Notice, in Fig. 9-11, that the control parameters now are simple string pictures, with a length of 2. This example works exactly the same as the previous one, as long as BOLDON (the Use variable) and BOLDOFF (a report label) are initialized properly before this line prints.

A final word about CONTROL statements: When you use Form 1, it is normally because you are using a label or Use variable to designate the sequence. This works fine, unless you have a sequence that is shorter than the length defined for the control.

Assume that you have defined a CONTROL(6),USE(BOLDON) statement. A statement like this would allow you to handle any printer's bold command, as long as it could be designated in six character or less. The program, however, will always specify six characters. That means if the sequence is only two characters for the current printer, four extra characters (usually spaces) are sent, as well. Naturally, this can mess up any formatting that you have established.

Only one possible remedy exists for this situation (other than never using an incorrect length). Most printers ignore null (0) characters when they are received. This means that you could use a statement like BOLDON = '<27>E<0,0,0,0>' to initialize the entire CONTROL statement length and achieve the proper results. If a printer does not ignore null characters, check to see if there are any non-printable characters that do not affect formatting.

Processing report structures

Once you have defined a report, you can begin to write the code necessary to process it. There are only a few statements that deal directly with the report structure and substructures.

The OPEN statement

The OPEN statement has the form:

    OPEN(report)

and will open a report structure's device, if defined, and prints the report header, if it exists. The report parameter is the label of a report or that of an EXTERNAL,REPORT statement.

The OPEN statement is not required, because the printing of any substructure will automatically open the report structure. If a device has been declared, however, it might be important for you to do an explicit OPEN. This is especially true if you have specified a filename for the device. You can examine the ERROR function after an OPEN statement to see if the device opened properly.

Remember, if the device fails to open, the report will be sent to the standard printer device.

The CLOSE statement

The CLOSE statement has the form:

    CLOSE(report)

and will close a report structure after printing any report footers, if defined. The report parameter is the label of a report or that of an EXTERNAL,REPORT statement.

Closing a report is important if a device is being used (like a filename) and/or if the report has a footer structure that might not have been printed yet. Additionally, it is a good habit to close your own reports, because executing a RUN, CHAIN, or CALL, or ending the program will close the open device but not print the report footer.

The PRINT statement

The PRINT statement has two forms:

    Form 1   PRINT(detail)
    Form 2   PRINT(string)

Form 1 of the PRINT statement causes the identified structure to be sent to the device specified by the report. The detail parameter is the label of a header, detail, or footer structure. PRINT will print all the lines associated with the structure named as a parameter.

Two things will be checked before a PRINT statement is executed. First, if the report has not been opened, an implicit open will occur. If a header structure exists, it will be printed before the structure. (Naturally, if the parameter of the PRINT statement is the header structure, it is only printed once.) The second check occurs when the parameter is the label of a detail structure. A check is made to determine whether there is sufficient room left (using the LENGTH variable) to print the detail without interfering with the footer. If there is not enough room, a page overflow will occur, causing the footer to print and then the header of the next page. (If the parameter is the FOOTER, it will be printed only once, on the current page.)

Form 2 of the PRINT statement simply writes the string parameter to the standard printer device (usually LPT1).

The NAME function

The NAME function has the form:

    NAME(report)

and returns a string containing the device name or file specification. The report parameter is the label of a report or that of an EXTERNAL,RE-PORT statement. This function can verify what device or file will receive the report.

As with any processing statement, it is important to check for errors that can occur. Errors should be generated if the report cannot be opened or if a PRINT statement fails, and can be returned from the ERROR function.

PATH NOT FOUND can be returned if the DEVICE attribute of the report structure has an invalid file path declared when you try to (explicitly or implicitly) open the report.

TOO MANY OPEN FILES can also be generated when the report is opened. Sometimes this error can be eliminated by increasing the number of files (set by CONFIG.SYS) that DOS allows you to open. Check your DOS manual to determine how to change your CONFIG.SYS settings. Another item to examine in response to this error is whether there are files opened that could be closed during the report operation. Don't forget to close your reports when you are done, because they use file handles too.

ACCESS DENIED can be set in a number of ways, but primarily will be one of two things. First, the report device cannot be opened if it is already opened by another task or report. The second most common situation that can cause this error is when you run out of disk space while sending the report to a file.

Now that you are familiar with the report formatter and its statements, you can begin to write the report processing statements. Referring back to the example you generated using the report formatter, Fig. 9-12 demonstrates how you might process this report. In this example, the records are read sequentially from the EMPLOYEE file until all have been read. The open is implied when the first PRINT occurs.

```
PAGENUM SHORT

         CODE
         OPEN(EMPLOYEE)
         IF ERROR() THEN STOP.
         SET(EMPLOYEE)
         LOOP UNTIL EOF(EMPLOYEE)
           NEXT(EMPLOYEE)
           EXECUTE(EMP:DEPT)
             RPT:DEPT = 'Accounts'
             RPT:DEPT = 'Billing'
             RPT:DEPT = 'Sales'
             RPT:DEPT = 'Service'
           .
           PRINT(RPT:MYDETAIL)
         .
         CLOSE(MYREPORT)
```

9-12. Source code for processing a report

Between reading a record and printing the detail, it is necessary to assign values to the label variables that do not have Uses. In this example, each record contains a department number, but the report should also include the department name. The EXECUTE statement is a simple way to make the proper assignment.

Notice that an explicit CLOSE statement was used on the report. This ensures that the last page of the report will contain the FOOTER. Naturally, if this report uses a device, it would be even more important to ensure that it was closed. Figure 9-13 demonstrates how this report might appear using some sample data.

Group break processing

Eventually, you will want to make a report that contains more than one detail structure. One example might be multiple detail structures for printing information before or after records that meet a certain requirement. These are often called *group break structures* because they apply to an entire group of records.

Most commonly, group breaks are based upon at least one key of a file that allows duplicate keys (DUP). If no duplicate keys are allowed, then there will not be any groups. If you want to group records based upon a

```
         Employee Name          Department
         - - - - - - - - - - - - - - - -    - - - - - - - - -
         Tim Witherspoon        Accounts
         Tom Dooley             Billing
         Bill Franks            Accounts
         Frank Conners          Sales
         Andrew McAuto          Sales
         Bobby Barron           Service
         Beth Turner            Billing
         David Page             Accounts
         Bev Curtis             Sales
         John Lewis             Billing
         Tim Barnes             Service
         Pam Lawson             Sales
         Doug Brown             Accounts
         Jill Simpson           Billing
         Roland Deal            Service
         Matt Skaggs            Sales
         Ann Pots               Billing
         Dennis King            Accounts




                              Page    1
```

9-13. Sample report of employees and departments

field that is not a key, you will probably have to first sort the records by that field.

Refer to the example that has already been explained, using the EMPLOYEE file. Any number of employees can be in a given department. Since this file is also keyed by department, it is possible to retrieve all the records for employees in a given department before moving on to the next. Knowing this, you can include more detail structures in the example to process the group information.

It is not difficult to add additional detail structures to the report. Place the cursor inside the existing report structure and press Ctrl–F. Now that the report formatter has been loaded, move the cursor to the blank detail structure. If you give this structure a name, like DEPTHEAD, it will become a part of your report. Notice that a new, blank detail has also been added. This makes it possible to add another detail structure, named DEPTFOOT.

Figure 9-14 illustrates how the worksheet will look after a few addi-

```
....:....1....:....2....:....3....:....4....:....5....:....6....:....7....:....8
MYHEADER━━━━━━━━━━━━━━━━━━━━━━━━━━━Header━━━━━━━━━━━━━━━━━━━━━━━━━━━━
                        Employees by Department
        ...............................................

MYDETAIL━━━━━━━━━━━━━━━━━━━━━━━━━━Detail━━━━━━━━━━━━━━━━━━━━━━━━━━━
                    ■■■■■■■■■■■■■■■■■■■■■■
DEPTHEAD━━━━━━━━━━━━━━━━━━━━━━━━━━Detail━━━━━━━━━━━━━━━━━━━━━━━━━━━
            ■■■■■■■■■■ Department Employee Names
        ......................................

DEPTFOOT━━━━━━━━━━━━━━━━━━━━━━━━━━Detail━━━━━━━━━━━━━━━━━━━━━━━━━━━
        .......................................................
        Number of employees in this department = <<#
        .......................................................
━━━━━━━━━━━━━━━━━━━━━━━━━━━━━━━━━━Detail━━━━━━━━━━━━━━━━━━━━━━━━━━━
MYFOOTER━━━━━━━━━━━━━━━━━━━━━━━━━━Footer━━━━━━━━━━━━━━━━━━━━━━━━━━━
                            Page <<#
....:....1....:....2....:....3....:....4....:....5....:....6....:....7....:....8
```

9-14. Worksheet display with group breaks

tions and a little arrangement. The objective will now be to print the employees by department. The header will designate the report title. At the start of a new department, the depthead structure called group header, should be printed. This will identify the area where the employees work. Next, all the employees of the stated department are printed through the DETAIL structure. When the last employee from a department has been printed, the deptfoot structure is printed. The group footer contains a count of the number of employees in the department.

Finally, each page is numbered by the page footer structure. The code generated for the report structure is shown in Fig. 9-15.

```
MYREPORT    REPORT          LENGTH(60),WIDTH(80),PAGE(PAGENUM),PRE(RPT)
MYHEADER                    HEADER
            ROW(+1,30)      STRING('Employees by Department')
            ROW(+1,16)      STRING('-{50}') CTL(@LF2)
                            .
MYDETAIL                    DETAIL
            COL(31)         STRING(20),USE(EMP:NAME) CTL(@LF)
                            .
DEPTHEAD                    DETAIL
DEPT        ROW(+1,20)      STRING(10)
            COL(31)         STRING('Department Employee Names')
            ROW(+1,20)      STRING('-{36}') CTL(@LF)
                            .
DEPTFOOT                    DETAIL
            COL(16)         STRING('-{50}')
            ROW(+1,19)      STRING('Number of employees in this department =')
            COL(60)         STRING(@N3),USE(COUNTEMP)
            ROW(+1,16)      STRING('-{50}') CTL(@LF)
                            .
MYFOOTER                    FOOTER
            COL(37)         STRING('Page')
            COL(42)         STRING(@N3),USE(PAGENUM) CTL(@LF)
                            CTL(@FF)
                            .                    .
```

9-15. Report formatter source for a report with groups

Notice, in Fig. 9-15, that the additional structures are still detail structures. Usually, making the structures and lines in the report formatter is the simple procedure of handling group breaks. Most of the work is done by the code processing the records. Example code that might be used to process the EMPLOYEE file using this report structure is presented in Fig. 9-16.

You can see, in Fig. 9-16, that group breaks requires more statements than a simple report. First, a variable to hold the current group settings is required. The variable SAVEDEPT is used to keep track of which department is currently being processed. As records are read, the employee's department is compared to this variable in order to determine whether the department is the same. If it is determined that it is the same department, the record is simply printed and the next record is read.

When an employee is read who does not have a department equal to the SAVEDEPT variable, it is time to print the group footer and a new group header. Additionally, the SAVEDEPT variable must be set to the new department, and all other necessary variables have to be updated to reflect the change in department.

Another important point to notice in Fig. 9-16 is that the first record of the file is read outside the loop. This is done for two reasons. First, the

```
                PROGRAM
EMPLOYEE        FILE,PRE(EMP)
NAMEKEY           KEY(EMP:NAME),NOCASE
DEPTKEY           KEY(EMP:DEPT),DUP
                RECORD
NAME               STRING(20)
DEPT               SHORT
                .  .

MYREPORT        REPORT      LENGTH(60),WIDTH(80),PAGE(PAGENUM),PRE(RPT) |
                            DEVICE('SAMPLE2.FIG')
MYHEADER                    HEADER
                ROW(+1,30)   STRING('Employees by Department')
                ROW(+1,16)   STRING('-{50}') CTL(@LF2)

MYDETAIL                    DETAIL
                COL(31)      STRING(20),USE(EMP:NAME) CTL(@LF)

DEPTHEAD                    DETAIL
DEPT            ROW(+1,20)   STRING(10)
                COL(31)      STRING('Department Employee Names')
                ROW(+1,20)   STRING('-{36}') CTL(@LF)

DEPTFOOT                    DETAIL
                COL(16)      STRING('-{50}')
                ROW(+1,19)   STRING('Number of employees in this department =')
                COL(60)      STRING(@N3),USE(COUNTEMP)
                ROW(+1,16)   STRING('-{50}') CTL(@LF)

MYFOOTER                    FOOTER
                COL(37)      STRING('Page')
                COL(42)      STRING(@N3),USE(PAGENUM) CTL(@LF)
                             CTL(@FF)


PAGENUM  SHORT
COUNTEMP SHORT                          ! COUNT FOR THE EMPLOYEES
SAVEDEPT SHORT                          ! STORE THE CURRENT DEPT
    CODE
    OPEN(EMPLOYEE)
    IF ERROR() THEN STOP.
    SET(EMP:DEPTKEY)                    ! SET TO RETRIEVE BY KEY
    NEXT(EMPLOYEE)                      ! FIRST RETRIEVE A RECORD
    SAVEDEPT = 0                        ! INITIALIZE SO BREAK OCCURS FIRST
    LOOP                               ! LOOP THROUGH ALL EMPLOYEES
      IF EMP:DEPT <> SAVEDEPT           ! IS THIS EMPLOYEE IN ANOTHER DEPT
        IF SAVEDEPT <> 0                ! PRINT THE DEPT GROUP FOOTER?
          PRINT(RPT:DEPTFOOT)           ! YES, PAGE HAS BEEN STARTED
          .
        SAVEDEPT = EMP:DEPT             ! START A NEW DEPARTMENT
        COUNTEMP = 0                    ! INITIALIZE FOR NEW DEPT TOTAL
        EXECUTE(EMP:DEPT)               ! INITIALIZE THE DEPARTMENT NAME
          RPT:DEPT = 'Accounts'
          RPT:DEPT = 'Billing'
          RPT:DEPT = 'Sales'
          RPT:DEPT = 'Service'
```

9-16. Sample program for a report with group breaks

```
      PRINT(RPT:DEPTHEAD)              ! PRINT THE DEPT GROUP HEADER
  .
    PRINT(RPT:MYDETAIL)               ! PRINT THE DETAIL RECORD
    COUNTEMP += 1                     ! ADD ONE TO EMPLOYEE COUNT
    IF EOF(EMPLOYEE) THEN BREAK.      ! STOP AT END OF FILE
    NEXT(EMPLOYEE)                    ! RETRIEVE THE NEXT RECORD
  .
  IF SAVEDEPT <> 0                    ! PRINT THE DEPT GROUP FOOTER?
    PRINT(RPT:DEPTFOOT)               ! YES, PAGE HAS BEEN STARTED
  .
  CLOSE(MYREPORT)                     ! CLOSE THE REPORT
```

9-16. Continued

record area had to be initialized so that the first group will be recognized. If this is not done, the first department's employee's will be printed without the group header. By initializing the same variable to an invalid value and reading the first record, you ensure that he first group will be processed properly.

The second reason that the first record is read outside the loop is implied in the first reason. You will not know that the department number has changed until you actually read the first record of the next department. This means that you have to check the break criteria before printing the record that you currently have in memory. Otherwise, you will misplace one record in each department. The first part of the loop will check for breaks, while the rest of the loop reads the next record.

One more point can be drawn from the example in Fig. 9-16. notice that the statement, IF SAVEDEPT <>, occurs in two places and, only when this is true, will the group footer be printed. The statement occurs inside the loop and after the loop, yet they serve the same purpose. Until the SAVEDEPT variable is given a value, no employees will be printed. Without this added step, you might print a group footer when no records have been printed. Additionally, the "outside" loop handles another situation. After you have read the last record in the file, the loop terminates. This means that the code that verifies a group change will not be executed because no more records can be read to change the department number. The final IF is included to ensure that the last group footer is printed before closing the report.

Using the same sample data that was shown in Fig. 9-13, the output for this new report by department is shown in Fig. 9-17. Every employee has been categorized by department and each department is preceded and followed by specific group information.

You can add more group levels with the same techniques. For example, if the file contains a DIVISION variable, you could break when the DIVISION changes. The report formatter could add the new group structure, and additional code could be added to watch for the division breaks.

More complex reports are built up from this basic approach—

```
                    Employees by Department
........................................................

        Accounts   Department Employee Names
        .........................................
                Tim Witherspoon
                Bill Franks
                David Page
                Doug Brown
                Dennis King
........................................................
        Number of employees in this department =   5
........................................................


        Billing    Department Employee Names
        .........................................
                Tom Dooley
                Beth Turner
                John Lewis
                Jill Simpson
                Ann Pots
........................................................
        Number of employees in this department =   5
........................................................


        Sales      Department Employee Names
        .........................................
                Frank Conners
                Andrew McAuto
                Bev Curtis
                Pam Lawson
                Matt Skaggs
........................................................
        Number of employees in this department =   5
........................................................

        Service    Department Employee Names
        .........................................
                Bobby Barron
                Tim Barnes
                Roland Deal
........................................................
        Number of employees in this department =   3
........................................................




                    Page    1
```

9-17. Sample report, employees grouped by department

formatting the report with the needed variables and strings, and then writing the file (or memory table) processing statements to ensure that the proper records are in memory when you print the detail lines. Because there is no direct connection between a report structure and the statements that process the files, the format of the report can vary dramatically without changing the processing statements.

10
CHAPTER

Memory tables

In this chapter, you'll learn how to format and use memory tables and how to declare them in your programs.

Programs occasionally require a user to select several items from a list of information. If the list is almost always the same (like a list of the states in the United States) then your first approach might be to create an array of the information and compile it into your program. Although this technique might meet your program's current needs, what if the list needs to change regularly? This is just one of the many uses of memory tables.

Clarion memory tables provide a flexible means of maintaining ordered lists in your programs. These lists are "built" by the program and added to from records read from a file, entered by a user, or any source of data that can contribute to the list.

A table itself can be thought of as a type of file that is kept in memory. Using this analogy, recall that to write to a Clarion file, you must have a file structure declared. The same is true for memory tables. A table structure declaration can contain the same types of data definitions as a file structure (BYTE, SHORT, LONG, REAL, DECIMAL, STRING and GROUP). These table "records" can be added, retrieved, and deleted from the table the same way records are processed in a disk file. Indeed, many of the statements that process table records are identical to those used with Clarion files.

Tables store their records in free memory, which is the amount of memory that remains unused after your program has loaded. It is possible to process the records in a table sequentially, forwards or backwards, or directly by relative record number. You can even access table records with a field's value, like keyed access to Clarion data files.

Advantages of memory tables

There are a number of reasons why memory tables can be more advantageous than files or arrays.

- Table records are stored in memory, which can offer faster access than reading from the disk once the table has been established.

- Unlike arrays, which require memory to store the data (even when the data is not in use), a memory table only uses memory as records are added. Additionally, when items are deleted from a table, the memory is released. Any time a memory table is no longer required, all the memory used by the elements can be released using the FREE statement.

- Records in a memory table do not have to be contiguous in memory. The elements are "chained" to each other by internal pointers, which allow forward and backward processing. This means that you do not have to predefine a specific location for the elements because they will be stored anywhere they fit. As you add and delete records, the chain maintenance is handled for you automatically.

- Arrays are limited to a total data size of 65,520 bytes per array. Memory tables have no such limit, although the size of an individual table record is limited to 65,520 bytes. The memory table itself can use practically all the memory available to the program in order to maintain a maximum of 65,536 total records.

- The elements in a table are chained together in a manner which is normally described as a *doubly-linked list*. Again, such a list offers the ability to process the elements forwards and backwards without the records being contiguous in memory.

- The chain also makes it possible to sort the list quickly. This speed is achieved because the data in the records do not have to be moved during a sort; only the link pointers are changed.

- Finally, unlike array elements which are constant in size, spaces can be clipped from the end of table records before being placed in memory. Thus, a table will use memory more efficiently by taking only the memory that a record requires. When possible, it obtains it automatically, without additional code on your part—another advantage in itself.

Disadvantages of memory table

There are not many disadvantages to using a memory table, but there are a few important points to remember:

- Memory tables are limited to available memory. If a program using a memory table is executed on a machine that does not have enough free memory, it might not be able to handle as complete a list as the program requires. Worse, if you write an application that uses a memory table to store stock numbers, for instance, there might come a day when your user adds so many new products to stock that your program will run out of memory.

- A small amount, 10 bytes, of additional memory is required to maintain the forward and backward chains for each element in the list. Although a table does not predefine space like an array, more space could be required for any individual element. However, the added overhead could be more than offset by the space-saving advantage discussed earlier.

- Memory used by a table is also used for file buffers and caches. If memory is required for a new table entry and not enough is available in the free memory pool, buffers and caches can be reduced to make room for the entry. This action occurs because memory tables have a higher priority during memory allocation than buffers and caches. A disadvantage, however, is that your program often relies on a buffer or cache to increase file performance. For specific information about memory priorities, refer to the Clarion *Language Reference* manual.

- Except when the program terminates, tables are not freed automatically. This is a very important point to remember. If a procedure or function declares and builds a local memory table, be sure that function frees the table before exiting. Likewise, free a table before using it to ensure that it is empty. There is no danger in using the FREE statement on a table that is already empty.

- If a memory table reflects information that is read from disk, any changes to records in the table will not change the records on disk.

Although you can write the table records back to the original file, handle two important cases carefully: if you have fewer records in the table than when it was first read from disk, you must do something about the "left over" records; when you write the records back, you must check to see if there are any conflicting keys when duplicates are not allowed in the file.

• Since tables are essentially memory files, the ERROR function should be used to detect errors in them. After each memory table statement, it is wise to check the error condition to determine if a problem has occurred. (This is not really a disadvantage, but is often overlooked.)

Uses for memory tables

Memory tables can offer many programming advantages over arrays and files. Other advantages can be found when tables are used in conjunction with files or arrays. The following paragraphs illustrate a few scenarios that might make use of a memory table.

Records from a file, *filtered* to select records that match a certain criteria, can be retrieved and stored in a table. These records can then produce a report or be displayed to the user. Depending upon the size of the file's record, it could be advantageous to store only a pointer to the file's record in the table. This pointer can be returned by the POINTER function. When a table record is selected, the appropriate file record can then be retrieved with the printer and a GET statement.

Tables can be sorted with any field defined in the table structure. This offers a flexible capability—sorting records in a file without having to define a key or use an external program.

Individual records in a memory table might be used to maintain running totals for batches of transactions, multiple data files, or other tables. These totals are available for reports or can be applied to other files.

You are probably starting to realize how important memory tables are, and how they can help you in your applications. To enable you to better understand tables, I will briefly describe each of the table statements.

Declaring memory tables

A TABLE structure declares a memory table. The syntax of the structure is:

```
label       TABLE,PRE(xxx)
              (data declaration statements)
```

The label of the TABLE statement names the structure, and must be used as a parameter in processing statements just like the label of a FILE statement. A prefix is optional in the TABLE statement. It can be useful if you intend to have names declared for the variables within the structure that are also used in another structure (like a file). Like all Clarion structures, the end of the table structure is designated with a period.

Statements (variable declarations) made within the structure serve to define the table's record area. The record area can be any size, from 1 to 65,520 bytes of data. Any combination of BYTE, SHORT, LONG, REAL, DECIMAL, STRING, and GROUP data types can be used to declare any variables you require within the table structure. Here is a table declaration for a simple phone list:

```
PHONELIST   TABLE,PRE(TBL)
NAME          STRING(30)
AREACODE      DECIMAL(3,0)
NUMBER        STRING(@P### - ####P)
```

Tables can be declared globally, for use throughout a program, or locally, limiting the scope to a particular procedure or function. When the label of a table is used during assignment, it is treated like a group. In addition to the example presented above, suppose this file structure has been declared the following way:

```
PHONEBK     FILE,PRE(PHN)
RECORD        RECORD
NAME            STRING(30)
AREACODE        DECIMAL(3,0)
NUMBER          STRING(@P### - ####P)
```

The statement PHONELIST = PHN:RECORD will transfer a copy of all the information found in the file record to the table record. Naturally, if the group definitions do not have a one-to-one correspondence, it is permissible to move individual items between structures.

Note that information is not actually stored in the table until a table processing statement, like ADD or PUT, occurs.

Tables used as parameters

You can define a table in one procedure that is not global, and still be able to pass the table to another procedure. You do this by defining the receiving procedure so that the label of the table is declared as an EXTERNAL,TABLE. Without the additional TABLE attribute attached to the EXTERNAL statement, the compiler will assume that only the information contained in the table record (which is treated like a group) is required.

Individual elements of the table's structure definition will not be known, however, unless they too are received as EXTERNAL declarations. The ability to use tables as externals can increase the usefulness of local table definitions by allowing another procedure access to the table. A portion of a program is presented in Fig. 10-1, demonstrating how to pass and receive a table and a table record variable.

```
            PROGRAM
            MAP
              PROC(SORT_TABLE)
                  .

NAMES           TABLE,PRE(TBL)
DATE              STRING(@P##P)
AGE               STRING(@P##P)
NAME              STRING(20)
                    .
                :
                :
            CODE
                :
                :
              EXECUTE (SORTMETHOD)
                SORT_TABLE(NAMES,TBL:NAME)
                SORT_TABLE(NAMES,TBL:DATE)
                SORT_TABLE(NAMES,TBL:AGE)
                  .
                :
                :
!--------------------------------
SORT_TABLE PROCEDURE(TABLE, TBLITM)
TABLE           EXTERNAL,TABLE
TBLITM          EXTERNAL
                :
                :
            CODE
            SORT(TABLE,TBLITM)
                :
                :
```

10-1. Passing a table and a variable as an EXTERNAL

If the label of a table is received, but the TABLE attribute is omitted from the EXTERNAL declaration, only the table's record buffer will be received. The label of a table structure must follow the rules of any valid Clarion label.

Processing memory tables

Thus far, I have made several analogies between tables and files. Tables, unlike files, do not have to be opened or closed. The table structure declaration is all that is necessary to initialize a memory table. Likewise, memory tables do not require key definitions. Any variable declared in the table structure can be used as a key, with the exception of variables containing the DIM attribute. The table can be sorted by including the label of the variable in the SORT statement. Additionally, if the table is already sorted, records can be added or retrieved in keyed order by simply including the label of the variable in the proper processing statement.

As records are added to or retrieved from a memory table, an internal pointer is maintained that identifies the current record. The logical record pointer is simply the sequential number of the record, as it appears in the list. The first record is position 1, the second 2 and so on. If a sort has not been performed, the record number will correspond to the order that the records were added to the memory table.

Don't confuse this record pointer with the forward and backward chain pointers mentioned earlier. Chain pointers are automatically maintained outside of your Clarion code.

There are several powerful statements with which you can process memory tables:

The POINTER statement

The POINTER function has the following form:

```
POINTER(table)
```

and returns a long value, equal to the logical record pointer for the last accessed record. If the table has not been accessed, zero will be returned.

Remember, the logical record pointer identifies the last accessed record (via ADD or GET). If you fill the table record with new information, that record will not have a new pointer value until it is added to the table.

The RECORDS statement

The RECORDS statement has the form:

    RECORDS(table)

and returns the number of entries found in the table as a LONG variable type. Because logical record numbers are the sequential number for each table entry, the last record in a table has a logical record pointer, equal to RECORDS(table).

The FREE statement

The FREE statement has the form:

    FREE(table)

and returns all the memory associated with a table's records back into the free memory pool. Whenever a table is no longer in use, or before filling the table, it is a good idea to use the FREE statement. Remember, it does not hurt to free an empty table. It could hurt, however, to not free a table that is no longer in use because that memory will not be available for the rest of your program.

Note that FREE does not change the table record area. If you need to initialize the record area of the table, use the CLEAR statement.

The ADD statement

The ADD statement, when used with tables, has three forms:

Form 1	ADD(table)
Form 2	ADD(table, pointer)
Form 3	ADD(table, key)

and includes the information currently held in the table record area as an element into the table.

As table records are added, the record area is first clipped of any trailing spaces and then copied into a freshly allocated memory area of the appropriate size. Therefore, you should place those string data items that are likely to be blank at the end of a table structure. This data is automatically inserted into the doubly-linked list that maintains the table.

Form 1 of the ADD statement simply adds the contents of the record area to the very end table. A table built using this method will be in the order that the records were added.

The pointer parameter in form 2 specifies the sequential location that you want the record to occupy in the table. For instance, if you want a record to be the first record in the table, you would use a statement like this:

```
ADD(table,1)
```

This would make the current record buffer the first table record, and the records that are already in the table would follow this one. If every record was added to a table using the statement ADD(table,1), the resulting table order would be the opposite of the order by which the records were added.

Variables, expressions, or constants can indicate the integer value for the parameter in form 2 of the ADD statement. If a variable is used, it must not be one of the variables declared in the table structure, or form 3 of the ADD statement will be assumed. Additionally, the value must indicate a position between 1 and the RECORDS(table) statement, or the entry will simply be added to the end of the table.

If a table has been sorted (or is being built sorted), the key used for the sort can be a parameter to the ADD statement, as shown in form 3. The key must be a label of one of the variables declared in the table structure. Groups can be used as keys, but arrays and array elements cannot. All other variable types can also be used as keys.

When a key ADD is requested, the table is searched to determine where the value of the current key should be placed. New records are added after all current records that have the same or lesser key values, but in front of those records that have a greater value in the key.

Adding by key is useful when the sort order needs to be maintained. If all the records of a table are added using this option, it will not be necessary to sort the table using the SORT statement (for this key). This is called building a table that is sorted "as you go."

The GET statement

The GET statement has two forms:

```
Form 1    GET(table, pointer)
Form 2    GET(table,key)
```

and retrieves a particular record from a memory table. The specific record retrieved depends upon whether the second parameter is a logical record pointer or a keyed value held in a table record element.

You can retrieve table records by pointer, form 1, simply by identifying the logical record number of the entry. The pointer parameter is an integer and can be represented with a constant, an expression, or a variable (as long as it is not one of the variables declared in the table structure).

A statement like GET(table, 10) would retrieve the tenth entry in a memory table. Make note, however, that if the value of the pointer is less than 1 or greater than the number of entries in the table, a new record will not be read and the error function will return "Entry not found" as the error condition.

Form 1 is the method most commonly used to process a table sequentially, forwards or backwards. Although tables are similar to files, the NEXT and PREVIOUS statements can be imitated with the GET(table,pointer) statement. Figure 10-2 demonstrates how to simulate sequential processing, forward (NEXT) and backwards (PREVIOUS), using LOOP statements.

```
NAMES          TABLE,PRE(TBL)
NAME             STRING(20)

   CODE
   :
   :
LOOP INDEX# = 1 TO RECORDS(NAMES) ! PROCESS FORWARD (NEXT)
   GET(NAMES,INDEX#)              ! GET NEXT RECORD
   :
   :
 .
   :
   :
LOOP INDEX# = RECORDS(NAMES) TO 1 ! PROCESS BACKWARDS (PREVIOUS)
   GET(NAMES,INDEX#)              ! GET PREVIOUS RECORD
   :
   :
```

10-2.   Imitating NEXT and PREVIOUS for table processing, using LOOP statements

GET(table,key), form 2, requires a label from one of the variable declarations in the table structure for a parameter. The same rule applies for a key parameter in GET as for the ADD statement. The label of the variable identifies which portion of the record you want to match, and the value currently contained by that variable is the match criteria.

Only exact matches will be found by the GET statement. The search for a particular keyed entry will stop when the first entry that matches the key is found, or when an entry is found that has a larger key value. Only if an exact match is found will the table entry be copied into the record area. Otherwise, the error function will return an "Entry not found" message.

You don't need to worry about matching records when trailing spaces have been removed from some of the records in the table. This is handled automatically for you.

An important point to consider about unsuccessful get operations. Remember, an internal pointer (which can be retrieved via the POINTER statement) is maintained at all times by the table. When a get by key occurs and the entry is not found, the pointer is set to the location where the key value contained in the record could be inserted into the table. This is a very useful feature if you want to insert the record when it is not already in the table. Figure 10-3 demonstrates the code to add only those records that are not currently in the table.

```
      :
      :
NAMES          TABLE,PRE(TBL)
NAME              STRING(20)
                      .
      CODE
      :
      :
   LOOP                          ! LOOP
     ACCEPT                      ! RETRIEVE USER INPUT
       :
     CASE FIELD()               ! EDIT FIELDS
     OF ?TBL:NAME               ! IF THE TABLE FIELD
       GET(NAMES,TBL:NAME)      ! TRY TO GET THIS RECORD
       IF ERROR() = ''          ! IF FOUND
          :
          :
         CYCLE                  !    JUST CONTINUE
       ELSE                     ! OTHERWISE
          :
          :
         ADD(NAMES,POINTER(NAMES))  !   ADD IN PROPER PLACE
       . .
      :
      :
```

10-3.   Using get by key and add by pointer to maintain a sort order

There is one significant difference between get by key and add by key. Remember, add by key will insert the record after any records that have duplicate key values. Get by key, on the other hand, will return the first record that matches the key value. Therefore, if a table contains duplicate key values, it will be up to you to perform the code to verify that you have indeed retrieved the correct record. Figure 10-4 demonstrates how the get by pointer statement can be used after a get by key to retrieve all the records that have duplicate key values.

Figure 10-4 demonstrates the table equivalent of a file's set by key and next by record. This can be used to position the internal table pointer

```
      :
      :
NAMES          TABLE,PRE(TBL)
NAME             STRING(20)
                       .
     CODE
      :
      :
     ITEM$ = 'Stephen'              ! ITEMS TO SEARCH
     TBL:NAME = ITEM$               ! NAME = SEARCH VALUE
     GET(NAMES,TBL:NAME)            ! RETRIEVE A RECORD BY KEY
     LOOP UNTIL ERROR()             ! LOOP WHILE NO ERRORS
      :
      :
       GET(NAMES,POINTER(NAMES)+1)    ! GET NEXT RECORD BY POINTER
       IF TBL:NAME <> ITEM$ THEN BREAK.! NO LONGER MATCHES
```

10-4. Using get by key to set the table pointer for sequential processing

to a particular location which then allows you to begin processing the records sequentially.

Here is another very important point to remember about get by key: Requesting records from a table by key presumes that the table has been sorted or built in a sort order. If this is not the case, the results will be unpredictable.

The DELETE statement

The DELETE statement has the following form:

    DELETE(table)

and removes the table record currently indicated by the internal record pointer. The record pointer is continuously updated by each ADD and GET statement that occurs in the table. If a get or add had not been performed, or the table is empty, the error function will return the "Entry not available" error message.

When using DELETE, it is important to ensure that the proper record will be deleted. For instance, if you do a get by key and fail to check the error function to see if the get was successful, the DELETE statement might not remove a record. On the other hand, if you do a delete immediately following an add, you will remove the record that you just added.

The PUT statement

The PUT statement has the form:

    PUT(table)

and updates (puts back) a table record already in the table. Put will copy the data in the table record area into the location indicated by the current table pointer.

Remember, the current table pointer is set by the statements GET and ADD. Like DELETE, the PUT statement does not change the pointer setting. If no record is currently selected, a PUT will fail and the error function will return "Entry not available."

A PUT statement handles the record much like an ADD. When possible, trailing spaces are clipped from the record area. Thus, a record will require less memory than it did in its former condition.

Sort sequences are not maintained by the PUT statement. If a table is built in a sorted order, it might be more advantageous to delete the old record and add a new one with the key parameter. This will ensure that the sort is maintained.

The SORT statement

The SORT procedure has the form:

```
SORT(table,key)
```

and orders a table into an ascending sequence, based upon the key's value. The key must be the label of one of the statements declared in the table structure, and can be either string or numeric data. The variable can be any type except an array or an array element. When the label of the table is declared an EXTERNAL,TABLE then the key label must also have been declared as an EXTERNAL.

Again, note that when a sort occurs, the items in the table do not move. Only the "links" in the sequence chains are changed, making the table sorting operation very quick.

The SORT statement acts much like the ADD statement when duplicate key values are encountered in the records. If there are duplicates, the order in which duplicates occur in the table is not changed. An added benefit is that you can perform additional sorts using a different key because the former sort order is retained. For example, assume a table has the following definition:

```
NAMES      TABLE
NAME         STRING(10)
AGE          SHORT
```

Also assume that these items are currently held in the table:

Bob	10
Andy	12
Bill	9
Carol	12
Tom	8
Tim	8

If you sort the table by the NAME field, the resulting table will have the following order:

Andy	12
Bill	9
Bob	10
Carol	12
Tim	8
Tom	8

If you sort the table again by the AGE field, the resulting table will now appear:

Tim	8
Tom	8
Bill	9
Bob	10
Andy	12
Carol	12

Examine what has happened. By sorting the table alphabetically, and then sorting the ages, you have a table sorted by age, with each age category sorted by name. Notice, however, that the final results depends upon the order that the key sorts were performed. If you sorted age first and then name, the table would be different. The resulting table be like this:

Andy	12
Bill	9
Bob	10
Carol	12
Tim	8
Tom	8

These sort orders point to the importance of determining which sort is of primary importance, and which is subordinate. Your primary sort should always be performed last. This is true even if there are more than two sorting criteria. Start with the least significant sort and work your way back to the primary sort.

As mentioned before, the sort command only sorts the records into an ascending sequence by the key specified. If you need a descending sequence, you can improvise with the following methods.

The first method for processing a table in descending order is to simply sort the table and then process the records in reverse order. This method might not be adequate, however, if the records need to be sorted ascending by one field and descending by another.

If the field that you need to sort in a descending order is a number, then one technique is to store the "negative" value of the number in the table. Negating the values will cause the largest values to become the smallest and the smallest values the largest. Suppose several records each have one of the values, -99, -9, -2, 1, 10, and 100 stored in the same field. If you negate them, the SORT command would order the records in the order -100, -10, -1, 9, and 99; which is the descending order of the records. All you have to do to negate a value is assign it into the table using the minus sign (TBL:VAR = $-$FIL:VAR) or multiply the variable by -1.

Negating the value of fields has a couple of disadvantages, however. First, it will not work on DECIMAL, STRING, or GROUP data types because of their internal storage format. Second, if you intend to use the variable, you must remember to convert it back to its original value.

Given these problems, it might be more appropriate to add an additional field to the table to hold the negated value for the sort. Naturally, the data type you choose will depend upon what kind of field you are trying to sort. SHORT, LONG, and REAL variables can hold their negated values. It might be best, however, to use a REAL variable for the negated data type when the sort field is DECIMAL.

There are a few points about choosing key values that you might find useful. First, it has been stated that the label of an array or an element of an array cannot be used as a key for sorting. However, you can "bypass" this with a group label. By including the array definition inside a group structure, you can indirectly use the values found in the array as a key. Whether this method can be used properly depends upon what kind of array you have. Likewise, if you want to use only a particular element of an array as a key, then use the OVER attribute to declare an alternate label for that array element's area.

Groups are treated similar to strings. Despite the variable types that are declared within the group structure (STRING, LONG, REAL, etc.), the entire group is treated as one variable. This treatment means that declarations of SHORT, LONG, and REAL variables are not sorted properly as part of a group because of the way these variables are stored in memory.

Therefore, if you want a GROUP to serve as a sort key, use only BYTE, STRING and DECIMAL data types within the group structure.

There are 3 possible error messages that can be posted by table function "Insufficient memory" indicates that not enough free memory remains to store the record. This can occur after an ADD or a PUT statement. "Entry not found" indicates that the record requested by a GET statement cannot be located. If the GET was by pointer then the value is greater than the number of elements in the table or less than 1. With a GET by key, this message indicates that no record has a matching key value. "Entry not available" indicates that a PUT or DELETE was attempted without a valid record pointer. Only after a successful GET or ADD, is a valid pointer BE available.

Conclusion

Memory tables can be a powerful tool for performing many programming tasks that involve lists of information that must be processed and manipulated.

PART THREE
Application strategies

11
CHAPTER

Organizing the application

One of the first principles presented in most introductory programming classes is "understand the problem that your program will solve before you start the programming." This is always good advice, but is often ignored. The more you understand about how a program needs to work, the less likely you'll be to rewrite sections of code because you forgot a crucial part of the design.

In practice, however, knowing everything about the application in advance might not be possible. One of the biggest advantages of Clarion is that it is forgiving. You can make radical changes to file definitions with the Filer, give screens a totally different appearance with the screen formatter, and quickly rearrange information in a new way with the report formatter.

One of the most important elements of your application you should identify in advance is the kind of user that will operate your programs. There is world of difference in design considerations for a program that only you will use as opposed to one that will be used by a computer novice. A program for a new user requires particular attention to how keystrokes are used, how screen and report information is presented, and how the program fits into the overall environment of the user.

A common question from students who are learning a new language and are starting their first true application is "Where do I begin?" There have been many books written on structured programming and systems analysis, all of which can teach you something about how to solve data processing problems with different program design techniques. The emphasis here, however, is how to design and create practical applications with Clarion.

Planning your files

With Clarion, the first place to start is usually with the file layouts. Although there are some methodologies that are useful and valid and use a different approach, beginning with the file design is practical with Clarion. In a way, Designer requires you to do this because you can't reference data from a file in a report or screen without having defined it first. When laying out your files, it is important to keep several questions in mind:

- Is there enough data in the files to produce the intended output, either in reports or onscreen?
- Is the data organized correctly for retrieval?
- Is the data stored efficiently?
- Will the layout of the file cause performance problems?
- Is the data on the disk secure from unexpected events?

It is rare when the data requirements for a given application provide no scheme or model from which to work. This scheme can consist of manual forms, memos, conversations, and reports, however informal, that are being used on a regular basis to accomplish the goal. This information can be invaluable in creating your file layouts.

The process of deciding how your data should be organized into files and how the files will be related in your program is sometimes called *normalizing* a database. There are many books that cover this topic in depth that are beyond the scope of this book, but I can provide you with a few useful principles.

The first step is to identify all of the data elements that the application requires. This involves making a list of all the data that needs to be displayed, either on reports or screens, in order to accomplish the goal of the application. You should then decide which data can be derived from other data. Derivative data does not need to be stored, but can be calculated. For instance, storing the dollar total amount for all items purchased in an order is unnecessary, because the total can always be derived by adding up the price for each item in the order.

After separating stored from derived data, give each data element a valid Clarion label. Then decide the maximum size required to represent each data item. This will determine the length of string variables and the data type for numeric values.

The next step is to store related sets of data in separate files. For instance, you might write an application that processes orders for products sold. You could have one large record that has all the information about the order, like the number and kind of items sold, and the customer information. However, using this approach might cause some problems. If the customer changes addresses, you might have to revise each order for that customer to show the address change. A better approach would be to have a file for orders and a file for customers, using a keyed customer number field to relate the files. Similarly, you might want a separate file for items purchased with an order number related to the record in the order file.

The next step is to identify the relationships for each file. These relationships allow the retrieval of related data by a screen or report, and are established primarily with keys or indices in Clarion.

In this order processing example, there is a relationship between the customer file and the order file. The relationship, however, implies some responsibility on your part. If an order record in the order file has a customer number that doesn't exist in the customer file, the integrity of the relationship between those files has been compromised. This could be caused by a customer record that has been incorrectly deleted, or by adding a new order with a non-existent customer to the order file. Although Clarion is responsible for making sure that the key and index files accurately reflect what data is in the files, you must make sure that your design will prevent this kind of problem.

Another step that will determine the definition of keys and indices for your files is listing the order in which the data needs to appear. If you want a listing of customers in alphabetical order for a report, you can key or index the file by name, even if there is no relationship to another file using this key.

The layout of files is often an iterative process. You might, therefore, decide to change the layout based on new information gained during development. Clarion allows you to add new keys and redefine them very easily.

Deciding on the user interface

Once you have a plan of how you want to structure your files, you can consider the user interface. This requires that you have a good understanding of the user. Depending on the user's level of sophistication, the level of help that you give your user (either with the F1 key or provided directly onscreen) will also vary.

For instance, if your intended user is a "casual" user—one who does not continuously use your program—then requiring him to remember many complicated function key assignments will require too much effort. This can be remedied by creating a program that "walks the user" through each step with a series of simple menus and clear, direct message prompts on screen.

On the other hand, if your application will be used by experienced data entry operators who process the same screen hundreds of times a day, the number of keystrokes required to process the data will be an important factor. A fact to consider in this situation is that the operator might not even glance at your screen after only a few hours of working with it.

Designer generated code (using unmodified models) produces programs that have a particular user interface. The programs produced by the Designer have simplicity as their main goal—in fact, one of Designer's main virtues is that all of its programs can be explained by simply describing the arrow, Esc, Enter, Ins, and Del keys!

There might be times, however, when a radically different interface is required. You might need to match the application to a manual method currently in use, and you need your screen designs to reflect that. You might need to make your program behave according to the same rules of an older program that all users are already familiar with. This often requires radical changes to keystroke assignments and the style of menus presented.

Creating a new user interface is not as simple as it might appear; it will certainly require a large amount of time for testing. The good news is that Clarion allows you the necessary control to create a user interface that is most appropriate for your application.

Screen design

At first, the layout of your screens might not seem very important. Because of all of the other factors you must consider during the design of your application, it is easy to regard screen appearance as just a matter of "cosmetics."

However, the layout of screens is of great importance. How a user first reacts to your software sets expectations that are very difficult to later change. You must remember that although you might have perfected some very complex algorithms to make the application work, your user takes this for granted, and only sees your screens, reports, and keystroke assignments. Also, many users regard the appearance of a program as an indication of the care and thought that has been put into the rest of the application. In fact, there have been many studies done to show how screen design effects users. One such study timed users' ability to complete a particularly complex screen. Then, after redesigning the screen in a more structured and consistent form, repeated the test. The average time required to process the screen was reduced from 8.3 seconds to 5.0 seconds. Although this might not seen significant, when you take into account that this screen could be processed by hundreds of users, hundreds of times per day, and that the life expectancy of a program can be several years, an estimated 79 years of user effort was saved simply by following sound screen design principles!

Again, there are several helpful books that have been written to address good screen design, but here I'll try to present the most important principles. Unfortunately, these are simply suggestions. Screen design is more of an art form than an engineering problem, and as such any rules you can state might have several perfectly good reasons to be broken for a particular application.

The first rule in screen design is "be consistent." For instance, if you decide to put the current date on all your screens, always put it on the same place. This prevents the user from either hunting for it, or glancing at it just to find out that it is not what they want.

This rule is more subtle than you might think. Consider the simple field layout in Fig. 11-1. Even though this screen might look simple, these fields create several implicit rules in the user's mind:

- All prompts capitalized the first letter of each word.
- Entry starts after a colon.
- There is no space between the prompt and the colon.
- Colons should be vertically aligned.
- Prompts are left justified with the colons:

```
First Name:              Last Name:
    Address:
       City:              State:      Zip:
      Phone:
```

11-1. Example field layout

If the user proceeds to a different screen and different design rules are used, he can become very irritated without even realizing why. In this example, the implicit design rules used are not nearly as important as how consistently they are followed from screen to screen. Another way of stating this rule is "Don't surprise the user." Consistency creates a feeling of comfortable familiarity in your programs.

The next rule in screen design is simplicity. The more information on your screens, the more effort is required to use them. In fact, one measure of simplicity is the actual number of characters on the screen. If you have a screen that has 50 fields so crammed together as to negate any kind of order it can become a nightmare for the user. If the same information is presented on two or three screens with a more simple organization, the user will never know how bad it could have been.

Information on the screen can have different levels of intensity. For example, in order to be consistent, you could have track borders around each screen, with the message "F1 – Help" in the upper left-hand corner, and today's date in the upper right-hand corner. While it is true that this is more information on the screen, the user does not normally need to notice the information, because its meaning was presented when the screen was first seen, and it doesn't require further thought. (Perhaps this explains why many users do not think to use the F1 key for help, even though there are explicit instructions to do so.)

Also, the main information on the screen should flow from left to right, top to bottom. Presumably this is because you read text this way, at least, in occidental cultures. Forcing a user to go against this convention just makes it harder for him to understand your screens. This is also why Designer-generated programs process entry fields in this order.

You should place fields so that related fields are kept together and distinct from other kinds of fields. This can be done in a variety of ways. You can keep field groups separate with blank spaces or tracking characters. Unfortunately, this approach takes up more space on the screen. Painting different background colors for separate groups is a way of distinguishing them without taking up any space on the screen.

The appearance, as well as the content of your screen, should be simple and consistent. It is generally a good idea to use simple, basic color combinations, which can greatly enhance the appearance of your programs with little effort. Clarion allows you to create screens that use color that will translate to a monochrome screen, so you can design for both. Don't go too far, however.

If you design the application so that the user must notice a color change in order to use a function that change might not be apparent on a monochrome screen. Also, it should be pointed out that there are a number of people who are color blind, and they may not be able to use your program.

Provide a simple way for the user to find out what the application is capable of and how to operate it. Online help is very important for this. Take the time to create good online help and your users will feel more comfortable with your programs before they even begin. Even without online help, if an operation is required, indicate it directly on the screen.

Give your screens a consistent, orderly, and uncluttered appearance. The simpler the screen, the easier time your user will have with it.

Use plain English for all instructions and messages. Don't use threatening or patronizing language, and be positive and helpful. Use simple words that state facts. There is also a tendency to use acronyms for everything, making it easier to fit information on a screen or report—resist it.

Make sure the terms you use are not ambiguous. Computer terms that are often taken for granted by programmers cause problems for other people. The word *default*, for instance, has a very different meaning for someone in finance or banking than for people who work with computers.

Make sure your screens are clear about what information is shown and what the user can do with it. Use carefully chosen prompts and messages to explain everything.

One last rule—always give your user a chance to change his mind. It must be clear to the user when an operation will cause a permanent change. You can use messages like the popular but vague "Are you sure?" to the more intimidating but explicit "Delete this month's work? Yes or No." Do not delete or change things without giving the user a chance to reconsider.

Report design

Many of the principles for presenting data onscreen also apply to reports. For example, consistency about how the data is formatted and clear descriptions about what the data means is just as important in your reports as on your screens. Also, like screens, data should be grouped into logical sections and reports should have an uncluttered appearance.

There are differences between screens and reports, however. Reports are seen by people other than the operator of the application, so the need for clarity is even greater. Also, reports can exist for long periods of time, while data onscreen is temporary. Including the date (and even time) of when a report is printed is almost always a good idea.

Reports also imply that a printer is necessary. Many people who work with computers rapidly gain a disdain for printers. It seems that they run out of paper, ribbon, or alignment at the worst possible time. Your user is no different. It is almost always a good idea to give the operator a chance to either change his mind about the report or halt the report to adjust the printer. This can be done very easily. For example, if the operator selects a report from a menu, instead of just calling a routine that prints all detail lines until done, you might open a pop-up window that looks like Fig. 11-2.

You can make the "Printing Report" string blink, which gives the user the idea that the computer is working. After you print each detail line of the report, check the keyboard function. If is false, continue with the report. If it is true, you can open another window like the one in Fig. 11-3, and call the ask procedure. This will prompt a keystroke from the user, and you can check to see if they want to quit the report (the Esc key) or continue. This simple function gives the user the ability to stop the report any time and adjust the printer.

```
 _____
|                                |
|      Printing Report           |
|                                |
|                                |
|   Press Any Key To Stop        |
|_____|
```
11-2. Printer busy window

```
 _____
|                                |
|      Printer Stopped           |
|                                |
|    Press Esc To Quit,          |
| Or Any Other Key To Continue   |
|_____|
```
11-3. Printer stopped window

One other good thing to do for your users is, if they are using forms or mailing labels that are difficult to line up before starting the report, offer a "test pattern" that prints a character on every position of the form or label. This lets them check form alignment. If they're using labels, it is usually a good idea to print more than one test label to ensure alignment.

Conclusion

This chapter has presented several rules about application design. If all of these rules seem a bit daunting, don't worry. Design is a process of making trade-offs. If you break any of these rules, just be sure that you have a good reason for doing so. The most important rule to remember is to always keep the needs of your user in mind — follow this and you won't go too far from the mark.

12
CHAPTER

Creating
the application

In this chapter, you will learn strategies for creating your own application, using both the Designer and the Editor to your advantage.

Many experienced programmers new to Clarion are often uncertain about the prospect of using a code generator to create applications. It is true that any code generator will probably produce code that is different from the code a programmer would write. It is also true that a programmer using a general-purpose language has much more freedom of choice about how the application will behave.

However, Designer works by taking four archetypal program components—the menu, table, form, and report procedures—and letting you combine them in hundreds of ways. It also lets you add your own custom source procedures by allowing Other procedures to be called in many places throughout the Designer.

Designer has another advantage—it uses a model file as a template for the code that will be generated, and this model file can also be changed by the programmer. This adds yet another layer of both versatility and capability to your design strategies.

Five basic approaches

A question that often arises when people learn Clarion is how to use Designer as part of the program development process. The *Clarion Professional Developer* provides you with five basic ways in which to do this:

- Use the Designer to create your entire application. If the features of Designer let you fulfill all the requirements of your application, there is no faster way to create and maintain an application.

- If you have unique requirements that Designer does not support, let Designer get you started. Do as much of the application as you can with Designer, let it generate the code, and take it from there. After you change the generated source code with the Editor, you will not be able to go back to Designer. It is an old programming proverb that "nobody writes a program from scratch; they always start with some working program and modify it." The only problem with this proverb was coming up with the working program. Now you can let Designer make it for you.

- Write the entire application with the Editor. While this gives you the maximum amount of freedom over the design of the application, it also requires more knowledge and effort on your part. Note that while writing an application with the Editor, you still have the screen, report, and help generators at your disposal.

- Let Designer and Editor code coexist in your application. This is why the Other procedure is included in Designer — it lets you use the Designer, and still include your own programming ideas. The Other procedures you include can be either written entirely with the Editor, or they first generated with the Designer, redefined as an Other, and then revised with the Editor.

- Make Designer generate the code you want by changing the way it generates code. That is, create your own model files. Perhaps you need to create a series of applications that require a different user interface than Designer generates, or you need special purpose routines not included with Designer. You might start by using the Editor to create a new model file, and then letting Designer produce all the applications you need.

These five basic approaches are listed in order of the amount of programming expertise you need. It takes more knowledge about both the Designer and the Clarion language to use the fifth approach than the first. Of course, the more you know about any tool, the more effective you can be when using it. Fortunately, Designer lets you gradually learn about all the different programming features of Clarion.

Breaking away

Thus far, you've seen a simple example of an application with Designer, and some examples of programs written with the Editor.

How do you combine code that you write with the Editor with the Designer's code? By using Other procedures, which are supported by Designer. The Other procedure is defined in the .APP file. When the Designer generates the code for the program, it will include the Other procedure in its map structure. It will not generate the code for the Other procedure, but expects to find it in the module file you name while creating the Other procedure.

You can call Other procedures by name from a menu, or as specified in the edit procedure, setup procedure, or next procedure lines anywhere in Designer. For instance, let's say that you need to write a procedure for the Bookstore application that simply totals the number of books on hand and prints a report. You might place a new menu item, displayed as "Print Total Books" on the main menu screen and name TOT_BOOKS as the procedure name. Now, the application summary window will show a new "ToDo" procedure. Place the cursor on the ToDo procedure, and press Enter.

After selecting Other as the procedure type, you will see the Other window, as shown in Fig. 12-1. The first line asks you for the name of the procedure. This should be the label of the PROCEDURE statement in your Editor written code, and also the name you used in the menu item definition above.

12-1. Other window

```
                              Other

          Procedure Name :TOT_BOOKS
          Description    :Report of Book Totals
          Modules Name   :TOTBOOKS
            Binary       :No        Yes  No
          Return Value   :No        Yes  No
            Data Type    :          Long  Real  String
          Procedure Calls:
```

The next line is a description of the procedure, which is used only for display in the application summary window.

The next line is the name of the module, or source file. You should call this TOTBOOKS and assume it will be in the same directory as the other application source modules.

The next line asks you if this will be a binary module. If you want to use a LEM procedure, you would say yes. Since you are writing this procedure in Clarion, select no.

If the Other procedure will be a function instead of a procedure, you can specify this by selecting the data type the function will return. Since you are creating a procedure, select no to the Return Value line.

The last few lines allow you to call procedures in the application from this Other procedure so that their reference will be indicated in the application summary window. Because the example will not call any other application procedures, leave this blank.

That's it for the Designer. Now generate the code for your application. When the program runs, it will expect to find a compiled module called TOTBOOKS.PRO to include with the application.

Now you need to create the Other procedure with the Editor. To do this, simply create a file called TOTBOOKS.CLA and type in the code shown in Fig. 12-2, then compile it. When the application runs, the user can select "Print Total Books" from the Main Menu, and your code will execute.

```
                    MEMBER('BOOKS')

  TOTAL             LONG

  TOT_BOOKS         PROCEDURE
                    CODE
                    TOTAL = 0
                    SET(BOOKS)
                    LOOP UNTIL EOF(BOOKS)
                       NEXT(BOOKS)
                      TOTAL += BOO:QUANTITY

                         .

                    PRINT(@LF5)
                    PRINT('          Total Number Of Books = ' & TOTAL)
                    PRINT(@FF)
                    RETURN
```

12-2. Sample Other procedure

Note that you only need to define local variables; Designer places all file definitions in global memory. You could also create a report structure and make a more sophisticated report using the report formatter in the Editor.

You can let Designer generate the original source code for an Other procedure and then modify it. Suppose you want to customize a form procedure. You would do this by creating the procedure with the Designer, and generating the source. Using the Editor, you would then edit the generated source code and put (using Ctrl-P) the code for the form procedure into the new source file. You would then edit the new source file that now contains only the source for the form procedure, and add the MEMBER statement at the top of the file.

Next, you would go back into Designer and, in the application summary window, place the cursor bar on the form procedure you just copied, and press the Del key. This will delete the procedure. Since the form procedure was called by a table procedure, it will still be shown, but its type is now a ToDo. Now press Enter on the procedure and specify an Other type, and fill out the Other window by naming the source file you created.

After generating the source and compiling the Designer code and new module, the program will run the same as before the change. However, now you can edit the new module (which Designer originally wrote) without Designer generating new code each time you change the .APP file.

Modifying the model

The last approach involves changing the model file. Although a detailed tutorial on customizing the model file is beyond the scope of this book, I will provide a starting point for you. First, you will need to understand what happens when Designer creates the source code. Also, if you are going to experiment with changing the model file, a few recommendations are in order.

First, print a hard copy of a model file, like STANDARD.MDL, and the file MODEL.DOC. MODEL.DOC has detailed explanations about each of the procedures used in the model file. Also, create a simple program in Designer that generates one of each of the procedure types. In this way, you can compare the model with the code that is actually generated.

Also, if you are making any changes to the model file, first make a copy of it with a different name and edit the copy. Remember, you can specify any name for the model file in Designer's base page.

Whenever Designer exits, it asks you if you want to generate source for the application. If you say yes, it opens the model file specified on Designer's base page, and begins reading it.

The first thing Designer needs to create is the program procedure. The data declaration area of this procedure is global, so all of the file definitions and memory variables must be placed here. It also defines some global equate definitions and the ACTION variable. (See Chapter 4.) In the code section, it will clear the screen, open your files, and call the base procedure you specified on Designer's base page.

When Designer creates the program procedure, it looks for the procedure keyword "*GLOBAL", starting in column 1. It then places the PROGRAM statement with a label that is the same as the name of your application. As Designer then reads each line from the model file, it writes that line to the new source file.

At this point, you can see that if you add lines of code to the model file, Designer will just write them to the new source file that is generated. This simple idea suggests many possibilities. For instance, consider the messages that are displayed in a form procedure, like "Record will be added." If you want to change these messages, simply edit the model file, using the Editor to search for the strings (using Ctrl-S and Ctrl-N), and then change them.

Designer continues to read and write lines until it comes to a line with another type of keyword, one that starts in column 1 with an @ character followed by a name. These are *procedure-call keywords*. When Designer finds a procedure-call keyword, it will substitute generated code for this line.

The code it substitutes for a procedure-call keyword can be generated from information in the .APP file, or it can be a procedure that is defined in the model file. For instance, the first procedure-call keyword in the model is @MODULES, which is placed inside a MAP statement. This procedure-call keyword causes Designer to list all of the modules and procedures (including Others) defined in the .APP file. Similarly, the @FILES keyword causes Designer to generate all of the file structure statements that are needed to declare the file definitions in the .APP file, and so on.

Some of the @NAME procedure calls are for procedures that are defined further on in the model file. The important thing to understand is that some of the generated code is written by the Designer from your .APP file, but most of it is simply copied out of the model file. The code which is generated by the Designer from your .APP file cannot be modified, but the source from the model file can be changed. Also, new lines of source code can be inserted anywhere in the model file.

For each procedure type (menu, table, form, and report) you define, Designer will substitute new procedure code for each. Some of the more common reasons for changing the model are:

- Changing keystroke assignments. Perhaps your users are familiar with other software packages, and you need to use other key assignments, for instance, Ctrl–Esc and Ctrl–Enter. You can change these very easily by changing the EQUATE statements on lines 6 and 7 of the model.

- Changing error handling. Perhaps you want to allow the user to stop printing reports after the report has started. You could define a small window (possibly in global memory so that it is accessible by all reports) that blinks "Printing – Press any key to stop." In the report procedure, you can then open the window before the printing starts, and after each record is read, check the keyboard function to see if the user has pressed a keystroke.

- Reducing code. Each Designer procedure type supports many different features and types of fields, and therefore generates the code to handle them. You can reduce the amount of code by creating simpler versions of the procedure. For instance, if you have a lot of simple menu procedures in your application, you might copy the entire *MENU procedure to the bottom of the model, rename it *SMPL_MNU, and remove all of the code supporting Ctrl–Enter, Ctrl–Esc, lookup fields, computed fields, etc. Then, when you create a simple menu, you can specify SMPL_MNU at the Model Name line of the procedure definition window. Remember, you cannot define any of these deleted features when using SMPL_MNU. By creating a simpler version, Designer will then generate only the code you want to see. You can still use the default (larger) version of the menu procedure within the same application by simply not specifying a model name for the menu.

Most customization can (and should) be handled with Other procedures. Once you create a new model file, you are responsible for it and will need to maintain it, which is a consideration when modifying the model file.

Conclusion

In this chapter you have learned how to use Designer's model files, how Designer generates code, and how you can create your own versions of the model files. The more you understand about Designer and its model files, the more programming power you will have.

13

CHAPTER

Distributing
the application

Clarion provides several options for the final form of your application.
Memory usage, program overlays, translation, and distribution are all
parts of considering the outcome of your application.

Using memory

As your application grows, you might reach a point where you want more
memory. On current PCs, there is an unfortunate architectural limit of
640K bytes of memory, without resorting to expanded or extended memory. DOS will reside in some of this memory, along with an "terminate
and stay resident" programs.

If you are writing your program to execute on the broadest range of
machines, you do not want to assume that your user has access to expanded or extended memory options.

The need for memory can arise for a variety of reasons. Perhaps you
have an application so complex that there is simply not enough room in

memory for all of the code. Perhaps you want to maximize file access efficiency with caches or buffers. You also might need to structure your application to use large memory tables.

There are several options you can use to get around memory limitations. One has already been presented — using the RUN, CALL, or CHAIN statements (see Chapter 6). These statements allow you to break your application into several distinct programs, which call each other. This technique uses memory to hold only the relevant part of your application at any one time.

You can also use these statements to implement menus for the user's entire system. There are many Clarion programs that present only a Main Menu, and can run other DOS programs like word processors, spreadsheets, etc., along with the Clarion application.

Although breaking your application into several programs can be a simple and effective solution to many problems, there are some important things to consider. It usually takes more time to save and load several small applications than one large one. (Loading time will be discussed in more detail later in the chapter.) Multiple programs can be more difficult to maintain than one program that has been written using well-designed modules.

Another important consideration is that global memory is not be shared by the program "parts." As each program is called, it is loaded into memory with its own global area, which has none of the data present from the calling program. You can circumvent this by writing the global memory to a file. As each program is called, it reads the data from the intermediate file into its own global memory. The drawback is that each program has one more file to open and read after it is loaded. DOS does not, alas, provide a better formal mechanism for programs to communicate with each other by sharing common areas of memory.

For many applications, these considerations might not present a problem, and breaking the application into several programs that are called or chained together is an effective technique.

Overlays

Another more refined way of breaking your program into manageable units is with overlays. Overlays are separate part of your program that do not need to be in memory at the same time. As your program executes statements that call procedures or functions in these overlays, they are automatically loaded into memory, with each overlay occupying the same area of memory; they are said to "overlay" each other. Overlays also have the advantage that they do not replace global memory, which is always present.

Clarion makes the process of creating overlays in your program simple. It is all done through the MAP statement, as discussed in Chapter 5.

Consider the map structure in Fig. 13-1. This structure contains groups of procedures that deal with clients, vendors, and inventory. None of the procedures in each group call any of the procedures in the other groups, making each group a good candidate for an overlay. The groups will become overlays, so that only one group will reside in memory at a time. In this example, each group requires about 60K bytes of memory. Therefore, to have all three groups in memory at once will require about 180K bytes of memory.

```
MAP
   MODULE('CLIENT.CLA')
      PROC(NEWCLIENT)
      PROC(CHGCLIENT)
      PROC(SHOCLIENT)
      PROC(PRTCLIENT)
      .
   MODULE('VENDOR.CLA')
      PROC(NEWVENDOR)
      PROC(CHGVENDOR)
      PROC(SHOVENDOR)
      PROC(PRTVENDOR)
      .
   MODULE('INVENT.CLA')
      PROC(NEWINVENT)
      PROC(CHGINVENT)
      PROC(SHOINVENT)
      PROC(PRTINVENT)
      .
```

13-1. Example map structure

Consider the map in Fig. 13-2. Here you can see the same procedures declared, but with a few more structures around them. The area structure declares the area of memory in which all of the overlays will reside, one at a time. Within this area, the separate overlay structures are declared so that when the program runs, it will know which procedures and functions within an overlay are also placed in a separate source module.

In the example, the Main Menu (in the program procedure) will call one of the procedures in one of the three overlays. If that overlay is not already in memory, it will be loaded into memory and executed. When that procedure returns the program to the Main Menu, the user can select a different menu item that calls a procedure in one of the other overlay groups, which will then be loaded into memory, and so on.

```
MAP
  AREA
    OVERLAY
      MODULE('CLIENT.CLA')
        PROC(NEWCLIENT)
        PROC(CHGCLIENT)
        PROC(SHOCLIENT)
        PROC(PRTCLIENT)
                    .

    OVERLAY
      MODULE('VENDOR.CLA')
        PROC(NEWVENDOR)
        PROC(CHGVENDOR)
        PROC(SHOVENDOR)
        PROC(PRTVENDOR)
                .

    OVERLAY
      MODULE('INVENT.CLA')
        PROC(NEWINVENT)
        PROC(CHGINVENT)
        PROC(SHOINVENT)
        PROC(PRTINVENT)
                .

            .

        .
```

13-2. Example map structure with overlays

How much memory is required for the area? It will be the size of the largest overlay, so that each one will fit. In the example, the area will be about 60K bytes of memory. This shows a savings of about 120K bytes of memory, minus any code necessary to load the overlays.

Overlayed programs can also help to distribute the load time of the program. If you have a program that runs as soon as the system is turned on, and is used all day, incurring the load time all at once during startup would be the most desirable. This way, the user will not encounter disk activity during the day. However, if the program will be run many times during the day for brief intervals, loading only parts of the program as needed might be a better idea.

The rule about making overlay structures is that you must declare them so that there is no possibility that a function or procedure in an overlay will call another function or procedure in a different overlay of the same area. That is, you must make sure that more than one procedure or function does not need to exist in memory at the same time.

Thus far, I have discussed memory usage without regard for whether the program is being executed by the Processor (CRUN or CPRO), or by an .EXE program created with the Translator. Overlays will work in either case, provided that the linker you use (not supplied with Clarion) will create overlayed programs.

The runtime environment

As mentioned before, your compiled programs can be executed directly with the Processor. The Processor comes in two forms, one which includes the symbolic debugger and help screen generator (CPRO), and one which does not include these built-in features (CRUN). CRUN can also be distributed with your programs. CPRO is the Processor on the main Clarion menu and is usually used during development so that you can compile and test rapidly. After the program is complete, you have to choose whether you want to distribute your programs with CRUN or as a translated program. There are advantages and disadvantages to both.

The Processor is a large file because it contains all the necessary code to execute any possible Clarion program you can write. Suppose you write a simple program that has one screen and one keyed file, that will add, revise, and delete records. After compiling this program, you see that the size of the compiler output file, the .PRO file, has a size of only six or seven thousand bytes.

However, in order to run the program, you also need all of the supporting routines that your program calls to process key files, open screens, process fields, provide automatic type conversion, support a variety of video monitors and video timeout, keyboard functions, etc. All of this supporting code is code that you didn't have to write (which is how Clarion makes you productive), but still needs to be present at runtime.

If you have a simple application that only uses 60 percent of the procedures and functions that Clarion provides, the Processor still includes all of them. However, it is also true that the more complex your application, the more likely you are to use most of Clarion's features.

Processor programs separate your code from the Processor's code. You have already seen that the amount of your code (from the compiler—the .PRO files) is relatively small. Thus, you can update new versions of your software by distributing only the smaller .PRO files.

Using the processor form for your programs pays off, especially if you need to distribute several programs. In this case, you need to distribute only one copy of CRUN and the .PRO files for all your programs. This can make a difference of several diskettes in order to include everything for your application.

Also, the CALL and CHAIN statements work differently if you use the Processor. Under the Processor, the CHAIN statement keeps the Processor resident, while swapping the smaller .PRO files in and out of memory. The result is a significantly faster load time over the .EXE-based programs using CHAIN. Likewise, the CALL statement also loads only the .PRO files, while the Processor stays resident.

Translating and linking

A translated program has the advantage of being a single file. It includes only those routines you need to run the program. Also, (and this might or might not be important) it is harder to tell which language your program was written in.

Translated programs also have the advantage of executing slightly faster than Processed programs, but this can be misleading. If a Processor-based program spends 95 percent of its time waiting for keystrokes, the printer, or the disk (as most do), so will a translated program. Also, the difference in execution speed between translated programs and Processor-based programs is slight. This is not because translated programs are slow, it's simply that the Processor is very fast.

As you saw in Chapter 2, the process of creating translated programs does most of the work for you. The Translator will prompt you for the name of the .PRO file that contains your program procedure. It also uses the other files generated by the compiler to determine what additional modules are necessary, and then translates these into .OBJ files.

The Translator also uses the information specified by your map structure to generate a file to be used by your linker. The resulting file, called the *automatic response file* (ARF), tells the linker which .OBJ files to include. It also specifies which Clarion libraries are needed to pull out the code your program needs.

Translator supports two types of linkers—those compatible with the Microsoft linker, and those compatible with the Plink86 linker from Phoenix Technologies. You select the type from Translator's base page. You can also specify the name of the linker if it is different from LINK.EXE

If your program has overlays, you will need to provide it with the name of a linker that will support overlays. The linker will then include any additional code needed to load the overlay portions of our program. If this overlay loader code requires 5K additional bytes (an estimate—see your linker manual for the exact amount), make sure your overlay area is greater than 5K bytes, or you haven't gained anything!

The Translator also allows you to pass additional parameters to the linker, called *switches*. These are specific options that your linker might require in order to link all of the program segments together. See your linker manual for examples of these.

As mentioned above, if you write a program using many of Clarion's features (like screens, keyed files, reports, etc.) you might have used 80 of the code in the libraries in your program! If you need to distribute two or three of this type of translated program, you will be distributing 80 percent of the library two or three times. In this case, a Processor-based approach might be more desirable.

Conclusion

The decisions you need to make about how your program is distributed allow you to decide the best method that fits your situation. Most other development systems offer only one choice. Once you understand how to make these decisions, they represent flexibility that allows you to respond to different environments.

Index

Index

Index